ADMIRAL HYMAN RICKOVER

Admiral
Hyman Rickover

Engineer of Power

MARC WORTMAN

Yale

UNIVERSITY

PRESS

New Haven and London

Yale University Press books may be purchased in quantity for educational,
business, or promotional use. For information, please e-mail sales.press@yale.edu
(US office) or sales@yaleup.co.uk (U.K. office).

Frontispiece: Vice Admiral Hyman Rickover aboard the USS *Nautilus*
on June 8, 1958, prior to its transit under the polar ice cap.
(Naval History & Heritage Command # 2014.91.01)

Set in Janson Oldstyle type by Tseng Information Systems, Inc.
Durham, North Carolina.
Printed in the United States of America.

Library of Congress Control Number: 2021940519
ISBN 978-0-300-24310-9 (hardcover : alk. paper)

A catalogue record for this book is available from the British Library.

This paper meets the requirements of ANSI/NISO Z39.48-1992
(Permanence of Paper).

10 9 8 7 6 5 4 3 2 1

For Jodi

You are the solace of my cares, light in the blackest nights, and company in lonely places.

I have long since learned that a man
may give offense and yet succeed.

—John Adams to Robert R. Livingston,
February 26, 1782

CONTENTS

CONTENTS

ADMIRAL HYMAN RICKOVER

INTRODUCTION

Something New in the World

In the afternoon of May 31, 1953, one of the largest and most daring technology ventures ever attempted was about to reach its culmination. Rising from the high desert flatlands of southeastern Idaho, a six-story concrete and steel blockhouse stood against the distant gray buttes and snow-tipped Rocky Mountains. Inside the National Reactor Testing Station, the Mark I STR, Submarine Thermal Reactor plant, was ready to make steam. When it did, for the first time, nuclear energy would drive an engine. Practical atomic power would be born.

The death-dealing "radiance of a thousand suns," as J. Robert Oppenheimer memorialized the atomic bombs, had ended the Second World War less than eight years earlier. The atom's awesome explosive force had etched an indelible nightmare vision on the world. That was about to change. Mark I promised to convert the same energy that incinerated Hiroshima and Nagasaki into controlled machine power.

Inside the Reactor Testing Station, a horizontal, ribbed, steel cylinder lay partially submerged in a forty-foot-high, 385,000-gallon, circular concrete tub of greenish saltwater. About as far from the seacoasts of North America as possible, this "land-submarine" duplicated the control room, power plant, and propulsion machinery of a real seagoing sub. When the clutch of tense men inside the hull turned the throttle, a chain nuclear reaction would produce enough heat to boil up the steam needed to turn a heavy steel propeller shaft.

In theory.

If successful, a second submarine thermal reactor, the Mark II, based on lessons learned from this prototype, would go into a real United States Navy submarine presently under construction on the Atlantic seaboard. All existing submarines cruised along the surface with noisy diesel engines or, if underwater, on electric power at slow speed for no more than a few hours before they needed to resurface to charge their batteries. However, these boats were easily hunted—and often swiftly sunk. But in principle, a nuclear submarine would be able to slide into the depths and maintain top speeds for weeks or even months without need for recharging fuel, air, or battery. Atomic-powered submarines represented a seafaring and naval warfare leap as fundamental as that from sail to steam. This oceangoing sentinel would in theory travel faster and longer underwater than any sub before—almost unceasingly, like a deep-sea satellite. Nuclear-powered surface ships, even giant aircraft carriers, might follow in the intensifying Cold War with the Soviet Union.

Nuclear reactors were not for warships alone. A new way to generate electricity was also in the offing. The same naval organization that built the Mark I reactor had also begun engineering the first dedicated, commercial-scale atomic power plant, an entirely new utility for electrifying the world. For the first time, humanity would capture the energy encased in an atom's nucleus to power humanity's dreams rather than its nightmares.

If the STR prototype worked, the 13,400-horsepower Mark II would push the twin screws of a submarine being built in Groton, Connecticut. Named *Nautilus* and designated USSN-571—*N* for "nuclear"—the sleek and foreboding black and olive-green vessel would surpass its science-fiction namesake that Jules Verne depicted in *Twenty Thousand Leagues under the Sea* eight decades earlier. President Harry Truman had expressed the wonder of what lay ahead at the *Nautilus*'s keel-laying ceremony the previous year. "This ship," he declared, "will be something new in the world. . . . Her engines will not burn oil or coal. The heat in her boilers will be created by the same source that heats the sun—energy released by atomic fission, the breaking apart of the basic matter of the whole universe."[1] Capturing atomic power to drive a ship beneath the waves for previously inconceivable distances was a notion as preposterous as a voyage to the moon.

But it was crazy in another sense as well. An out-of-control nuclear chain reaction would melt the reactor cauldron until it exploded, shooting radioactive steam out across the Idaho countryside, surely killing the men inside the land submarine's hull, as well as poisoning the landscape. If it failed, whatever hopes the United States harbored for harnessing the atom's power would be dashed. Given the already widespread skepticism—"a nice toy, but it will never be practical" was a typical refrain heard among the Navy brass—the public backlash to such a catastrophe would put atomic propulsion off the table probably for decades, if not forever.

Inside the land sub's maneuvering room—the power plant's operations center—members of the *Nautilus*'s future crew sat at three side-by-side consoles.[2] Civilian engineers in shirtsleeves watched over their shoulders in the cramped quarters. Standing among them, United States Navy Captain Hyman George Rickover wore civilian clothing—per usual. A wisp of a man at barely five and a half feet tall and 125 pounds, Rickover's elongated, slender neck and small, silver-haired head pushed out of his oversized collar like a turtle's head from its shell. His sparrow's face and piercing hazel eyes bore an almost querulous expression. He spoke in a high-pitched, nasal voice with a twang from the Chicago streets, punctuating his sentences with frequent curses, sometimes directed at the people he spoke to. He never uttered a word of praise.

Rickover was born Chaim Godalia Rykower fifty-three years earlier in the Polish shtetl of Maków-Mazowiecki, then part of tsarist Russia. Past biographers have disputed Rickover's birthdate, contending that he may have altered it to ease his way into the Naval Academy. He did not, but like many central European immigrants, he never knew his true birthdate. He came to believe that he was born on January 27, 1900, the date later inscribed on his gravestone at Arlington National Cemetery. But newly unearthed documents show that he was born a little over a month earlier, December 24, 1899.[3] Six years later, his devoutly Orthodox family came to America to escape antisemitic violence and grinding poverty. With their names Americanized, they eventually settled in Chicago. In 1918, Rickover won an appointment to the United States Naval Academy in Annapolis. Few among his fellow midshipmen liked the "little Jew," as one described him. But he "survived"— his word—four years of hazing, marching, antisemitism, and hard study. He held on in a service that tried to shake itself free of him. By now he had already amassed thirty-five years in the Navy.

Rickover projected none of the commanding physical presence of the stereotypical naval captain. But nobody in the Mark I's maneuvering room doubted his authority. He combined in himself leadership of both the US Navy Bureau of Ships Nuclear Propulsion Program *and* the Atomic Energy Commission (AEC, predecessor to today's Department of Energy) Division of Naval Reactors. The federally funded military-civilian bureaucratic hybrid was known simply as Naval Reactors. Behind it lay Rickover's fearsome drive for power. His indomitable will, ruthless determination, and engineering insight had brought the submarine thermal nuclear reactor and *Nautilus* program to this point.

Plenty of doubts remained about whether the Mark I STR would explode when it powered up. Panicky engineers suggested starting it up remotely. Rickover killed that idea. He even rebuffed controlling the start-up from the balcony over the hull. Should anything go wrong, he would suffer the consequences along with the rest. Ever watchful for political advantage, Rickover gave the chief of the AEC, Thomas E. Murray, the honor of opening the throttle. Rickover nodded to Murray. Murray turned the handle. A nervous staffer leaning in behind him readied to shut it down.

The silent men listened for the sounds that would answer their fears and dreams. Those sounds came right away. Hissing steam hit the turbine in the land sub's power plant. The whine of spinning gears pierced the engine room. The red-and-white striping of the thick propeller shaft slowly began to snake and turn. From outside came the sound of churning water as a heavy wheel began to spin like a propeller through the sea. The men listened in silent awe to the first machine noises produced by harnessed atomic energy.

Relief and excitement passed across the men's faces, having arrived at the culmination of a years-long path. They practically levitated within the steel shell. Yet, having achieved something no human had ever done before—the invention of a new form of power—Rickover remained outwardly impassive. But he knew they were witnessing a unique event in humanity's existence, the invention of a new, perhaps inexhaustible form of energy.

Later, as the atomic-powered water wheel turned and turned, a gaping submariner gestured toward the reactor: "She just sits there and cooks."[4] The Age of Atomic Power was born.

Also born was the legend of the engineering and organizational wizard Hyman Rickover. Shipyard workers would install the Mark II, and the *Nautilus* would go to sea in less than two years—meeting his astoundingly short timeline. The *Nautilus*'s first operational voyage went farther and lasted longer than any previous underwater run by a factor of *ten*. Three years later, *Nautilus* transited beneath the North Pole. Its "discovery" of the under-ice Northwest Passage would captivate the world almost as much as the moon landing did a decade later. It also put the Soviet Union on notice that US warships would soon shelter beneath the polar ice within missile range of its northern cities and tracking distance of warships exiting its ports. A new dimension in national defense and warfare had opened.

Secretary of the Navy Dan Kimball termed the *Nautilus* "the most important piece of development work in the history of the Navy." Edward L. Beach, a renowned nuclear-submarine captain, author, and measured critic of Rickover's, called it "unquestionably the greatest engineering advance ever experienced by warships, . . . a totally new sort of warship."[5] Even before the real submarine went to sea, Rickover had already won almost mythical status.

Dubbed "the father of the nuclear Navy," Rickover would go on to build ship after ship—underwater and surface vessels—powered by nuclear energy. The development of nuclear ships, the largest and most complicated machines yet built, transformed the US Navy. Once acoustic-silencing technologies eliminated nearly all noise, US nuclear subs were almost impossible to detect and track and could stay down for months at a time. The geopolitical and military implications were immense. Subs could transition from their previous peacetime roles of collecting intelligence, trailing enemy ships, and watching and waiting for possible conflict. Before the end of the decade, submarines would carry strategic nuclear missiles deep below the world's oceans, ice floes, and littorals; smaller attack submarines could follow Soviet ships, which ran in constant fear that a hidden hunter-killer lurked nearby.

In the Cold War's terrifying calculus of mutually assured destruction, possessing what became a fast-growing strategic and tactical nuclear fleet, ever quietly in motion, meant that the Soviets could not attack the United States or its allies without facing certain catastrophic retaliation. Once the Soviet Union acquired a large fleet of its own nuclear subs, the underwater "silent services" held both nations back from direct armed conflict that could potentially escalate into nuclear war.[6]

Nuclear propulsion also proved transformative for surface ships. Aircraft carriers and their atomic-powered escorts could steam at flank speed over the world's oceans to crisis spots, without being slowed by accompanying oilers or the need to put into port, and, once on station, they could remain in combat operations indefinitely. Nuclear power reduced response time to crises and expanded the fleet's global range while enhancing national leaders' strategic options. A few months after the launch of the *Nautilus*, Rickover summed up what nuclear propulsion meant: "We can now go *where* we want, *when* we want."[7] Although Rickover did not live to see it, the collapse of the Soviet Union resulted in no small measure from the Soviet's inability to sustain its costly technological race against Western and particularly US nuclear fleets. As the world's nuclear fleets continue to sally forth, Rickover's maritime revolution continues to inform geopolitical strategy in the world's capitals.

In addition, after the world's first nuclear-propelled vessel went to sea, Rickover also opened the first civilian atomic central power station. In late 1957, a "beached" naval reactor inside a riverside power plant at Shippingport, about twenty-five miles above Pittsburgh, began illuminating the region's homes and powering its factories. Shippingport became a nuclear utility "university" and laboratory, founding the global nuclear-power industry. Most of the world's current 450 reactors utilize the same basic technology that Rickover pioneered there.

Rickover has emerged as arguably the greatest engineer in military history and among the most influential engineers ever. Before the *Nautilus* went to sea, Rickover was already a household name. The project made headlines from coast to coast, a book appeared about him, and *Time* magazine put his face on its cover. Hollywood soon followed with undersea fantasy movies featuring atomic submarines and a hit television series, *Voyage to the Bottom of the Sea.* A play based on Rickover's life ran briefly on Broadway. Even the sophomoric *Mad* magazine got into the act with a cartoon spoofing "Hymie Rickover and His Atomic Submarines."[8]

Beneath the technological marvels, bureaucratic ingenuity, and pugnacious persona lay startling productivity from the unprecedented engineering organization Rickover pioneered at Naval Reactors. More than thirty years before the high-tech revolution remade the US workplace, Rickover instituted the "flat" research-and-development organization. Nothing quite like Naval Reactors existed anywhere in 1950s corporate America, certainly not in the Navy. At Naval Reactors, he abolished rank and uniform: naval officers worked for civilians, and knowledgeable young engineers argued with senior staffers over technical questions. "There is no hierarchy in matters of the mind," Rickover said, and he insisted that all were "permitted to do as they think best and to go to anyone and anywhere for help. Each person is then limited only by his own ability."[9] One of his technical leaders described Naval Reactors as "almost like an idealized university setting."[10]

Rickover presided over an island of brainy, work-until-the-job-gets-done, shirtsleeved nonconformity inside what was perhaps the most regimented, hierarchical, and polished organizational culture in US society. When somebody brought in a copy of the *Naval Regulations* book, Rickover yelled at him, "Get the hell out, and burn it!"[11] Rickover ignored the chain of command and all but locked the Navy out of Naval Reactors. He almost never dressed in uniform, preferring civilian clothes even on the most ceremonial occasions. His fellow officers heard him loud and clear when he scoffed, "Well, for Chrissake, what the hell is there about standing up and saluting and dressing up in uniform? You can put dummies to do that job."[12] When the Defense Department called for an organizational chart for the 350 or so men and women who worked for him at his Washington office, he sent back one filled in with Chinese characters.[13]

Navy and government officials bristled at Rickover's rebellious nature, indifference to the chain of command, and frequent workarounds. More tradition-bound Navy officers detested Rickover and all he stood for. A secretary of the Navy portrayed Naval Reactors as "a personality cult," with Rickover described as a Stalin inside the Navy. Admiral Elmo R. Zumwalt Jr., onetime chief of naval operations, the service branch's highest officer and member of the Joint Chiefs of Staff, reportedly said that the Navy's two greatest enemies were, first, the Soviets and, second, Rickover. Rickover was, wrote Zumwalt, a "malady that afflicted . . . the Whole Navy," undermining the concept of a unified service branch. The powerful Vietnam-era secretary of defense Robert McNamara wanted to court-martial him.[14]

Rickover's virtues and vices were as tightly coiled as the fuel rods inside his reactors: his obsessive drive to get things done according to his own vision made everything he undertook a holy crusade, with Naval Reactors his knightly roundtable foraying out against blockheaded Navy commanders, bumbling bureaucrats, and profiteering contractors. He deliberately made enemies and never forgave a slight. He felt incessantly aggrieved by the "stupid people" in the Defense Department and Navy "cheerleaders" who were "not knowledgeable enough to instruct or to see that the work has been done properly" yet who expected to oversee his engineering program. "It's like setting a blind man to lead the seeing," he hissed.[15]

He fought them all tooth and nail. When someone could not outmaneuver or outargue him, he went in for the kill. He took perverse pleasure in making people squirm. "He liked to be difficult," recalled Admiral Charles Duncan, a deputy chief of naval operations and chief of naval personnel. "He liked to get into a fight and, of course, to win, and he would go to any lengths to win."[16] After a run-in with Rickover, few dared stand in his way.

He delighted in being unreasonable in his demands and ruthless in wielding power. "People say I am like Captain Bligh," he archly observed to his authorized biographer, Francis Duncan. "I am disappointed. I consider myself more like Attila the Hun."[17] As the years went on and he grew virtually unassailable, he became if anything more irascible and obnoxious. The people who admired him most and worked years, even decades, for him sarcastically referred to him as "the KOG," the "Kindly Old Gentleman."[18] He was anything but.

He often saved his "best" insults for an offender's intelligence—and he found plenty who did not measure up. In parting words to a small group of prospective nuclear commanding officers who had successfully completed their grueling practical and written examinations after three months of intensive training in 1977, he offered no pats on the back or reassuring words. Instead, he jumped his then-seventy-seven-year-old body up on a tabletop, stomped with rage like an angry djinn, and screamed at the top of his lungs, "I understand genetics. If you make a mistake with my nuclear plant, it's because your mother was a street whore who trawled for tricks with a mattress on her back!"[19] Shaken officers hated the tongue lashings, but they would never forget their scarifying message: "On penalty of all you hold dearest, do not fail to live up to my standard of perfection."

They did not. According to US Navy public records, the nuclear Navy never experienced an incident resulting in an uncontrolled radiation release. By contrast, the Soviet and successor Russian Navy has suffered multiple accidents, causing numerous radiation-poisoning injuries and deaths and environmental contamination that lingers.[20] Rickover's safety record continues in the Navy: with US nuclear subs having logged more than sixty-nine hundred reactor-years of operations and traveling more than 162 million miles on nuclear power by the end of 2017, with tens of thousands of sailors living just feet from a reactor for months at a time, no ship reactor had released radioactivity above surrounding levels.[21]

Within twenty years of the first powered run of the Mark I STR and the triumph of the *Nautilus*, Rickover's nuclear Navy had grown into an empire. By the mid-1970s, Naval Reactors controlled or oversaw six massive shipyards and the nuclear laboratories at Westinghouse, General Electric, and Combustion Engineering, with their tens of thousands of employees, along with around one thousand smaller contracting firms, five nuclear prototypes for testing and training purposes in three states, and a nuclear power school in a fourth. Rickover's Navy was operating more than 120 nuclear-powered warships, including attack and ballistic-missile submarines and surface ships, among them the largest aircraft carrier and biggest and most complicated military machine ever built, projecting US Cold War power globally.

And just about everyone thought of it as "Rickover's Navy." As transformative as the hardware he built were the officers he trained to command his machines. During his thirty-five years as chief of Naval Reactors, Rickover personally selected about five thousand officers for nuclear-power training out of some fifteen thousand prequalified interviewees. His eccentric, sometimes abusive, even borderline-illegal, and always intimidating interviews—including embarrassing personal questions and hours-long banishment to a broom closet for any young officer whose answers fell short in his estimation—were designed to throw a candidate off balance. He did this literally, too, by infamously sawing off a couple of inches from the front legs of the interviewees' chair. The young men who entered Nuclear Power School took a demanding course of study in nuclear-reactor physics, engineering, and operations knowing in the raw end of their nerves that Rickover held them on a very short leash, which he would keep taut their entire careers.

Rickover's Navy finally overtook "the Whole Navy" when he drove a comprehensive revamping of the faculty and curriculum of the venerable US Naval Academy. Distressed that so many among the midshipman candidates he interviewed were not capable of success in his nuclear program, he cajoled and lobbied and finally toppled the Academy's long-standing mission of preparing midshipmen for broad, multidisciplinary command. Pressure from Rickover caused academic ability and achievement in technical and scientific disciplines to displace traditional prerequisites for military leadership: personal bearing, tactical acumen, social graces, and command presence. The laboratory overtook the parade ground in Annapolis. After that cultural sea change, the warrior-technocrat increasingly took charge.[22]

Rickover's vision for educational reform did not stop there. He warned that the nation's entire education system was failing and falling behind those of its Cold War enemies and economic competitors in the dawning technological age. The admiral became an educational critic and philosopher, compiling congressional testimony, speeches, and other writings into three books lambasting US schools for wasting precious resources and time on sports, socializing, and other nonacademic pursuits. He derided educators who nurtured students for social success— "life adjustment . . . to make every child happy"—which he called "a hopeless endeavor."[23] He urged the federal government to institute national educational standards for schools decades before any were developed. "To be undereducated in this trigger-happy world," he warned, "is to invite catastrophe."[24]

Despite Rickover's heading a fourth-echelon naval bureau with responsibility for propulsion and electrical power generation in at most a third of all Navy ships, through his iron-bound control of technical education, nuclear-officer selection and training, and atomic-powered propulsion construction and operational safety, he gained a virtual stranglehold on the entire US Navy. Admiral Duncan, a close observer and sometimes Rickover combatant for nearly two decades, described him as "a genius at orchestrating power."[25]

Rickover's willingness to wage and win every fight at any cost made him countless enemies. But those friends he did have, above all in Congress, were more powerful; they protected and promoted him, placing him outside his enemies' reach. Captain Edward Beach wrote, "I have heard a Chief of Naval Operations, in the full regalia of his own four stars, say, 'You fellows may think I'm running the Navy, but you are wrong. I work for Rick, like everybody else.'"[26] Duncan agreed: "if the CNO challenges Rick it will be the CNO who falls."[27] And several CNOs learned this lesson the hard way.

At the zenith of Rickover's power, the doors to the White House were flung open to him. Future president Jimmy Carter titled his campaign autobiography *Why Not the Best?* after a soul-penetrating question that Rickover asked Carter in 1952, when Carter was a young naval officer interviewing for the nuclear-officer training program.[28] "With the exception of my father," Carter claimed, "no other person has had such a profound impact on my life." He declared Rickover more than once "the greatest engineer who ever lived."[29] With Carter in the White House, Rickover's influence extended to the pinnacle of world power.

But Rickover's dazzling ascent almost never happened. On the day after Truman celebrated the *Nautilus* at its June 14, 1952, keel-laying ceremony, the Navy declared war on the man behind the most revolutionary technological advance in its history. A selection board composed of admiral-rank—flag—officers refused to promote Captain Rickover into their ranks. Less than a year later, with the Mark I about to begin its first chain-reaction test, a second board reconsidered his promotion and again said no. Under Navy up-or-out rules, he would have to retire at the end of June 1953. In effect, the Navy *fired* Rickover while he engineered the colossal submarine-reactor and *Nautilus* programs and the world's first commercial-scale atomic electric power plant project. Although he was able to turn back the Navy's effort to oust him and would go on to defend his tenure for another thirty years, his service-branch home had made clear it did not want him or his revolution.

The roots of Rickover's all-out war with the Navy lay deep in his past, long before he joined the service branch, stretching back to the day when he first stepped onto American soil, in 1906. Even when he was a welcomed guest in the White House and on Capitol Hill, he never stopped fighting to secure his place in the United States. Now, when he achieved the postwar world's dream of harnessing the power inside the atom, the Navy intended to toss Hyman Rickover overboard. He would never leave his fate to the mercy of others again.

1

The Lucky Bag

SIX-YEAR-OLD CHAIM RYKOWER, his sister Faiga, age eight, and their twenty-nine-year-old mother, Ruchia, huddled together amid the din of thousands of immigrants filing through the Ellis Island Great Hall. The forlorn family waited with their cloth bundle of possessions. Women and children without money could not enter the United States legally and after ten days were sent back to where they started. If Ruchia's émigré husband, Abram, did not show up shortly, the trio would be put back on a ship.

US immigration authorities hung numbered tags on the Rykowers when they arrived in New York Harbor on March 26, 1906. Ten days later, the tags still hung there. The family tried not to give up hope, but that morning officials stamped "DEPORTED" next to their names on the immigrant registry.[1] They could see the Statue of Liberty and, across the harbor, the bustle and smoke of Manhattan's waterfront and the astounding thicket of buildings beyond. They feared this would be the closest they would ever get to the promise of the New World.

Since steaming into the Port of New York aboard the passenger ship *Finland*, the Rykowers, their names eventually Americanized to Hyman, Fannie, and Rachel, had spent each day scanning faces outside the Registry Room doors.[2] Like thousands of other Jewish immigrants who had gone through Ellis Island since their arrival, the Rykowers had left their former lives behind, bringing only what they could carry. Almost two months earlier, in the hard Polish winter, Ruchia had wrapped a pot and utensils, a pair of candlesticks, and several days' supply of kosher food in a sheet. Leaving the shtetl of Maków-Mazowiecki in Russian Poland, Ruchia and her children journeyed westward in a canvas-covered wagon. As they rolled through the windswept countryside, a regiment of Russian paramilitary horseback soldiers—Cossacks, as the Jews called them—rode past. Eight decades later, Hyman still remembered his terror when, he said, "they whipped the sides of our wagon and the horses." The Rykowers eventually reached Antwerp. Hyman's first sight of ships and the sea was not auspicious: the scared boy burst into tears.[3] From there, they crossed the Atlantic in the bounding *Finland*'s teeming, fetid third-class belly. They had only salted herring and bread to eat. Chaim ate his first orange when it was tossed from the upper deck into the hold.

The night before the ship entered New York Harbor, the ship's purser gathered the steerage passengers. He explained to the immigrants that they must communicate with their loved ones to meet them at Ellis Island. He offered to telegraph ahead. Ruchia should not have trusted him.[4] As a result, they appeared headed back to Maków.

For generations, Yiddish-speaking Jews like the Rykowers had lived in Maków, an eight-hundred-year-old cathedral and market town and light-industry center on the grassy banks of the Orzyc River. According to an 1897 census, Maków's 4,480-person shtetl comprised about 65 percent of the town's total population. The Jews were separated from their Catholic neighbors by streets, religion, language, and legal and property rights. The rickety Jewish parts of town were little different from hundreds of other Polish shtetls.

Maków's Jews built a lively if impoverished community.[5] Judaism governed their lives. Many of Maków's Jews were followers of revered Hasidic rabbis who had established Talmudic study centers there. Eighty years after leaving Maków, Rickover recalled studying at a *heder*, a Jewish day school—Polish law barred Jews from state-sponsored schools—starting at age four. "School hours," he said, "were from sunrise to sunset, six days a week. On the seventh day, we attended the synagogue a good part of the day."[6] Rickover's lifelong habits of concentrated study, argumentation, and long days and weeks of work began early.

Back home, Ruchia's husband, Abram, had been conscripted into the Russian army. He deserted at the risk of execution—evincing an antiauthoritarian streak that he passed on to his son—and returned to Maków. His income tailoring barely supported the family.

Maków's Jews faced another threat beyond poverty. Fearing growing political unrest, Russia's Tsar Nicholas II had scapegoated Jews in recent years. He directed his provincial paramilitary forces to harass and suppress them. Pogroms swept through many Polish shtetls and urban ghettos. Hunger and antisemitism pushed many Jews to leave for other countries, particularly the United States. Most of the Jewish people would stay on in Maków, until, in November 1942, Nazi forces exterminated the shtetl's last residents.[7]

Abram Rykower joined the gathering wave departing for the New World. The twenty-one-year-old arrived alone in

New York City on December 1, 1896.[8] Although the exact dates are uncertain, he then returned to Maków sometime in the latter part of 1897 before sailing back to America a few months later. He started naturalization proceedings in early 1898.[9] In the first months of the following year, he visited his family at least once more, during which time he and Ruchia conceived their son Chaim, the future Hyman. Then Abram left Maków a final time, reentering the United States via Canada on February 16, 1901.[10] As Abraham Ricover, he would become a US citizen on September 6, 1906.[11] Eventually, the family's name further Americanized to "Rickover."

Abraham saved up enough money to bring his wife and two children to join him. However, on the night before the *Finland* reached New York Harbor, Ruchia gave the purser the last of her money to contact her husband for her. The purser probably pocketed it, for Abraham never received the telegram and did not know they had arrived.[12] Penniless, they waited the maximum ten days in the immigration terminal facilities.

Finally, luck intervened. According to Rickover, a man who knew his parents from Poland came to Ellis Island to meet his own wife. "He saw my mother sitting in a large hall with her bundle of possessions," Rickover recalled. The man ran back to find Abraham. "He came just in time to retrieve us." Almost eighty years later and a world-famous four-star admiral known for his many bruising battles with corporate shipbuilders, he could joke ruefully about the near miss: "During my naval career, many contractors have probably cursed the man who reported my arrival and thus prevented my being shipped back to Poland."[13]

When the future Hyman Rickover stepped onto US soil for the first time, he understood with a six-year-old's sense of vulnerability that his place in his new homeland was not assured. He would spend a lifetime forging his own form of unbreakable security in the United States.

* * *

For the reunited Rickovers, the future now looked promising. They soon settled in the Brownsville section of Brooklyn. Just a few months later, Abraham and a business partner bought a small apartment building, a move they believed would bring them a measure of stability.[14] Despite speaking no English, Hyman started public elementary school. He loved it. His father tailored, and his mother washed clothes at a Catholic hospital. One day hospital nuns offered her a stack of back issues of a church magazine for her bright son. They were, Rickover remembered, "my first gift. I read them avidly." Those magazines served as primers that, he said, "greatly helped me learn English."[15]

A third and last Rickover child, daughter Hitel, given the American name Augusta, was born in New York City in 1908. By then the family could ill afford another mouth to feed. Abraham's business partner died, and his widow walked away from the shared mortgage, leaving Abraham to cover it. The bank foreclosed on Abraham's apartment building.[16] The family sank back into poverty.

Abraham Rickover started over again. Sometime in 1909 or 1910, he headed west once more to seek opportunity, leaving his family behind. Settling in Chicago, Abraham found work as a tailor at a men's clothing manufacturer, where he, some years later, rose to managing the shop floor.[17] He eventually bought another income-generating apartment building. With his finances rebuilt, in 1911 Rachel brought the three children to Chicago. The family moved into an apartment in a narrow, three-story, stone building on South Hamlin Avenue in the North Lawndale section on the city's West Side. They rented out one of their three rooms to tenants. That room would make all the difference in young Hyman's future.

* * *

Known as "Little Jerusalem," Lawndale was home to the country's largest Jewish community outside of New York City. Unlike the teeming Maxwell Street, Chicago's equivalent to New York City's Lower East Side, Lawndale's apartment buildings and small houses had plots of grass fronting airy streets and wide boulevards. Three synagogues were just a short walk from the Rickover apartment, one immediately next door. Each day after grammar school, Hyman studied at a Jewish school. At age thirteen, he had his bar mitzvah.[18]

Life became more stable, yet Rickover rarely spoke about his Chicago childhood with warmth. Poverty still plagued Rickover's Yiddish-speaking family. His mother sometimes went without food so the rest of the family could eat. The lessons of want stuck with Rickover; later in life, he made a virtue of living parsimoniously to a fault, avoiding waste and, until late in life, possessing few personal luxuries except stacks of books at home.

He was, he said, a fiercely "stubborn" child. His father had a temperament to match. Rickover recounted the time his father "had to chip away his front teeth in order to force medicine down."[19] If home life was often harsh, Chicago's streets could be worse. The threat of antisemitic violence was pervasive: several times Irish Catholic children jumped the slight boy, yelling, "Christ killer! Christ killer!" as they beat him.[20]

Even before moving to Chicago, Rickover started working. Around age nine, he spent part of each day holding up a lantern for a neighbor in his basement ironwork shop. He also stocked shelves at a small grocery and made deliveries by horse and wagon. After his last grammar-school grade in 1914, his family expected him to go to work full-time like his older sister. That summer he delivered telegrams by bicycle and streetcar for a local Western Union office.

At the end of the summer, the company offered him a regular delivery job, from three in the afternoon until eleven at night. He jumped at the chance because he could attend high school while working. However, he had to lie about having attained the legal minimum age for nighttime work. He listed his birthdate as August 24, 1898, on his high school enrollment forms, leading some biographers to suspect mistakenly that he later changed his birthdate to January 1, 1900, to appear younger when he applied for nomination to the Naval Academy.[21]

That fall he started John Marshall High School. Rickover's work ethic was reinforced over the next four years—as was a certain embarrassment at his limited formal education in world culture. "Each week of the years at high school," he said, "I worked more than 70 hours a week, with no vacation during the entire time. I remember those high school years vividly. Trying to study a book while delivering Western Union telegrams was difficult. It would have been wonderful to have had the opportunity for more study, for reading good books. But I did not have that opportunity."[22] He held on his entire life to a front-page 1916 Chicago newspaper photograph taken late at night, showing him in the foreground delivering telegrams at the Republican National Convention while behind him a future US president and then-senator Warren G. Harding delivered a keynote address from the stage.[23]

Despite working an exhausting full-time job, the teen carved out enough hours for study to discover a lifelong passion for history and a love of literature. In the style of education at the time, he memorized long passages from classical writers, Shakespeare, and English poets. He often recited John Milton's sonnet "On His Blindness," also known by its first line, "When I consider how my light is spent . . ." The poem concludes with lines that would resonate throughout Rickover's life:

Thousands at his bidding speed
And post o'er Land and Ocean without rest:
They also serve who only stand and wait.

Sleepwalking at times through the school day, Rickover stumbled early on but made almost straight A's as a senior. At his Marshall High graduation ceremony in February 1918, the class gave him the honor of wearing the class mantle embroidered with the word "Knowledge." Already noted for his quick wit, he gave a short, mostly humorous, if juvenile, speech to the graduating seniors and their families. Rickover was even then aiming his deadpan jokes at their brunt's intelligence. In his talk, he described the preceding and following senior classes as "large in number but small in brain."[24] The elfin, easily-picked-on Jewish immigrant found a ready weapon in comic mockery. He would later hone his cutting humor to a saber's edge that he wielded with a hussar's lethal delight.

In March of his junior year, two weeks before the United States declared war on the Central Powers and entered World War One, Rickover joined his high school's military training program. He began drilling one day a week at school and fantasized about attending the Army's or Navy's military academy.[25] But for boys like Rickover, the service academies might as well have been on Mars. Those institutions catered mostly to sons of the elite who had attended preparatory schools. Rickover's only choice after high school appeared to be more work. Then, family life, school, work, and military preparation came together in an entirely fortuitous way to open the young Hyman's small and doleful world to his seemingly unreachable dream.

Rickover frequently delivered telegrams to the district office of US Representative Adolph J. Sabath. A Jewish immigrant from what is today the Czech Republic, Sabath would eventually serve twenty-three terms. Neither the telegraph boy nor the congressman could possibly envision how their lives would intertwine to build the *Nautilus*.[26]

Sabath was a wily political operative. At home, Rickover's family rented a room to Joseph Rothstein, an older distant relative. Rothstein happened to serve on Lawndale's draft board. A wealthy, politically connected area resident asked what Rothstein could do to keep his son out of the Army. Rothstein struck a bargain: he would make sure the man's son got an exemption in exchange for Sabath's nomination of the Rickover boy to the US Naval Academy. Sabath forwarded Rickover's name.[27]

At about the same time that Rickover graduated from high school, he heard that the Academy would consider his nomination. But first he had to pass a demanding series of admissions exams, with a minimum passing score of 2.5 out of a possible 4 in each of a half dozen academic subjects. Testing began in about a month and a half. Knowing he would have a tough time passing, Rickover spent $300—much of his savings—for a specialized prep course in Annapolis. After one session, he realized that he lagged so far behind that the course alone would never get him through the entrance exam. He stopped going to class, forfeiting the tuition. Instead, he devoted every waking hour to memorizing material he anticipated would be on the tests. In mid-April, he took the three-day test. Then he went back home to work and await the results.[28]

His scores arrived two months later. He squeaked through, making the minimum 2.5 on the algebra test and not much better in a couple of other subjects. But they were good enough. He would enter the Naval Academy as a plebe (first-year student) in the class of 1922. In learning that he would indeed get the opportunity to pursue "a dream that had previously appeared out of reach," he experienced, he recalled, joy for the first time in his life. He would not feel so moved again for another thirty-five years.[29]

* * *

Rickover walked through the Academy gates for the first time on June 29, 1918, beginning a summer's immersion in midshipmen life, naval culture—which at the time included table etiquette and waltzing—and seamanship. The last of Rickover's savings went for uniforms, books, and supplies. Then he stood before the Academy's superintendent to swear the US Navy induction oath and enter his full name in a registry. Rickover paused. He had never publicly used his given middle name, Godalia, a Hebraic word meaning "God is great." He considered a moment before entering, "Hyman George Rickover." After this, a small number of intimates would call him "George," including his future wife. Navy friends and work colleagues called him "Rick"; almost nobody called him "Hyman." And "Hymie," a term that antisemites used to label Jews, was out of bounds.

Rickover was in the Navy, an outcome that in hindsight was as unlikely as a mule winning a thoroughbred horse race. He would never leave.

With more officers than ever being prepared for the world war, Rickover and the 963 other plebes composed the largest class in Academy history up to that time and more than the entire prewar midshipman brigade. Filing up the white granite steps and through the bronze doors into Bancroft Hall, the center of midshipman life, Rickover entered the thousand-seat mess hall, where he took his place at the long rows of tables draped with white tablecloths. A Christian prayer was said. After that, white-jacketed Philippine waiters rushed about and set a plate in front of him, heaped with more food than he had ever seen before. As if to mark his break with the past, his first Navy meal was ham—his first non-Kosher food. He told himself it was "rare roast beef." The pragmatic Rickover adapted.[30]

His time at the Academy almost ended before it truly began

when in early fall he was possibly exposed to diphtheria and put into quarantine. During this time, the worldwide influenza pandemic struck, halting virtually all activities outside classrooms. Eight midshipmen died of the flu. Although healthy, Rickover was not allowed to leave the hospital for nearly the entire fall.

Adding to his woes, Rickover feared forced cuts following the November 11, 1918, Armistice ending the war. He was determined not to lose out on his education. The Academy curriculum encouraged rote learning, memorization of information on specific maritime and military situations. Classes were bone-dry chances for midshipmen to display what they had memorized. Although students had to drill their textbooks into their heads, study was not allowed after lights-out at ten in the evening. Rickover did not care. He retreated to the shower room, where he repeated formulas and phrases and memorized diagrams late into the night.

If his grinding study habits did not isolate him from his classmates, poverty did the rest. Many midshipmen came from well-to-do families. A large number were sons of naval officers. They brought dates from Washington and Baltimore to tea dances and made the social rounds of rising young officers. Rickover could not afford to date or go to the movies on his one-dollar-per-month plebe stipend. Athletics held an important place in Annapolis; he had never played sports and found he had no talent when he tried. Rickover told Clay Blair for his 1954 biography that he "finally withdrew to the privacy of his room, . . . [where] he read almost constantly."[31]

As a Jewish immigrant, he also stood apart from the brigade. Rickover was one of just seventeen Jews in his plebe class, less than 2 percent of entering students.[32] A massive Episcopalian chapel stood in the figurative and literal center of campus. All midshipmen attended Christian services there—absent Jews and Catholics who worshiped off campus. Plebes endured hazing such as beatings, orders to do calisthenics until they collapsed, and other minor tortures at the hands of upperclassmen. Jews endured worse: silence. According to a student at Annapolis around the same time as Rickover, "All Jews lived in Coventry," midshipman lingo for being shunned. Jews were almost never spoken to in casual conversation or even acknowledged by fellow middies except by way of insult.[33] Openly antisemitic taunts were apparently infrequent, although Rickover recalled that a midshipman cursed him for eating the last piece of bread at a meal and then hissed, "What can you expect from a Jew!" Rickover challenged him to a fight. When they met the next morning in the gym, Rickover said, "[I] got the hell beat out of me."[34]

Although Annapolis was probably no more antisemitic than the rest of US society, a clearly antisemitic prank directed at one of Rickover's classmates spilled beyond the Yard. Leonard Kaplan, one of Rickover's few Jewish classmates still "surviving" after four years, was vying for the 1922 class's top rank, an enduring title in a Navy career. However, he rose to the top through hard study, behavior that most midshipmen condemned as "cutthroat."[35] Jerry Olmsted, Kaplan's principal rival for the number-one spot, also happened to edit the school yearbook, *The Lucky Bag*. Student photos and biographies appeared in the yearbook, two per page. To twist the nose of his rival, Olmsted put Kaplan's picture and biography alone on a page next to an obviously antisemitic and slovenly caricature, nicknamed "Porky." Kaplan's biography listed him as "Educated in the Convent of Zion . . . [and] Zion City Collech." His activities included "Coventry" for all four years in Annapolis, and the biography mocked "the mental effort or coercive force to bone [study] out of hours." The unnumbered page was perforated for easy removal; the index did not list Kaplan's name at all. Once his page was removed, his four years of Coventry in the Navy Academy would last forever, at least in the book of

Annapolis memories. When word got out about the incident, newspapers around the country ran stories about it, eventually bringing down a formal reprimand from Acting Secretary of the Navy Theodore Roosevelt Jr.[36] But Olmsted still graduated number one.

In later years, some people came to believe that Rickover, not Kaplan, was the target of the ugly prank, but his more typical picture and biography exude none of this venom. Rickover's *Lucky Bag* write-up pointedly noted his striving "to bring himself up to the plane of a worth-while and credit-bestowing profession" and his unwillingness to "smile" at Academy humor. However, the biography acknowledged both his "loom[ing] large" in the classroom and "his favorite pastime of helping the other fellow."[37] Rickover never felt that being a Jew affected his grades or classroom experience, but even sixty years later, he condemned his mistreatment by other middies, "because," he told an interviewer, "I was Jewish." Out of the original seventeen, only Rickover and six of his Jewish classmates would survive their four years in Annapolis.

Through his time there, his grades improved every year. He performed particularly well in his English classes and stood solidly in math and science courses, though he demonstrated no special gifts. But he studied and read incessantly. In the end, he finished a more-than-respectable 107th in the largest class to graduate the Academy up to that time, 540 officers.

But Rickover loathed what he later derided as a "lousy boy's school." He reviled the "juvenile rituals" that constituted the life force of the Academy—marshaling companies and drilling on the Yard, displaying martial bearing, playing football or leading cheers, demonstrating social graces, and exuding a pleasingly virile personality. Rickover seemed largely devoid of the stuff Annapolis prized in an officer.

Admiral James Holloway Jr., who graduated the Academy three years before Rickover did and later served as its superintendent, thought Rickover's Annapolis experience fed into his famously combative personality. He said, "Rick had his heart on his sleeve a long time because, [as] a little Jew in the Naval Academy, [he] probably got kicked all over the place, and he had to be over-aggressive to overcome it, which he was."[38] Rickover never forgave his fellow middies. Well over age eighty, he recalled, "When I had high rank in the Navy, one or two of those—I was going to use the word bastard—came around and asked me for favors for them, those who had treated me that way. I wouldn't do it."[39]

Rickover never lost that spite—whatever success he had in the service—and it proved an enduring motivation. It was the first of many chips on his shoulder, and he would use it to build an unparalleled Navy career. But his struggles to make his way were just beginning.

2

$\blacklozenge\!\cdot\!\blacklozenge\!\cdot\!\blacklozenge$

Mastering Power

RICKOVER'S GRADUATING CLASS rank was high enough to win him the billet he requested, destroyer duty in the Pacific. After a period at home in Chicago, in September 1922 Rickover reported to the destroyer *La Vallette*, homeported as part of the Battle Fleet (predecessor to the Pacific Fleet) in San Diego. Freed from the "juvenile rituals" he had loathed over the preceding four years, he took immediately to shipboard life.

An advanced power plant sent the sleek greyhound, one of the latest four-stackers in the fleet, speeding over the ocean. Rickover quickly discovered a fascination with the inner workings of the ship. He spent every spare minute below deck, charting out the web of machinery, cables, and piping that ran from there throughout the ship. They became something akin to what poetry had been for the schoolboy Rickover. Rather than simply read blueprints for the ship, he spent hours in its hot, cramped bowels deciphering what pipe and wire ran where and drawing and memorizing the tangled skein. Taking notice of his interest, the ship's commanding officer designated him engineering officer after just six months. At age twenty-three, he became the youngest ensign in the Pacific squadron in charge of a destroyer's engine room and its thirty-six-man "black gang" (a holdover term from the coal-fired era, when coal grime coated the boiler crew) who kept the fiery machine running. The black gang almost immediately tried to put one over on the young officer.

La Vallette was slated to join a fleet exercise shortly after Rickover took engineering command. Hours before the ship was to leave port, the chief machinist mate reported to him that a steam condenser tube had cracked and would need replacing. *La Vallette* would have to stick at the pier until the part could be found and the repairs made. Sitting down to lunch in the officers' wardroom, Rickover suddenly realized that the entire black gang had gone out drinking the night before. He rushed below to scrutinize the "crack." Somebody had etched a pencil line on the tube. The enlisted men wanted to keep the ship in port long enough to sleep off their hangovers. Rickover rang up the bridge: the ship could get under way immediately. He turned his fury on the bleary-eyed black gang. After that incident, he would never again accept deficiencies identified in inspection reports without personally verifying conditions.

Navy officer assignments typically lasted a year to a year and a half. Following a lengthy hospitalization for a hernia and time away to attend a torpedo-school course, Rickover rotated to the battleship *Nevada* in October 1925. The twenty-five-year-old ensign was soon put in charge of the ship's electrical systems. When the Navy offered a replacement control system for the aging battleship's guns but no budget to install it, Rickover volunteered to take on the project.[1] He later acknowledged his "brashness" in trying to rewire five hundred telephones and multiple switchboards from mast-top spotting posts to the bridge through plotting and magazine rooms to firing stations. The work overwhelmed his small crew. With the *Nevada* set to leave port, it looked like she would not have working guns. The shipyard's electric-shop foreman, a civilian, appreciated the young officer's tireless work. He offered his skilled crew's help. *Nevada* set sail on time, with a new fire-control system. And Rickover witnessed the power that civilian chiefs exercised in shipyards, a power that, in later years, he always made sure to keep under his own control.

At sea, Rickover made no attempt to hide his indifference to naval etiquette, rank, and the company of fellow officers. He often retold the story of having been ordered to attend a reception for a visiting admiral on another battleship. Rickover came aboard, saluted the admiral, and walked across the deck and down a gangway to where he had arranged a launch to meet him.

Despite his unorthodox attitude toward rank and lack of interest in socializing with other officers, his commanding officers gave him high marks. As the *Nevada*'s captain wrote, despite "having no outward signs of qualities of leadership," Rickover got results.

Rickover wanted a deeper technical education. On July 1, 1927, he reported back to the Naval Academy for a year's coursework on advanced engineering fundamentals. In Annapolis, he studied in his usual monomaniacal fashion, devouring math and science textbooks and memorizing formulas and theorems. Before the end of June 1928, he completed his coursework and learned that he had been promoted to lieutenant.

From Annapolis, he went to Columbia University in New York City for a year's graduate study in electrical engineering. The experience would change his life—in many determinative ways. Most of the forty-one naval officers studying at Columbia lived off campus, but Rickover chose to room in Columbia's International House, a residential hall at 500 Riverside Drive housing several hundred students, three-quarters from foreign countries.[2] The multicultural and intellectual atmosphere there, he told his authorized biographer Francis Duncan, "suited him perfectly."[3] So did the year of study in a great liberal arts university. First, though, he had to unlearn the Navy's way of education.

One of Rickover's favorite Columbia engineering professors, Charles Lucke, a noted thermodynamics expert and authority on combustion engines and a World War I Navy veteran, criticized Navy officers taking his courses for being "an aggregation of photographic memorizers" who failed to grasp the significance of what they studied.[4] Lucke got through to Rickover. Over the year, he began to understand that scientific principles comprised more than a preset kit of facts and formulas. He learned how to apply theories, prove a hypothesis, and experiment to solve technical problems. Rickover became a creative engineer at Columbia.

While there, he also marinated in the so-called Technocracy Movement, a loosely knit circle of like-minded academics centered in New York City, among them several engineering professors whom Rickover encountered at Columbia. They championed the idea that Machine Age society needed to adapt to the rigors of new and ever-more-complex technologies. And technocrats would lead the way. They asserted that, as Rickover wrote many years later, "the men who can handle the intricate mysteries of complex scientific and engineering projects" should maintain "professional independence," remaining free to control advancing and sometimes dangerous technologies as "a safeguard for [their] employers and the general public," who could not comprehend such mysteries.[5] The technocrats should form a priestly caste in the modern world. The movement's adherents criticized corporate executives' conspicuous displays of consumption and advocated eliminating waste and inefficiency.

The Technocracy Movement's guiding ideas resonated with Rickover. He saw US affluence as the country's downfall, encouraging laziness, reliance on misunderstood technologies, and improvident waste of resources. A few years later, in the depths of the Great Depression, he wrote that the economic misery would serve as a sort of tempering fire that he hoped would "continue . . . a little longer": "We shall have a fine country if it does."[6] He lived an ascetic lifestyle at home and work, convinced that comfort bred complacency. When traveling on government business in later decades, he stayed in associates' homes or bunked in shared naval quarters rather than spend taxpayer money on a hotel room. He refused to buy better furnishings or replace broken flooring in his Navy office. He thought luxuries would encourage laziness among staffers. He openly criticized the big shots inside and out of government for their slack and spendthrift ways.

After his year at Columbia, he was ready to make use of his engineering degree in the Navy and to think about the wider implications of the philosophy he had imbibed. And he was in love.

Shortly after arriving at Columbia, Rickover spied an evidently bright and urbane woman, pretty, with dark-brown hair, talking in an outspoken manner with a light German accent at an International House colloquium. He made sure to meet her. Three years younger than Rickover and two inches taller, Ruth Masters was born in Washington, DC, of socially prominent German-immigrant parents. After their early deaths in a car accident, relatives raised her in a German town near the border with France. During World War I, she could hear artillery fire from the Western Front and saw the wounded being carried from the trenches. Horrified by the experience, she came to

Columbia to study international law in hopes of promoting peace and order among nations. "She was the smartest person I ever met," Rickover would later tell their son.[7] He was smitten. At first she was unsure of what to make of the Navy officer, but he won her over.

The otherwise deeply private Rickover opened his heart to Ruth. In a letter written a year after they met, he shared insights into his uncompromising nature. In a world where success "is in great measure due to 'self-advertising,' etc.," he told her, "I cannot create false impressions, even in small matters. . . . These many years I have refused to conform, combating continually the natural tendency to become engulfed in the ordinary."[8] Rickover assured her that he valued those same qualities in her: "I respect and admire your independence and your integrity. I shall never encroach upon these."[9] He proposed to her a working partnership in marriage, with a vision she appreciated: "to combine your work with my work."[10]

His work, though, required extended separations. With surface-ship command opportunities fallen sharply in the postwar Navy and few friends who could help him, Rickover transferred to submarine service, where, he expected, chances for winning a command were higher. Also, submarine school in New London, Connecticut, and the Navy's main sub-base in nearby Groton were a manageable train ride to visit Ruth in New York City. After finishing his master's program in spring 1929, he attended sub school and, on June 21, 1930, went aboard the S-48, a diesel sub. He soon moved up to XO, executive officer, S-48's number two. Any other sub officer could have told him that this was a misbegotten billet.

The chief engineer of the badly designed S-48, William D. Irvin, later a rear admiral, said that the boat "had a faculty for getting into trouble every day of the week. Everything that could go wrong went wrong."[11] With Rickover aboard, first came fire: subs at the time ran underwater on a mattress-size pair of batteries. Much like a car battery, if improperly charged, they oozed sulfuric acid, gave off toxic fumes, and too frequently caught fire, a source of terror for the crew screwed down tight inside the hull. While on a training run off New London on the evening of September 15, 1930, black smoke billowed out of the battery compartment. The captain ordered everyone topside and the boat sealed; they prepared to abandon ship. But Rickover took it upon himself to inspect the "cans." Donning a gas mask, he descended into the smoke-filled battery compartment. Struggling to breathe, he found that the batteries were not damaged but had set deck boards on fire. He put out the fire.[12]

Then came water: several times the vessel listed badly and suddenly before diving. Finally, after nearly failing to pull out of what Rickover called a "scary" dive, frightened officers drafted a joint letter asking the Navy to withdraw S-48 from operations. Rickover would not sign it. He wrote to Ruth afterward that he felt, "if we are assigned a duty to perform, it is up to us to accomplish it, no matter how much extra effort, lack of sleep, etc., it may involve."[13]

The S-48 was dispatched to the Navy's Panama Canal base at Coco Solo to patrol the canal's Pacific side. When a sailor fell overboard and started to drown, Rickover dove in to rescue him. The secretary of the Navy awarded him a special commendation for heroism.[14] S-48 sailed on.

Not only was "pigboat" duty dangerous, but in the tropics, the hot, rank, stale air made breathing difficult; relentless drops of condensation fell everywhere; quarters were mildewed and beyond cramped. He wrote Ruth, "I hope that never again in my naval service will I ever be subject to conditions such as these."[15] When he had the opportunity two decades later, he made sure that seagoing accommodations were far better for submariners.

Between poor living conditions and dangerous equipment,

life on S-48 grew tense. He complained about the dullness of the officers, carping to Ruth that "a philosophical thought never enter[ed]" their "heads."[16] Chief engineer Irvin recalled that Rickover and the skipper "would argue and argue and argue all day long" about the boat's many problems. Irvin and Rickover also fought, but Irvin acknowledged that Rickover "turned out invariably to be right."[17] According to a submarine officer of the period, Captain Edward L. Beach, "[Rickover's] crew . . . hated him . . . [and] would rather be anywhere else than under him." Beach wrote that Rickover "was a despot who could never be satisfied." Fair or not, the Navy's tight-knit submarine community, wrote Beach, "wanted no part of him."[18] At the end of Rickover's S-48 tour, he was "surfaced," sent to a shore billet, a singular snub for a submariner. With no chance for a regular command, Rickover and the Navy came up with another plan for his future.

In March 1933, Rickover read newspaper reports about academic research under way "to obtain sub-atomic energy." He worried that breaking the atom's nucleus apart might prove, he wrote Ruth, a "Pandora's Box; where a great deal of misery was let loose by learning too much." He never lost this fear.[19]

Ruth visited Rickover at Coco Solo, and they toured around Panama. She returned to Columbia and, after a stint at the Sorbonne in Paris, became the first woman to earn a doctorate in her field. Finally, on October 8, 1931, the couple married in a simple church ceremony in the historic Connecticut town of Litchfield. Rickover's interfaith marriage was a blow to his Orthodox parents. He saw his family rarely after this. They would never meet Ruth or their grandson, Robert. During a visit with them two years after his wedding, Rickover wrote Ruth, "I have outgrown much that is here—and I feel a great deal out of place."[20] Reflecting three years later on growing antisemitism at home and in Germany, where the Nazis were seizing absolute power, he told Ruth that many Polish Jews "are a rather poor type." He thought that "the impact of 20th century progress upon an alien medieval people" made them perpetual outsiders, seemingly blaming lack of Jewish assimilation for the hatred aimed at them.[21]

Despite his estrangement, Rickover felt filial devotion. During his parents' struggles to stay afloat in the Great Depression, he took out a personal loan and sent them money to keep them from losing their home. Later Rickover pointed proudly to his father's continuing to work as a tailor, despite having achieved a measure of financial comfort, almost up to the day of his death at age eighty-five in 1960. Eight years later, Rickover's mother, ninety-one, died. He traveled alone to their Chicago funerals.[22]

Although Rickover was no longer a practicing Jew, biographers and others have mistakenly asserted that he converted and "considered himself an Episcopalian" for the rest of his life. Their mistake is understandable; even their only child, Robert, thought his father had converted—though neither his father nor his mother, he insisted, "was remotely interested in Episcopalianism."[23] They sent him to a Presbyterian church for confirmation, which they considered "a social thing," and he recalled that the ceremony was the only time his father came to church.[24] Although Hyman Rickover often spoke about a person's need for faith and drew on a wide range of Jewish, Christian, and other religious texts in his writings and speeches, he never publicly proclaimed adherence to any religion. But he read steadily on Judaism and Jewish life and donated all the money he made from his books and speeches to a Chicago Jewish orphanage. Eleonore Rickover, the devout Catholic whom he married after Ruth's death, insisted that he always remained a Jew.[25]

* * *

Ruth and Hyman's marriage proved conventional only in that she soon abandoned most of her professional ambitions for the sake of her husband's peripatetic career. In a service in which families were regularly uprooted and found community and social support among other service families, neither husband nor wife socialized with fellow Navy officers and their wives. Other naval couples, recalled Robert, were "the last people they'd want to hang out with."[26] Instead, during the early years of their marriage, they read, collaborated on academic research projects, and, when she could travel to his postings, explored exotic back roads and towns together.

He helped where he could in turning her dissertation into a book on the application of international law in national courts, one of the first works of its kind. Her hand is obvious in his article about the impact of submarines on international sea law that ran in the Navy's most prestigious journal, *Proceedings*, in 1935. She also helped him translate a major German treatise on First World War submarine warfare, published by the Naval War College in July 1936.[27]

However, Ruth quickly accepted that her career must suffer for the sake of Hyman's, telling him, "It is more important to be happy than [for me] to save or to have a career."[28]

With Rickover thwarted in his ambitions to command his own sub, he accepted orders in July 1933 to transfer to the Philadelphia Navy Yard, where he inspected materials procured from private industry for submarines. In the interwar period, the work might have been a dead end, except that as part of President Franklin D. Roosevelt's capital construction programs for exiting the Great Depression, the Navy started work on four new subs. Rickover's experiences with poorly engineered batteries aboard S-48 led him to advise private manufacturers on design improvements that reduced battery weight while increasing power.

On April 13, 1935, Rickover rotated to another battleship, the *New Mexico*, as assistant engineering officer. The ship's young and less experienced chief engineer was happy to hand off much of his authority to the thirty-five-year-old Rickover.[29] Rickover now oversaw some 280 men, spread across multiple below-deck divisions. As an early step, he set up something of an engineering school for ensigns fresh out of the Naval Academy, turning their first posting into a practical classroom—a practice he would make permanent at Naval Reactors. He knew already that getting the right personnel would help determine the engineering department's success. He carefully went through the lists of fresh ensigns prior to their arrival and made sure to interview those with the highest marks and class standing; he had the ones he wanted assigned to engineering. He institutionalized this rigorous selection process more than a decade later at Naval Reactors.[30]

As he had done for himself aboard his previous ships, he locked away the engineering blueprints and required each ensign to draw out his division's layout and learn it by heart. He tested them, including how their systems affected all the others on the ship. He had them "working like the devil trying to learn," he wrote Ruth. He then took the unheard-of step on a battleship: he gave the "georges" responsibility for crucial shipboard systems. Word soon got around about this taskmaster who pushed his men to the limits of their endurance. But Rickover also heard that behind the scenes many of the new ensigns were "trying to get into the Engineer Department because they realize that instead of treating them like school boys (as they are frequently treated elsewhere on the ship) I give them responsible duties to perform."[31] He learned that the best officers, the ones he wanted, craved responsibility, and the more responsibility entrusted to them, the more willing they were to work the long hours necessary to achieve high standards. Such experiences, he said, convinced him that responsibility bred performance and that "where responsibility ends, performance ends also."[32] Those who worked for Rickover never doubted that they would be held personally accountable for their performance.

At the time, oil fired virtually every shipboard system — from propulsion to heat and hot water, electricity for lights, gunnery control, and freshwater evaporators. The more oil a ship used, the more frequently it needed to slow to refuel from an oiler or go to shore to refill its fuel bunkers, which, in a crisis or conflict, would reduce its all-important tactical mobility. Thus, oil consumption was the primary yardstick for measuring a ship's efficiency, operational readiness, and rankings in the fleet's engineering race for a coveted red E emblazoned on a ship's stack. When Rickover stepped aboard, *New Mexico* stood in eighth place out of fifteen battleships' engineering departments. That *had* to change. Rickover's zealotry for reducing oil burned on the ship soon sparked tales repeated around the fleet. In the process, Rickover discovered that engineering held, in effect, almost unbreakable power to push *all* officers and men — no matter their rank — to their limits.

He removed lightbulbs until, he told Ruth, the ship was "as dark as hell," even in port. He found valves that reduced water pressure until shower and sink faucets at full blast produced only a trickle. He shut off half the radiators and then inspected quarters to find shivering sailors and officers who dared turn them back on, even chewing out the ship's captain for turning up the heat in his stateroom. When a visiting admiral and his staff came to a meal in the wardroom in heavy coats and scarves to protest the lack of heat, Rickover refused to relent.

Rickover dedicated "every waking moment" to his job, almost never taking shore liberty, recalled an ensign from the ship. *New Mexico* won that *E*, and it stayed there throughout Rickover's tour.

In March 1937, Rickover finally got his command when he was promoted to lieutenant commander. Hearing the news, he "swore terribly," his wife reported. With his rank, seniority, and success aboard *New Mexico*, he expected better. What he got was the USS *Finch*. The twenty-year-old, antiquated mine-sweeper was presently being used to tow targets for gunnery practice and haul freight off China's coast as part of the Navy's Asiatic Fleet. Rickover's first sighting of the *Finch* on July 17 in Tsingtao (Qingdao) harbor was truly disheartening. Rust flaked off its decks, and the hull had holes; garbage floated in the bilge. Its sun-addled crew showed complete indifference to their ship's sorry state. When Rickover headed to sea for the first time at the helm, its engines broke down. Rickover intended more out of the *Finch* and set his crew to work refurbishing it. However, the sailors bristled under the new skipper's heavy hand; they hated the long hours under the scorching summer sun scraping rust and painting the iron decks and hull so much that someone daubed "madhouse" in red undercoat paint on the hull.[33] The work had not progressed far when orders came for the ship to go into action.

In what proved to be the beginnings of World War II in Asia, Japanese forces had invaded China just ten days be-fore Rickover reported to *Finch*.[34] Fighting had now reached the outskirts of Shanghai, the great commercial metropo-lis. In August 1937, *Finch*, with its hull an unsightly mottled red and gray, steamed down the coast to Shanghai. Knowing about a fuel shortage there, Rickover loaded *Finch*'s decks with barrels of gasoline. That proved a dumb mistake. The initia-tive that Rickover thought would be welcomed, he lamented to Ruth, instead brought him a reprimand for coming alongside other Navy vessels carrying "liquid dynamite" that "a stray bullet might explode."[35] After the ship's dangerous cargo was thrown overboard, *Finch* ferried US Marines and Western officials and press in and civilians out of the city while shells flew overhead. A *Chicago Tribune* reporter wrote about the hometown captain's bravery under fire. "During the shelling," the story ran, "Lieut. Hyman G. Rickover of Chicago remained on the bridge to move the ship out of the danger zone." Rickover seemed to relish the danger: he blithely reported that "the Japanese displayed poor marksmanship."[36]

Despite his bravado, Rickover won few points for his brief time as a skipper. The gasoline incident and the ship's splotchy appearance went on his report. His imperious ways and antisocial character won him no Navy friends. He understood that the Navy would probably never give him the command that he felt was his due. His seagoing career dead-ended, he changed tracks. He transferred to Engineering Duty Only (EDO) status.

The Navy designated a small number of officers EDO—specialists in ship design, construction, maintenance, or repair. While prestigious, EDOs were not eligible for ship command, remaining on shore duty permanently, posting at naval yards, in laboratories, or in the Washington, DC, engineering bureaus.

For Rickover, being an EDO did not look much more promising than seagoing duty at first. In late October 1937, he moved to the Navy's only ship-repair yard in the western Pacific, at Cavite outside Manila. Rickover had not expected to stay there long, but the Navy delayed his anticipated move to the Bureau of Engineering in Washington, DC, several times, until August 1939. Rickover had little to keep him occupied. One plus was that Ruth joined him, giving the couple their first chance to set up a home. They also had time to travel.

They explored throughout Southeast Asia. "George," as Ruth called him, "brooded" over atlases. They ignored other

Westerners' advice to travel in colonial comfort, preferring, she explained, "by inclination and by reason of our limited financial resources," getting about by small boat, rickshaw, jitney, even water-buffalo cart and elephant back, while staying mostly in cheap hostels and eating street food. Wherever they went—bustling capitals, ruined ancient temple cities, sun-worn port towns, and almost unreachably remote, preindustrial tribal villages—Ruth recounted, "We talked with everyone—natives as well as resident whites." Westerners were so rare in some places that crowds gathered and stared at them. Ruth took it all in stride: "Compared to them," she recorded, "we whites are simply bundled up in clothes and so, of course, they are curious to see how we really look." As they crossed national borders, Hyman displayed "a constitutional inability to see eye to eye" with local officials, she found. In Japan, where war tensions kept the travelers under constant surveillance, Rickover could not resist making fun of the questionnaires they were asked to fill out at their stops. Ruth recalled what he wrote: "[that] our parents were infants when we were born [or that] they were in their nineties. Sometimes we claimed to have twenty children." Once, Rickover entered "Mohammedan" when filling out a hotel form. When the surprised clerk asked about it, Rickover "said in an offhand manner that quite a few American naval officers were converting to Islam since this was a virile religion, and, what with Japan arming herself and acting warlike, it behooved American service personnel to be prepared." Ruth found it all "nerve-wracking."[37]

After Hyman returned to Cavite, the adventurous Ruth continued for two more months solo, exploring throughout Southeast Asia while skirting war zones in China. In early spring 1939, she returned to the Philippines, and shortly after that, she headed off through Asia toward home. Rickover left Cavite in late May 1939 for his EDO post in Washington, DC. He traveled to Yunnan, the Chinese end of the Burma Road, and then continued by truck down the mountainous jungle route. Almost no Westerner had driven the tortuous 720 miles of mountainous road over which nearly all weapons sent to the Chinese forces in their war against Japan now traveled. He kept copious notes along the way; upon reaching Washington in mid-August, he typed up a single-spaced, sixteen-page report, among the first US military assessments of what proved a vital lifeline once the war with Japan began. Naval Intelligence planners sent word that they found Rickover's report very useful.[38]

Ruth stopped in Germany on her way to the United States for a visit with her adoptive mother. The women were together in Switzerland on September 1, 1939, the day Hitler invaded Poland and the Second World War began. Rickover was already at work in Washington when he heard the news, and he expected that the United States would soon be swept into war. It was a development that would reignite a naval career that had seemed on the verge of sputtering out.

The couple moved into a one-bedroom apartment at 4801 Connecticut Avenue in the Upper Northwest in Washington, DC, near Rock Creek Park, where they would remain for more than thirty years. They kept the place spartan, displaying items collected from their travels and little decoration other than shelves of books. Reading materials gathered in piles throughout their home. Both read constantly and widely. He regularly clipped and marked articles and other documents, often having nothing to do with naval or engineering matters, for distribution to his office staff and family. He filled scores of notebooks with writings of his own. Many items would find their way into his public speeches and testimony to Congress in the decades to come. A few years after the birth of their son, Robert, in 1940, they acquired a small upstairs apartment to serve as his bedroom. Until he left for college, they never owned a television set. The couple rarely entertained except occasional dinners with a small circle of friends, drawn almost exclusively from the civilians they knew. Although Rickover was often away, Ruth interacted little with her neighbors. A building resident, a congressman, remarked of her, "I guess you could call her a hard person to get to know."[39]

For about a decade, Ruth worked as an in-house legal scholar for the Carnegie Endowment for International Peace. Under her maiden name, in 1945 the Carnegie Endowment published her *Handbook of International Organizations in the Americas;* other work she did for the Carnegie Endowment provided part of the legal foundations in establishing the World Health Organization.[40] Rickover often traveled for work, sometimes for weeks on end, but when at home, as Robert grew, he and his father went for long walks through Rock Creek Park on Sundays before dinner. Robert recalled talking as they strolled "about pretty much any topic, current events, ideas, things we had read."[41]

Rickover started work at the Electrical Section on August 15, 1939, inside Main Navy, the massive World War I–era complex that served as headquarters for the high command. The drab three- and four-story wings of the unadorned masonry-and-glass complex covered much of what is now the Washington Mall. Main Navy stretched along the Reflecting Pool in front of the Lincoln Memorial and stood next to the identical War Department Munitions Building. Together they extended a third of a mile along B Street, today's Constitution Avenue.

A little less than a year after Rickover's arrival, the Bureau of Engineering merged with the Bureau of Construction and Repair to form the Bureau of Ships, often shortened as BuShips, headquarters for construction and repair of what would become a globe-straddling fleet in World War II. In wartime, BuShips grew to twenty-five hundred naval officers and enlisted men and employed thirty-eight hundred civilians who together oversaw hundreds of labs, 465 shipyards, and thousands upon thousands of industrial suppliers, with close to four million of their own employees. Wartime BuShips was responsible for design, procurement, construction, maintenance, and repair for 110,000 vessels, from amphibious landing craft and submarines to behemoth battleships and carriers.[42] And every ship electrical system—power, illumination, wiring, circuitry, communication, sonar, radar when it developed for ships, and other equipment—ran through the Electrical Section, BuShips' largest division.

Rickover arrived as BuShips' assistant chief. The headstrong engineer caused trouble at Main Navy from the outset. Shortly after arriving, he learned about the warring Royal Navy's outboard cable system that minesweepers used to deliver an electromagnetic pulse able to detonate floating magnetic mines at a safe distance. He believed that the system would protect ships far better and take up less onboard room than the US Navy's existing inboard degaussing (demagnetizing) system designed to keep ships from attracting and triggering magnetic mines. He acquired a splice of the patented British cable and reverse-engineered it to construct a Navy prototype. Despite lacking any authority to award a contract, he sidestepped normal procurement procedures and offered General Electric executives $12 million to produce high-voltage generators for the new minesweeping system as a priority order. The company balked, concerned about possible infringement on the British patent and Rickover's lack of a standard purchasing order. Rickover threatened the executives, "If you don't get to work on it, we will have to find ways to force you to do it." They went to work. When BuShips' alarmed procurement officers learned about the order, they ran to BuShips' chief with their concerns over Rickover's sidestepping procedures. Rickover was put on notice; it looked like the end of his career. But when BuShips' shipbuilders learned about the minesweeping system, they realized how valuable it would be for protecting the scores of new vessels coming off the slipways. They immediately settled the contract. Before the end of the war, most US minesweepers had the system on board, undoubtedly saving countless lives. Instead of losing his job, Rickover won praise for his initiative.[43]

In December 1940, he finally got a worthy "command," becoming head of the Electrical Section when his boss moved to another post. A year later, the nation was at war. Two years after that, in June 1943, Rickover was promoted to captain, one rank below rear admiral. Nobody meeting him would know it; he almost never went in uniform to Main Navy. "Engineers work in overalls!" he once scolded a new staffer who came to his office in a suit.[44]

Rickover made immediate changes to the Electrical Section. He blamed "laxness during eras of peace" for the Navy's electrical systems, which were known to break down, short-circuit, and even catch fire when tossed about in storms and live-fire exercises. He also bemoaned the lack of trained personnel ready to join the fast-growing organization. He needed experienced engineers, but the standard rotation of officers "represented considerable loss of 'know-how' to the Section." He also thought "considerations of naval rank . . . hampered or prevented" putting more technically qualified individuals in positions of authority. By tradition, civilians did not boss Navy officers. To overcome these deficits, Rickover stepped out of the Navy from deep within it.[45]

Rickover gathered expertise wherever he found it, forcibly "borrowing" numerous engineers from industry. He instituted expertise as the primary basis for standing among personnel. When he joined, the section had about 25 staff members, who were, excluding clerical workers, mostly naval personnel. By the end of his time there in March 1945, the section had 18 naval officers and 219 civilian engineers, including younger college

47

graduates trained up in the section, along with 106 clerical personnel handling the mountainous paperwork involved in administering hundreds of millions of dollars in contracts—equal to many billions today.

Within a month of the December 7, 1941, attack on Pearl Harbor, the Navy had seven hundred new vessels of every description on order—eventually reaching tens of thousands—and each one required multiple electrical systems. Rickover's office oversaw design, procurement, and installation of tens of thousands of generators, heavy-duty batteries, and electric motors and hundreds of millions of feet of armored wire and cable running through hundreds of thousands of switchboards, relays, and circuit breakers, along with sundry millions of pieces of electrical equipment like interior lighting, even bulbs and flashlights.

He made wholesale changes in the section's organization. Prewar, section administrators oversaw phases in a ship's life cycle—design, procurement, installation, maintenance, and repair—and yet, according to Rickover, nobody held actual responsibility for getting the best, most effective equipment into boats and making sure that it did what it was designed for under war-fighting conditions and that, when damaged, it could easily be repaired or replaced. "It didn't make sense to me," Rickover said in later years. "I changed the system." He placed technically trained and experienced individuals in charge of systems and equipment from design to repair. He assigned general responsibility to individual division heads for every piece of electrical equipment going into surface boats and submarines, as well as for auxiliary vessels and some important specialty systems such as minesweeping and submarine batteries. Despite the press of building thousands of ships of all types, he kept technical design control in house and gave Electric Section personnel responsibility for their systems' performance in the field. Rickover said, "I made one man responsible for his entire area of equipment—for design, production, maintenance, and contracting. If anything went wrong, I knew exactly at whom to point."[46]

But as the Electrical Section grew, Rickover needed a way to maintain his own oversight, to identify and cut off problems before they erupted into crises down the line. He devised a system that would remain a hallmark of his management for the rest of his career. At the end of each day, the clerical staff collected pink-colored carbon copies of every page of correspondence, even drafts in process, along with internal memos, produced in the section. Known as the "pinks"—even when photocopiers came into use—Rickover took the copies home evenings and weekends to read. He penned notes, sometimes revising drafts and even correcting grammatical mistakes. The pinks gave him insight in detail throughout the entire organization and kept staffers on their toes. The next morning or not long after, he shared his comments on the pinks and flagged issues for further review.

The pinks also helped him to identify promising young engineers at lower echelons within the organization. He sent them out into the field to inspect contractor factory work, shipyards, and war-damaged vessels. Engineering sciences advanced at a breakneck pace in wartime, drawing lessons from battlefield experience and research laboratory advances, so he placed a premium on continuing education. For instance, he instituted a series of weekly lectures that all personnel, including clerks and secretaries, could attend. In this way, he found and developed the talents of several of the men—and later women—whom he would bring back to work with him in the future.

Rickover personally inspected as many battle-damaged ships as he could, including a stint in 1942 at Pearl Harbor, where he devised a faster method for rebuilding the saltwater-ruined electric motors from the *California*, one of the badly damaged battleships sitting partially submerged for months in the muddy seawater after the Japanese attack. Some observers said his work speeded up her return to the fighting fleet by as much as a year. He drew other insights from inspecting ships postcombat. Blast waves blew out electrical circuits, disabling ships even without a direct hit. Electrical equipment needed to meet far higher standards to survive high-powered modern explosives. The section developed two-thousand-pound test hammers to simulate explosions' effects on equipment. Early on, Rickover had an eight-inch shell fired into an eight-inch-thick armor plate with a Westinghouse switchboard mounted on the other side. After the switchboard flew apart, he ordered Westinghouse to reengineer one capable of withstanding the blast. Rickover even arranged for gear tests on board a destroyer at sea. Overruling the skipper's objections, Rickover ordered that the ship steam slowly over its own exploding depth charges to make sure its equipment never stopped working.[47] It was a risk he deemed worth taking. When contractor representatives brought in smaller components, Rickover sometimes hurled them against an office radiator to see if they broke. He handed back the shattered parts with a curse, promising to withhold payment until they could withstand field conditions.

The section covered big and small gear, even replacing standard incandescent bulbs, which blast waves shattered, with lower-energy, shatterproof fluorescent fixtures. At the section's urging, the Navy switched from prewar standard blue to red light for low-light operations, a color that was harder for an enemy to detect at night yet provided better visibility for sailors. All these changes saved lives, and the Navy knew it. Rickover's fitness report from the period lauded his accomplishments, concluding that he "made as great a contribution to the successful preparation for the carrying on the war as any officer of the Navy's Shore Establishment. The value of his contributions to the improvement of our ships is inestimable."[48]

Rickover's time in the Electrical Section also taught him lessons in getting his way within Main Navy. He identified champions for his program in the chief of naval operations' office, often spurning BuShips' chain of command. Despite dissenters within BuShips, he went directly to the CNO's office to procure letters approving his programs and budgets and dared BuShips' procurement officers or those in other sections whose budgets had been cut to fund his to fight him. Few did.

He also recognized that he could dictate to industrial contractors beholden to his section. Typically contracting companies received a list of items to be delivered, engineered the materials, and faced scrutiny only upon delivery. Rickover upended those practices by contracting for gear designed by the section and then dispatching inspectors—some of whom considered themselves "Rickover's spies"—to factories and shipyards to oversee the work in progress.[49] Some inspectors took up residence in the field—a practice he would make permanent in later years. Spotting problems, they immediately sought redress or reported back to Rickover any issue they could not resolve. Even with such interference in the contractors' business, he refused to excuse missed deadlines, failure to meet specifications, cost overruns, or faulty installations, and he had no misgivings about delaying other Navy projects if that was what it took to meet his demands. One of his civilian senior engineers, Chancy Whitney, said, "He was ruthless if he thought someone was trying to screw him or the Navy." By acting as what Rickover called "a tough customer," he believed he represented the Navy's and the nation's best interests, whatever the Navy or government might think. While at Main Navy, Rickover's lack of collegiality and indifference to social norms became legendary, and most other engineering officers took an intense dislike to him. "He'd rather arouse a guy by saying something nasty than make a friend," Whitney said. "He loved to make enemies."[50]

He had plenty of them, but he found his supporters, perhaps most importantly Rear Admiral Earle W. Mills, then assistant chief of BuShips, who considered him a uniquely effective engineering administrator. Rickover knew that those who had power trumped the complainers. His talent for currying favor from those who held real power would later become almost an art form. Mills protected Rickover when others were after him and called on him to handle thorny special projects—most significant, unsnarling major logistical breakdowns at the Navy's massive Mechanicsburg, Pennsylvania, supply depot. Tie-ups in locating parts among the millions of different pieces stockpiled there were causing serious delays in construction and repair at shipyards around the country. That was costing lives. By the time Rickover departed, he had cleaned out a veritable Augean stables, reducing order fulfillment that had previously taken months to days.[51] Mills would not forget what he did and postwar would play a key role in determining Rickover's future.

With the war moving toward its endgame, Rickover wanted to be part of the action and applied for transfer to a battle zone. He was dispatched in late March 1945 to the Pacific theater to plan, build, and operate the Navy ship-repair base site on Okinawa for the anticipated invasion of Japan. As Rickover prepared to head out for his new command, several company executives sent notes wishing him success. He tossed the letters away, hissing, "If I were on fire, they wouldn't piss on me."[52]

As soon as the Okinawa site was liberated, he dove into his new yard's construction. With "unlimited scope for my ideas," he wrote Ruth, the "days go by without my knowing it." The repair base would include piers, dry dock, industrial ways, shops, and depots, plus housing and support facilities for some five thousand men. On August 6, 1945, though, the atomic bomb fell on Hiroshima; three days later, a second bomb incinerated Nagasaki. Rickover wrote Ruth that day, "we are too busy to worry too much about it." Rickover's Okinawa tenure was marked as always by conflict. He had been handed a command with an existing staff of officers and engineers, and he told Ruth how poorly they measured up. "Most of the stories and articles of the great officers of the Pacific war," he wrote on November 18, "are a lot of rot if Okinawa is any example." Those veterans of the Pacific war complained about Rickover's domineering ways in planning and constructing the base. Without Mills, the repercussions mattered.[53]

As work progressed, Japan's surrender made Rickover's plans for the yard on Okinawa largely superfluous. The Navy reduced the port to the scale needed to support the occupation force. Even that was not to be. In late September and early October, two successive typhoons blew away Quonset huts, cranes, industrial sheds, construction materials, almost everything Rickover had built to date, sixty-nine structures in all. Just one building remained in a scene of total devastation. Rickover's repair base quickly returned to minimal inhabitability, but island residents were less fortunate. He was particularly appalled by conditions he saw at a leper colony, which had previously been mistakenly bombed by US forces and was now reduced to abject misery. Rickover dispatched food, medicine, clothing, a generator, and other supplies to improve conditions. He also took it upon himself to teach a class of island children.[54]

Rickover soon rotated out. The commander of the Navy's Okinawa operating base, Rickover's immediate superior, with whom he often clashed, wrote a fitness report rating him poorly in "Ability to command," "Use of ideas and suggestions of others," and other important leadership categories.[55] With that blot on his record, Rickover had little reason to hope for a flag-rank future in a far smaller postwar Navy.

World War II was over, and the US Navy had performed splendidly. In October 1945, the Navy sent massive flotillas on jubilant victory parades to multiple port cities on the West and East Coasts. Once the euphoria died down, though, the fading horizon for the Navy's national-security mission became obvious. Most wartime shipbuilding programs were halted; the active-duty fleet was reduced to 10 percent of its wartime size. Shore-duty engineers, including Rickover, were assigned the dreary task of mothballing thousands of ships, few of which would ever sail again. In December, Rickover left Okinawa for the West Coast to inspect the tedious, haphazard work going on in the shipyards laying up two thousand ships for the Nineteenth Fleet reserve.

What he witnessed infuriated him. One of the officers who encountered him there recalled that Rickover's anger boiled up at the sloppiness that predominated. He even complained about food waste. "Rickover peered in all the garbage cans," he said. "Boy, he was really caustic." On one ship, the captain joined Rickover on his final inspection tour. Deep in the bow, they looked down into the freshly painted bilge compartment. Rickover motioned. "Somebody give me a quarter." He tossed it down into the tank. White water splashed up around it. The tank had been painted without bothering to pump out the accumulated bilge water beforehand. Rickover "blistered" the captain's ear. "He wasn't just going to take it for granted," said one of those who admired Rickover after hearing stories about his inspections that went through the fleet; "he was going to see what the hell was going on." But, he recalled, Rickover's zealousness left "some people very upset."[56]

White-haired, forty-six years old, with a wife and young son at home, Rickover had no idea what would come next after this exasperating temporary duty. His postwar Navy career seemed to have run onto the rocks. After almost twenty-seven years in the service, he had made few friends and many enemies. The Navy, too, was caught up in a bitter battle over its future role in national defense. Rickover's naval career seemed rudderless. "What do I do with the rest of my life?" Rickover fretted to a colleague.[57]

3

The Two Hats

As a us-dominated postwar world unfolded, some Pentagon war planners raised an unavoidable question: What use was a navy in the Atomic Age? Just two airborne atomic bombs had driven Japan to surrender; the German rocket technology that had rained missiles down on London would surely carry atomic payloads before long; and then there were the jets that the soon-to-be independent US Air Force would one day fly. What seagoing defense could stop them? A few months after the war ended, a *New York Times* headline summarized the Navy's quandary: "Navy to Test Atom Bomb. Admirals Seek Answer to Query, Is the Fleet of Today Obsolete?" In the dawning age of aerial strategic and perhaps tactical atomic weapons, the Navy risked being beached.[1]

After the Navy fleet's port-to-port victory parade, Admiral Chester Nimitz, a former submarine operational commander, architect of US victory in the Battle of Midway, and wartime commander in chief of the Pacific Fleet, spoke at the October 5, 1945, victory celebration in Washington, DC. "The beginning of a new atomic age," he speculated, might prove to be the single most important outcome of the war. The military would have to rethink national security planning radically. "To stand guard against the possible scientific attack of the future," he said, "naval and military men . . . must be as familiar with technological research and development as they are with the use of weapons at sea and in the field."[2] A new type of officer, a warrior ready to fight at the frontiers of science and technology, would have to emerge.

Many observers, though, believed that the terrifying force bottled up inside the atom would sink the Navy. But that explosive energy hinted at a new concept of maritime power. Nimitz, soon named chief of naval operations, would help Rickover fulfill that as yet vaguely conceived possibility.

Scientists had long sought answers to the mysteries behind the vast storehouse of energy packed inside the atom's nucleus. Since the 1920s, physicists—among the most famous Niels Bohr, Werner Heisenberg, Enrico Fermi, Leo Szilard, and of course Albert Einstein—had experimented with and theorized about the results they observed after shooting protons and neutrons at various elements, especially naturally radioactive metals, above all uranium. Studies showed that when struck, uranium atoms emitted energy in the form of heat and radioactivity. Capturing this fire without smoke offered mind-boggling possibilities for energizing the world. One idea seemed especially alluring: atomic-powered ships. As early as 1924, the *New York Times* enthused that this "new and immeasurable source of energy" could be developed "to send the largest ocean liner across the Atlantic Ocean."[3] But great scientific mysteries remained.

Then, on January 26, 1939, the visiting Danish physicist Bohr announced a momentous discovery at a scientific gathering of some of the world's leading nuclear physicists in Washington, DC. In December, the Berlin laboratory of the nuclear chemist Otto Hahn had bombarded uranium with neutrons. Drawing on the theoretical explanation by the physicist Lise Meitner, Hahn's longtime collaborator, an Austrian Jew who had left Germany for Sweden, the experiment found that the neutrons split the heavy uranium nucleus, producing two lighter elements, barium and krypton. This creation of the two elements—fission, as the process was soon called—also shot out several additional neutrons and produced a measurable energy spike. Splitting just a single atomic nucleus of the unstable isotopic form of uranium could produce about two hundred million electron volts, enough to make a small pebble jump, about two to three million times the energy produced by burning a molecule of coal or oil. Given that just one gram of uranium held trillions and trillions of atoms, the findings suggested that nuclear fission held the potential to generate unimaginable amounts of energy.

The discovery of fission also indicated two radically world-altering possibilities: controlled nuclear fission that produced enough heat energy to drive ships and power electric utility stations; and explosively uncontrolled fission, an atomic bomb. Many questions resisted obvious answers, but the scientists on hand discussed scientific pathways for exploring both possibilities.[4] With war tensions rising in Europe, the Pandora's box that Rickover had feared six years earlier now opened before the conferees' eyes.

A month and a half later, on March 17, 1939, the previous year's Nobel laureate, Fermi, an Italian physicist who had moved to the United States in January, came to Main Navy, where he met with Ross Gunn, the chief physicist at the Naval Research Laboratory (NRL), and other Navy scientists. They discussed what nuclear fission might mean for the military.

Fermi talked mostly about an atom bomb, but the naval engineers on hand "immediately," wrote Gunn, wanted to know
whether controlled nuclear fission could provide "an answer
to the submarine propulsion problem." Theoretically a "fission
chamber" engineered to fit inside a submarine could boil up
steam, without the need for air, to power extended underwater
operations.[5]

An enthusiastic Gunn went right to work. Within two
weeks, the Navy allocated $1,500 for research, enough to get
started on the first US-government-funded fission study. That
was almost six months before two other European emigrants,
Einstein and Szilard, wrote their later famous August 2 letter to President Franklin D. Roosevelt urging him to build an
atom bomb before Nazi Germany did. By June 1, Gunn had
laid out the basic problems his team would have to solve to
engineer a practical "fission chamber." First steps included
producing U-235, the unstable isotopic form of uranium, to
power reactor studies. U-235 is typically present at a ratio of
just seven parts per thousand of the stable U-238 in raw uranium. A better method was needed to isolate U-235 than existing costly, slow chemical separation processes. Gunn and colleagues at the NRL settled instead on liquid thermal diffusion,
a newer method in which a column of steam heat surrounds
an inner column of purified uranium salts to force its U-235
out. Gunn shortly lured Philip Abelson, the young research
physicist who pioneered the method, to join the NRL. After
building a prototype at the Washington Navy Yard, Gunn and
Abelson designed a far larger plant with dozens of columns at
the Philadelphia Navy Yard, where they could draw on plentiful steam to power the process. The pair had their U-235 production plant up and running by 1944. Then the NRL fission
project crashed into a roadblock set up by the highest authority
in the land.[6]

* * *

After reading the Einstein-Szilard letter, Roosevelt eventually established a centralized Army command to commence atomic-bomb research. When the nation went to war, the Army cordoned off a top-secret zone in Oak Ridge, Tennessee, for its atomic-weapons development program. Known as the Manhattan Engineering District (Manhattan Project was the name for the overall A-bomb production effort), the site drew on Tennessee Valley Authority power plants for the massive amounts of electricity required for producing fissile material. The district quickly grew to 60,000 personnel (out of 130,000 total people working on the project at its peak). The Army wanted to keep tight control over knowledge coming out of the Manhattan Project and, despite the Navy's head start on separating U-235, barred NRL scientists from the district.[7]

In summer 1944, finding the Manhattan District's existing methods for producing fissionable material too slow, the Army muscled into the Philadelphia plant, from which it requisitioned the NRL's five thousand pounds in total of enriched and raw uranium. That added about 20 percent to the Manhattan District's existing total. District scientists also copied out the NRL's thermal-diffusion plant blueprints, which they used to throw up a sprawling plant of their own with hundreds of steam columns in Oak Ridge.

Gunn, embittered at the forced break in his program, later blamed interservice rivalries for the one-way flow of information and contended that the Manhattan Project had "prolonged the war by many months" by "miss[ing] no opportunity to scuttle the NRL program." While that is disputable, a postwar review found that the addition of the NRL's U-235 stockpile and its liquid-thermal-diffusion system to the Manhattan Project pushed up completion of the A-bombs by at least a week.[8]

* * *

After the war ended, Gunn hoped to restart the NRL's nuclear-propulsion program; the lab held a symposium on nuclear propulsion on November 19, 1945, focused on building a submarine power plant. On March 28, 1946, Abelson and two colleagues issued a wildly optimistic report that claimed that "only about two years would be required to put into operation an atomic-powered submarine."[9] Several people in the Navy, probably including Rickover, read the report, but in the postwar wind-down, nothing came of it. At the time, the Manhattan Project still held a monopoly on atomic research, and its focus remained on producing as much U-235 as possible for testing and stockpiling bombs before the Soviets got their own atomic weapons. Not long after that NRL report came out, Gunn and Abelson, finding little support for their nuclear-propulsion studies, abandoned the program.[10]

Meantime, the Navy faced a more pressing matter: its survival. Congress invested significantly in building A-bombs, creating the new Air Force, and bolstering Army ground forces along the hardening European East-West border. The Navy's budget seemed extraneous and faced outsized reductions. To shore up the Navy's atomic interests, the chief of naval operations made a halfhearted gesture, opening up a small office, the Atomic Defense Section, in a dark, back hallway at Main Navy. But even that office quickly became embroiled in the "Revolt of the Admirals," as the political brawl to win a share in strategic weapons development and deployment became known. The Navy ultimately lost that fight.

In a failing effort to keep up with the newly independent Air Force, the Navy spent much of its limited research and development budget demonstrating the practicality of carrying atomic bombs weighing several tons aboard aircraft carriers. Planners contended that in a war the monstrous weapons could be armed and loaded onto airplanes large enough to carry a bomb yet small enough to fly off a carrier deck. Given such a seagoing task force's vulnerability to air attack, the Navy found few backers. After a bitter interservice political mud fight, President Harry Truman gave the Air Force sole control of atomic-weapon delivery and strategic defense. In a world where the nation's likeliest potential enemies in future wars barely engaged in sea commerce and possessed navies that posed little threat to the United States or its allies, the Navy and its "command of the seas" mission were sinking.[11]

In 1946, the Navy asked the Army to let it send personnel to the Manhattan District "for a program leading to the powering of its ships by atomic energy." The War Department agreed that a small Navy contingent could look into experimental atomic-power-reactor work going on there. The Bureau of Ships selected a seven-member team to dispatch to Oak Ridge that summer. Rickover's name was not on the list.

Captain Albert Mumma was to oversee the Oak Ridge engineers. He loathed Rickover. An Engineering Duty Only officer, Mumma would later become chief of the Bureau of Ships and nominally Rickover's boss. Despite their many conflicts and long-standing rivalry, Mumma supported the nuclear Navy program, particularly for surface ships. Still, he called Rickover "a dolt" when compared to the engineers he had selected for the Oak Ridge team. In addition, he said that Rickover lacked "the management skills that are required to get the maximum out of people and to motivate people other than by fear."[12] His views were common among line officers and EDOs; also common was blindness to Rickover's ability to engage and inspire bright minds to achieve practical goals. In selecting a BuShips team for the Oak Ridge assignment, Mumma crossed Rickover's name off the list.

However, Admiral Earle W. Mills, now chief of BuShips, remembered Rickover's accomplishments in the Electrical Section and his effectiveness while on the special assignment un-snarling the Navy's Mechanicsburg supply depot. Mills had studied the possibilities of nuclear power for ships during the war and was eager to push ahead. He knew, however, that along with the tremendous scientific hurdles to be surmounted, po-litical and bureaucratic inertia would hold back anything so revolutionary as an entirely new form of ship propulsion. He considered Rickover an excellent engineer, but even more im-portant, he knew the man: his unpleasant temperament, mono-maniacal drive, hatred of bureaucrats, and fierce work ethic had smashed through some of the heaviest barriers in wartime. Over Mumma's objections, Mills put him on the Oak Ridge list.

While still inspecting the mothballed Nineteenth Fleet on the West Coast, Rickover received word that he was bound for Oak Ridge. At first he figured that the Navy had found some remote billet where he could be fenced away. He possessed only the most rudimentary knowledge of nuclear physics, knew next to nothing about the Manhattan District and experimental re-actor work going on there, and had few insights into the Navy's intentions. He wrote Ruth that he was headed for "some proj-ect connected with [nuclear energy], somewhere in the U.S.": "I don't know what that means."[13]

In assigning Rickover to the Oak Ridge Naval Group, as it was known, Mills conceded to Mumma that Rickover would not have charge over the other men, despite being the ranking offi-cer. They would instead report to an Army officer while there. That lasted just a day after Rickover set foot in the "Atomic City," the vast, fenced complex deep in the East Tennessee hills and woodlands.

Arriving in June 1946, he went to see the Army officer over the Naval Group. Rickover explained that since he held seniority among the men, he should be the one to prepare their fitness reports, their career-determining periodic evalua-tions. The Army officer did not mind handing off that personnel duty at all. When the Naval Group assembled for the first time, Rickover archly informed the others, despite their not reporting to him, "I just thought you might be interested to know that . . . [I] will prepare your fitness reports." They were working for Rickover, whatever the Navy might say. Gaining control over the Navy team at Oak Ridge, he told his biographer Francis Duncan, was a first small step that eventually brought him complete authority over naval nuclear propulsion.

He moved into a four-bedroom Oak Ridge house, which he arranged to share with several industrial engineers there to build an experimental reactor known as the Daniels Power Pile. The planned reactor was named for one of the men sharing the house with Rickover, project leader Farrington Daniels. As part of the Manhattan Project, Daniels had been on Enrico Fermi's group that had stacked graphite bricks into a spherical lattice "pile" layered with uranium beneath the University of Chicago's football-stadium bleachers. Lifting out control rods by rope pulley released the uranium neutrons, which started up a low-level, self-sustaining fission chain reaction. The crude pile lacked any coolant or shielding.[14] Strides had been made in reactor construction since, but Daniels's ambitions to build a functioning power reactor at Oak Ridge were doomed from the start. The project suffered from a minuscule budget, little support from the nuclear-astute bomb makers still at Oak Ridge, and few among the thirty or so engineers from academic labs and industry on hand beside Daniels having insights into how to build a practical fission reactor. That was not going to stop Rickover.

One of the team, John W. Simpson, recalled feeling "dismayed" when he drove up to the house where he was to stay. He saw Rickover standing on the porch. "Wherever Rickover was," he knew from personal experience, "things would be hectic." A fellow Naval Academy grad who had left the service and now worked for Westinghouse, Simpson had suffered many Rickover dressings-down while producing ship switchboards under contracts with the Electrical Section. Rickover, he said, was a man who "made Simon Legree look like a scoutmaster." Simpson suspected that Rickover already knew where he wanted to take the nuclear Navy even before arriving at the Manhattan District. Simpson and the other engineers in the house were integral to Rickover's plans. Besides Daniels and Simpson, the other housemates included Harry Stevens from General Electric and Sidney Simon, a young engineer from the National Advisory Committee for Aeronautics (NACA, precursor to NASA). All the men would help Rickover build the future nuclear Navy.[15]

Rickover intended to learn what he could from the scientists and engineers who worked on the breeder reactors producing atomic-bomb materials. However, none of the Manhattan District's atomic knowledge existed in an organized form for Rickover's team to study. "I have to figure out myself just what to study," he wrote Ruth.[16] He soon devised a training program for the Naval Group. Mumma had chosen highly educated naval engineers, including four who had attended the Navy's postgraduate engineering program at MIT: Louis Roddis Jr., James Dunford, Raymond Dick, and Miles Libbey. They would later join Rickover when he moved ahead with his nuclear-propulsion program.

Rickover assigned each man to take educational responsibility for different fields. They needed to learn as much as they could about engineering radiation shielding, developing metals for encasing fissile materials and the machinery controlling the chain reaction that could stand up to radioactive bombardment, identifying the most efficient coolant for heat transfer, and designing piping, components, motors, and controls appropriate for operating a reactor in a ship's tight quarters. Given how little was known about power-reactor fundamentals, their learning curve was steep. As went for everyone who worked for Rickover, hours were long. They attended lectures given by staff and visiting scientists, met with on-site experts, and taught each other while keeping a close eye on the Daniels Pile and other concept reactors. The Naval Group team members wrote up detailed reports about their specialty areas until they had compiled the first handbook ever devoted to atomic power reactors. Mumma expected those reports to come back to BuShips through him; Rickover, almost certainly intentionally, infuriated his titular commanding officer by sending them directly to Mills.

Rickover knew the limits of his knowledge and abilities. "His studies of technical matters were hard work," Dunford later said of him; "it didn't come particularly easily, so he asked questions and always took particular pains to surround himself with technically excellent people."[17] When Rickover introduced himself to the physicist Edward Teller, later known as "the father of the hydrogen bomb," he said, "I am Captain Rickover. I am stupid."[18] But he intended to "own" any future naval nuclear-propulsion program and worked with clear purpose. Rickover was not a scientific genius, but he understood what he needed to know and what he did not. He quit Simpson's evening lessons in advanced reactor physics because, he said, "I already know more than any of the company presidents or government officials I'll have to deal with." He did not want to waste time. Simpson thought he was right. In his assessment, "He was not a technical detail person." He was "a master politician and an expert at getting things done; at deciding which technical option to back."[19]

Rickover realized quickly that the Daniels Pile, which was still in the design stage, would have almost no practical implications for a naval ship.[20] A reactor consists of nuclear fuel in its core, through which a circulating liquid or gas moderator or coolant passes. That circulating coolant keeps the nuclear chain reaction from overheating and, heated up, then transfers heat energy to a separate, adjacent circulating nonradioactive water system. That water, boiled into steam, drives a turbine. Although nonexplosive, the helium-gas coolant system planned for the Daniels Pile looked difficult to contain in a sub and too inefficient to power a turbine large enough to propel a ship. But if not helium, the Navy Group needed to find the right coolant to use to moderate and transfer reactor heat within the tight confines of a submarine hull. Among the many coolant possibilities already being studied were various other gases, molten sodium, which the Argonne National Laboratory outside Chicago had begun to develop, and both heavy and light pressurized water — along with scores of other possible liquid metals such as mercury. Rickover thought demineralized ordinary water would prove simplest for cooling and heat transfer for a sub reactor; for unlike other potential coolants, if a reactor ran low on water at sea, more was right there. But nobody knew which of the two most advanced coolants being studied, molten sodium or pressurized water, would work; so Rickover, as he often did, opted to develop both to find out which worked best.

Among other frontier challenges the Naval Group faced was figuring out what metals to use in shielding crew members standing within a few feet of a sub reactor and the materials for encasing the radioactive uranium fuel inside the reactor. The shielding needed to ensure safety yet could not be so thick inside a seagoing hull as to become impossibly heavy or large. While at Oak Ridge, Rickover decided that unlike Army and Air Force weapons studies that sometimes subjected military personnel to high levels of radiation, the Navy reactor shielding should prevent exposure of its ships' crews to radiation beyond normal safe civilian limits. That would increase the weight and bulk needed to shield a reactor, but his unbending concerns for safe operation — tied to the need to send naval vessels into urban ports, public fears of radiation, and his certainty that the brightest young officers would not serve if they worried about radiation sickness—proved foundational for the program's future public support.

Watching the struggles encountered by the Daniels Pile program engineers, Rickover was certain that the Navy needed its own dedicated reactor program. He wanted a practical reactor, not another research program. He watched the small, underfunded effort flounder and was not surprised when, a year later, the newly constituted civilian Atomic Energy Commission (AEC) shut the program down. The bomb physicist and AEC and Department of Defense adviser J. Robert Oppenheimer grumbled, "It seems as though every reactor is always two years off." But that failure opened the door for Rickover and his naval reactor. A disappointed Farrington Daniels watched as Rickover convinced Oak Ridge to convert the Daniels reactor program to a submarine reactor project. Daniels acknowledged that Rickover "saw the power vacuum, sailed in with the Navy, and went off with the atomic submarine."[21]

Even if the science remained inconclusive, Rickover wanted a submarine powered by a reactor. He believed broader awareness of the Naval Group's project would generate more support for its efforts. Starting New Year's Day 1947, the AEC would open its doors. It would oversee everything about the atom, from gathering raw uranium and refining it into bomb material to research on atomic-technology applications. On Capitol Hill, the new joint House-Senate Committee on Atomic Energy would oversee the AEC and its activities. As such, no branch of government or private company could go into the nuclear business alone, and the new AEC and its congressional overseers could help or hinder any Navy nuclear effort. For now, all the AEC's uranium production and attention were going toward amassing armaments and developing new types of bombs while stringing along small experimental energy projects. The Navy, fearful of losing out on the big budgets and missions, focused on winning a role in the strategic weapons programs.

However, a few visionaries saw potential in nuclear fission for changing the Navy's mission entirely. Among them was a bright young aide assigned to the Atomic Section, Captain Edward L. Beach, a much decorated World War II submarine commander who was, he later wrote, "convinced that [nuclear power for subs] was the wave of the future." He served as a conduit to CNO Nimitz for the man Beach called "this extraordinary but strange, disliked, difficult little Navy captain. . . . In a sense," he recalled, despite not being under Rickover's direct command, "I was one of 'Rickover's boys' from then on . . . and of course he used me, as he did everyone else he could."[22] Beach would, like many among the Navy's most ambitious and smart officers, circle around the bristly Rickover for the remainder of his career.

With Beach as an intermediary, Rickover argued that the Navy needed stronger advocacy for nuclear propulsion. In late November 1946, he had checked into the Naval Hospital in Bethesda, Maryland, for a hernia operation. In his monomaniacal way, he quickly ordered his scheduled surgery postponed, took over an office space near his hospital room, and brought secretaries out from BuShips and Roddis up from Oak Ridge to write a report on the Navy's outlook on nuclear propulsion. The Rickover and Roddis report asserted that a submarine nuclear power plant could be in operation in five to eight years and that nuclear engines could drive every class of ship within fifteen years. As the gurney rolled Rickover into the operating room in late December, he called out final edits to Roddis and charged him with getting the document into the hands of CNO Nimitz.

Thanks to Beach, Nimitz read the report on January 9, 1947.[23] Before World War II, Nimitz had overseen several submarine engineering advances including the US fleet's conversion from oil to diesel fuel. He understood that nuclear propulsion would overturn all existing submarine concepts—and probably much else in naval affairs. And he recognized in Rickover the character needed to have a realistic shot at carrying out that revolution. The next day, the CNO wrote a letter that endorsed the report's goal of designing and building "nuclear power plants for eventual installation in submarines to give unlimited submerged endurance at high speed." The report with the CNO's backing declared that "the atomic submarine is militarily desirable." Nimitz called on the Navy to "initiate action with view to prompt development, design, and construction of a nuclear-powered submarine."[24]

However, the Nimitz letter sat on his desk until the following December before being sent on to the secretary of the Navy, who would have to approve it and then transmit it to the secretary of defense. That was to become Nimitz's last official action as CNO.[25] Although he wanted a true submarine to become part of the future fleet, he knew that the Navy had no resources and no expertise outside the Naval Group at Oak Ridge. Despite the delay, once the memo went out, Rickover told a reporter, "That letter was my hunting license. Without it, *Nautilus* would have been just another of the dozens of worthwhile Navy projects that die of old age trying to get through channels."[26] Nimitz's most enduring legacy as CNO may well have been his last-hour endorsement of Rickover's nuclear-propulsion report.

Word of the Rickover-Roddis report when it finally appeared proved electrifying at Main Navy. Rickover and his group enjoyed a new reputation for their expertise and for pushing the Navy into an uncharted technical frontier. With the Navy in danger of becoming a military stepchild among the three service branches, some observers thought Rickover's idea offered a more hopeful future. Most of his fellow officers, though, scoffed at the patently crazy notion of sticking what they could conceive of only as an atomic bomb inside a submarine. Enraged that Rickover had once again circumvented the chain of command by sending the report directly to the CNO's office, Mumma confronted Rickover in the BuShips mess hall. Scuttlebutt about their ugly shouting match flew from office to office along the long corridors of Main Navy.[27]

Pleased to have support at the highest levels of the Navy, Rickover nonetheless worried that this "sincere but cautious" interest in nuclear propulsion left nobody within BuShips or the CNO's offices—not Mills, not Nimitz, not Mumma, not even the Atomic Section—to make "prompt development" of nuclear propulsion a reality. With scant U-235 to be had, few atomic experts available, and wobbly political backing, costly investment in a nuclear-reactor program for submarine propulsion seemed a far stretch. Rickover went to General Electric's leading industrial atomic laboratory in West Milton outside Schenectady, New York, to learn about reactor engineering in progress. GE ran large AEC contracts for breeder reactors to produce weapons-grade nuclear material in Hanford, Washington, and had also begun preliminary studies together with Argonne's national laboratory on a small liquid-sodium reactor designed to produce more plutonium for bombs and, as a by-product, generate electricity. Rickover confirmed in West Milton that a submarine reactor problem he believed to be "95 percent engineering" remained a scientific research program that might never come to practical fruition.

He was convinced that getting a submarine reactor built depended on the Navy's willingness to make it a priority and win support among the commissioners at the new AEC. Through the summer of 1947, he continued the Naval Group's education. He led five members on a tour of every major atomic research and development facility in the country. They met with most of the leading authorities in the field, including Walter Zinn, Argonne's director; Glenn Seaborg and Ernest Livermore, leading scientists at the University of California's Berkeley Radiation Laboratory (later the Livermore National Laboratory); and Teller, at the Manhattan Project's Los Alamos lab, where he was now working on the hydrogen bomb. The scientists whom the Navy Group engineers met encouraged their reactor-program work but saw any future for it as foremost a political and not scientific question. Livermore told Rickover that to succeed they would need "real cash" behind the project—$100 million or more, an inconceivable sum at a time of naval budget cutbacks. That much would be necessary if he expected to attract scarce nuclear-engineering talent and convince industrial partners to invest in such a monumental undertaking. Zinn urged him to start by constructing a land prototype for a submarine thermal reactor. He had a personal interest in the work because Argonne was likely to win a contract to pilot the project. Rickover was skeptical of handing off any prototype work because he feared Argonne would focus on scientific and not practical results.

After meeting with the Naval Group, Teller wrote a letter to Lawrence Hafstad, then a Department of Defense research administrator and soon to become the AEC's first director of reactor development. He was, he wrote, "very much impressed" by the group's efforts. Teller told Hafstad that its "detailed, concrete and down-to-earth plan" was not being taken seriously enough; it deserved federal support.[28] But even the influential Teller's pleading fell on deaf ears.

By the end of that summer, the Naval Group's work seemed at a dead end. The Daniels Pile project at Oak Ridge was being abandoned, while the Navy's interest in nuclear-submarine technology barely registered within the new AEC. Even Mills appeared to give up. He finally broke up the Naval Group, scattering its members to other BuShips branches. He brought

Rickover back to Main Navy, where his rival Mumma still had overall charge of nuclear programs. Mills gave Rickover a meaningless post as assistant for nuclear propulsion—with no staff under his command. Rickover moved into an office befitting his downtrodden status: lost along one of Main Navy's endless corridors, he set up his office in a refurbished ladies' room. The wash basin remained in the wall, as did the plumbing fixtures for the toilets. "Well, you can see that I rate pretty high around the Bureau," Rickover told visitors.[29]

With the exception of Edward Beach in the CNO's Atomic Defense Section, "no one else . . . was doing anything at all," Beach observed.[30] A submarine veteran who later captained a nuclear sub, William R. Anderson, wrote, "What Rickover was proposing seemed impossible to nearly everyone at all levels of the Navy."[31] Rickover had once again been "surfaced." The possibility of a nuclear-propelled submarine seemed as remote as sending a rocket ship to the moon. But the relentless Rickover was not beaten.

Working from the BuShips' nether reaches, Rickover took what he called an "orthodontic approach," like pulling teeth, pursuing every channel to find a way to force nuclear propulsion onto the agenda. Much of his effort went into getting BuShips chief Mills to go before the distracted AEC to advocate the Navy's position. Early feelers showed that Oppenheimer, who now chaired the long-range atomic objectives panel for the Department of Defense and the AEC's General Advisory Committee, agreed that building a nuclear-sub reactor was a realistic goal. But he still believed that doing it remained at least ten years off. Rickover convinced Mills to go before the commissioners to demand more support for a naval reactor. After yet more hesitation, they finally agreed to budget funds for power-reactor research but only at the Manhattan District and Argonne National Laboratory. Rickover doubted those labs could overcome the practical engineering challenges he knew remained. He was convinced that only by issuing large-scale industrial contracts with set timelines would real progress get made.

He also faced competing submarine-technology priorities within BuShips. Many in the underwater-warfare branch favored shorter-horizon projects to improve diesel performance, such as adapting German World War II snorkeling technology to US boats. The projects siphoned off engineering budgets and personnel. Except for Mills's fitful embrace of the sub-reactor idea, the rest of the brass shrugged off an atomic submarine, which would be "a nice toy," one Navy official said, "but it will never be practical."[32]

And so the AEC's and Navy's distracted, skeptical, go-slow approach remained in force. But then the Cold War suddenly thrust Rickover's fanciful nuclear-submarine project into the Pentagon's and the nation's strategic forefront in a big way.[33]

At the end of March 1948, Soviet tanks cut off Berlin from West Germany and the rest of Western Europe, raising the possibility of armed clashes with the United States and its western European allies. Previously overlooked, the Soviets had also overleaped US control of the seas by deploying submarine snorkeling technologies using captured German technology, engineers, and subs. On June 16, 1948, Mills and Rickover met with the full membership of the AEC to promote nuclear propulsion as a counter to this new threat. The AEC still balked at the Navy's desire to move reactor development away from Argonne and Oak Ridge. Frustrated by the foot-dragging, Mills was finally convinced that he needed a ruthlessly single-minded, sharp-elbowed officer to promote nuclear propulsion. On July 16, he went all in: he designated Rickover as the Navy's liaison officer to the AEC for naval reactors in the agency's newly formed Division of Reactor Development. On August 4, he went a step further by creating a Nuclear Power branch within BuShips' research division, putting Rickover in charge. Mumma lost his nuclear role to Rickover. Over the course of less than a month, Rickover had stormed out of his former ladies' powder room to take complete charge of naval reactor development, a program that necessarily encompassed both the AEC and the Navy.[34]

Wearing his two brand-new hats, Rickover did not wait to receive his formal orders. He quickly drew in a staff of twenty from BuShips, including several of the engineers he had worked with at the Electrical Section, among them I. Harry Mandil, a Navy Reserve officer and engineer who would become one of his chief subordinates for decades to come, and most of the original seven members of the Oak Ridge Naval Group. He hired some of his staff through the AEC and others through the Navy, but all were part of his hybrid Navy-AEC group. It soon became known as simply "Naval Reactors." Rickover's shop took up quarters in offices on a long, drab corridor in a dilapidated wooden Navy building, known as Tempo 3, one of the "temporary" annex buildings thrown up during the war along the Reflecting Basin where the Vietnam War Memorial stands today. Enclosed walkways over the Reflecting Basin connected Tempo 3 to Main Navy. Rickover refused to refurbish NR's ripped linoleum floors, painted-over windows, inadequate air conditioning that did little to relieve the wilting summer heat, or its badly beaten-up furnishings. Contractors who came to see him understood that he would not tolerate their profiting excessively at taxpayers' expense. He also thought it helped make sure his staff focused on their jobs. When more than a decade later one of his aides asked to replace a broken desk and chair, he barked back, "Title on the door, rug on the floor, a good desk and chair, and the next thing you know you think you're a big shot and nothing gets done!"[35] Nobody could accuse him of wasting government money.

Separated from Main Navy and across B Street (today's Constitution Avenue) from the AEC's building, Rickover relished his newfound independence. He finally *owned* nuclear propulsion. But nuclear propulsion's future was based on theoretical possibility and stalled power-reactor research projects.

In late fall of 1948, the AEC finally consented to move forward with the power-reactor development program. It agreed to fund reactor development along two tracks, supporting the sodium reactor at General Electric's Knolls Atomic Power Laboratory in West Milton, New York, and a water-cooled program at the Argonne National Laboratory outside Chicago. The latter would move for engineering to Westinghouse's new Bettis Atomic Power Laboratory going up on the grounds of the former Bettis Airport outside Pittsburgh. The Atomic Energy Commissioners still did not believe nuclear propulsion was on the near-term horizon, expecting that the programs would lead first to a civilian electricity plant and even that only years or even decades later. But Rickover was determined to force Argonne, GE, and Westinghouse to make his program their top priority.

He traveled back and forth among the three main contractors, cajoling their leaders into making commitments to build a practical nuclear reactor for submarine propulsion within his demanding timelines. Zinn at Argonne dug in against making a submarine thermal reactor his laboratory's priority. He favored developing concept reactors for additional scientific study. His ringing arguments with Rickover echoed through Argonne's halls. With multiple large AEC contracts in hand and a powerful corporate parent, GE's lab leaders—even Harry Stevens, who had shared the Oak Ridge house with Rickover—bridled at his efforts to dictate the pace and focus at Knolls.

Rickover pinned most of his hope on Bettis. Not long after

the Naval Group had assembled at Oak Ridge, Rickover met with Westinghouse's CEO, Gwilym Price, hoping to win his support for engineering a submarine reactor. Believing the atom would eventually lead to creation of a valuable civilian power business, Price agreed to establish an Atomic Power Division with Rickover as its first customer. On December 10, 1948, the AEC and Westinghouse formally agreed to a $6 million contract to design and build a nuclear reactor for installation within an operating submarine "within the shortest practicable time." For Westinghouse, this foray into naval reactor development was a bold first step into the still nascent nuclear industry.[36] Unlike GE, which had several far-larger AEC contracts, Naval Reactors was Westinghouse's sole nuclear business. Rickover thus enjoyed almost total leverage over the company's new Atomic Power Division.

Price understood what he had taken on in putting a branch of his company under Rickover's thumb. He went all in on his bet that Rickover would get his nuclear submarine built and, in doing so, would light the way for the company to pursue a much larger future civilian power prize.[37] He designated Charles Weaver the new division's first director. A sharp young marketing executive with an engineering background, Weaver knew Rickover and his ways well, having worked on Electric Section contracts during the war. Price gave Weaver "carte blanche" to staff up Bettis with the company's top engineers. Among those on the original Bettis team was Rickover's Oak Ridge housemate John Simpson, who moved over to Bettis as an upper-level technical manager and would remain closely involved with Rickover. Bettis eventually hired thousands of workers to fill its fast-building AEC facilities. Rickover in turn sent his Navy engineers to Westinghouse to give a series of seventeen weekly nuclear-engineering lectures. Price and as many as forty-five other executives and engineers attended the course. The "atom school" caught the attention of the *New York Times*, which reported on the company course where Navy officers were "professors."[38]

Much of this activity took place before Rickover received his formal orders in February 1949 to report to the AEC's fledgling Division of Reactor Development as his principal naval duty while also heading BuShips' Nuclear Power Branch. Rickover was just an Engineering Duty Only captain of a small branch within a division of the massive Bureau of Ships, yet he had managed to gain sole command over the nation's major nonweapons reactor program. (The Army was also studying nuclear fuel for powering airplane jet engines, a program that would later establish a similar relationship with the AEC. Despite immense investment, no atomic jet ever got off the ground.) As the bridge between two masters and the force holding them apart, Rickover held a singular position of power, and he intended to exploit it to the fullest. He would exercise all his skills as a ruthless political infighter within the government and as a "tough customer" forcing contractors to do his bidding.

Playing the AEC and the Navy off each other, he could draw funds from their separate budgets. From his AEC post, he would literally write a letter requesting Navy support for a project and then answer himself on behalf of the Navy. "If the Navy doesn't like what we're doing," he told a Navy staffer, James Dunford, "we'll do it with our AEC hat."[39] Neither side could withhold information from him—while he could act on the basis of what he alone knew without the scrutiny of one or the other boss. When superiors within BuShips resisted his demands for project support, he pulled funds from his AEC budget and then insisted that the lagging Navy get on board or face public humiliation—and vice versa. "This wasn't just a possibility," Simpson witnessed. "It often happened."[40]

In pursuing something new and untried, on a tremendous scale—harnessing an entirely new technology and building up an industry to engineer and manufacture it—Rickover enjoyed almost complete autonomy to attack problems as they arose. He could define what the organization needed, and he accepted that any failure would fall entirely on him. Amassing authority and power, Rickover was in a position to inveigle each part of the government to back *his* nuclear-propulsion program and to compel contractors to meet *his* project specifications and time-line. "Anything that delayed the schedule . . . was tantamount to treason," recalled one unhappy Westinghouse executive.[41]

On August 19, 1949, Admiral Louis Denfield, who had succeeded Nimitz as CNO, signed a memorandum drafted with Rickover's help. The document formalized building a nuclear submarine as a Navy program, calling for a new boat to be ready for operational evaluation in 1955. Rickover told his Naval Reactors associates that he was aiming to have a boat go to sea by January of that year. That seemed not just unfeasible but ridiculous. Designing and issuing a new uniform in the Navy could take longer than that.[42]

A decade after the discovery of fission and Gunn and Abelson's first fledgling and ultimately thwarted steps to develop a naval reactor for submarines, Rickover *owned* the nuclear Navy. But he needed to win Congress's budgetary backing and the president's political support to push his program toward his early-1955 launch-date goal. The Soviet Union shortly helped Rickover's cause once more.

On September 23, 1949, President Harry Truman announced the momentous news that the Soviets had exploded an atomic bomb. They succeeded as early as four years ahead of previous US intelligence estimates.[43] With fresh urgency, Congress furiously debated nuclear-weapons policy throughout the fall and winter of 1949–50. Rickover found a friend in Senator Brien McMahon from Connecticut, chair of the new Joint Committee on Atomic Energy, the powerful body responsible for AEC policy and budget. Electric Boat, often referred to as EB, in the river town of Groton, opposite New London in his home state, was the largest submarine manufacturer during the war. On February 9, 1950, Rickover met with the committee's subcommittee on reactor development. He testified in civilian clothing, as he would thereafter whenever he went to Capitol Hill—openly flouting Navy orders that he wear uniform. In what the *New York Times* characterized as a "highly secret" session, he explained to the subcommittee's members, Representatives Carl Durham, Carl Hinshaw, Henry "Scoop" Jackson, and Melvin Price, the advantages a nuclear submarine could offer US forces.[44] He also asserted that the Soviets were, in all likelihood, developing one of their own. He wanted to build two US nuclear subs, designed to test the two different reactor coolant technologies—pressurized water and liquid sodium—and briefed them on a five-year timeline for getting them operational.

Rickover's largely unscripted testimony, delivered without the Navy's prior approval and without accompanying deputies, surprised the committee members. They appreciated his candor and laughed at his witty barbs directed at superior officers and the Navy's slow, bureaucratic ways. His views resonated with members who had frustrations of their own with a Navy that was dragging its feet in the face of a budget-cutting Congress's calls to modernize and streamline the fleet. His maverick style and insistence that he could deliver a nuclear sub in half the time others claimed would be possible won their support. Each of the congressmen would become among his longest-standing backers. If the Navy leadership distrusted and did not know what to do about Rickover and individual officers despised him, Congress fell in love with him.

Captain Rickover was "a tremendous little guy," McMahon

told a reporter.[45] "He's a dissenter," Jackson enthused. He found Rickover "a nonconformist in uniform" and "a breath of fresh air" and tagged him "a genius."[46] Jackson would soon win a Senate seat from Washington State and emerge as a powerful voice for the nuclear Navy. Rickover befriended the rest of the subcommittee members and made numerous other friends in Congress over the coming years. He could rely on their support when he made his frequent end runs around the Navy and Pentagon leadership. In the coming years, his highly anticipated annual testimony to the Joint Committee on Atomic Energy and later to the Armed Services Committees in the House and Senate became known as the "Rickover lecture," for his unconstrained responses to questions and wide-ranging discussion of whatever was on his mind. Rickover was a brilliant extemporaneous speaker able to recall a vast amount of relevant historical and philosophical examples bearing on contemporary issues and to explain technical issues and statistical evidence, and his oral testimony to congressional committees typically ran for one to two hours. But afterward, his staffers would edit, amend, and elaborate on the transcript, before submitting it, often at twice the length or more of his spoken remarks, for publication.[47] Congressmen who might skip subcommittee meetings, particularly on abstruse technical matters such as naval ship propulsion, made sure to be on hand for his testimony. They knew the feisty naval engineer would say something surprising enough to make news, and they could get their names into the newspapers back in their districts.[48]

Rickover, for his part, developed a significant respect for the senators and congressmen, many of whom he came to know personally. He rejected any relationships with his staff or contractors outside work but enjoyed friendships on Capitol Hill without embarrassment. Senator McMahon would remain a strong backer until he succumbed to cancer two years later. Adolph Sabath, the Chicago congressman who had nominated

Rickover to the Naval Academy more than thirty years before, again came to the aid of his district's son, pushing Rickover's submarine until he, too, died in 1952. But others would come forward to support him for decades. The full Joint Committee accepted Rickover's arguments for building both nuclear subs at the galloping pace that he proposed.[49]

Even before Rickover went to Congress to win support to build the nuclear submarines, he raced ahead. The Navy had employed two shipyards as the primary manufacturers of subs during World War II: along with Electric Boat, the private yard on Connecticut's Thames River, the Navy still operated its Portsmouth Naval Yard on the Piscataqua River in Kittery, Maine. During the war, EB had been closely associated with GE as the principal supplier of its subs' power and electrical systems. In the last year of the war, the EB sheds, docks, and ways were turning out new submarines at the rate of one every two weeks. Since the war, though, EB's massive yard had all but closed, laying off most of its workforce. When Rickover approached EB's general manager, O. P. Robinson, about building a hull for GE's liquid-sodium-reactor-powered sub, he jumped at the chance, readily agreeing to Rickover's terms.

Portsmouth and Westinghouse had held a similar relationship during the war, again turning out and repairing subs powered by Westinghouse electric motors at breakneck speed. On January 12, 1950, Rickover and his NR colleagues Dunford and Roddis, both from the Oak Ridge Naval Group, along with Bettis's general manager, Charles Weaver, went to the Portsmouth yard, where they met with Rear Admiral Charles McShane, its commander. The visitors proposed that the yard build a land prototype of the Bettis pressurized-water-reactor engine and the sub to house the real thing. The yard was busy with modernizing wartime submarines, but Rickover told them he did not expect his project would need a significant staff buildup for another year. McShane was inclined to take on the prestigious project, but he turned to his planning officer, Captain John Scheibler, asking him to weigh in on the proposal. Scheibler knew Rickover at the Naval Academy (graduating two years after him) and as a fellow EDO at BuShips and did not want to work with him. McShane accepted Scheibler's negative recommendation and refused the project.

Rickover was stunned and angry. Biting his usually profane tongue, he asked McShane, "Do you mind if I use your phone?" He reached across the desk and dialed O. P. Robinson at EB. "O. P.?" he said. "Will you help me build the prototype for the first nuclear submarine? The damn Navy yard isn't interested. I'll need some of your best people. You will? Great! I'll be down there tonight. We'll settle the details." Rickover and the others went that very night to Robinson's house, where they reached an agreement in principle that EB would design and build both prototype reactors, the Mark I for the Westinghouse pressurized-water reactor to be engineered at Bettis and the Mark A for the General Electric molten-sodium reactor at Knolls. EB would also have responsibility for design and construction of the future submarines to house the first nuclear power plants. Although generally preferring dual-track programs to keep contractors in competition, Rickover was actually pleased. EB's desperation for work meant that the company would have to bend to his terms and work organization. Even years later and after Portsmouth had handled many nuclear-sub projects, Rickover would often remind BuShips' officers that their own yard had refused to build the world's first nuclear submarine.[50]

Rickover still lacked the Navy's final go-ahead for the nuclear-submarine program. At the end of March, he went to make his case before the Navy's General Board, the secretary of the Navy's then-powerful advisory committee composed of late-career flag officers. He played his two hats to the limits, appearing before the board members not as a fellow Navy officer but in a business suit as head of the AEC's Division of Reactor Development naval reactors program. He told the admirals that failure to build the subs would reflect badly on the service when the AEC completed the boats' propulsion plants but had no subs in which to install them. Previous plans had called for the first nuclear sub to serve as a test bed—a research vessel—rather than as a war-fighting ship. Rickover feared that going the experimental route would delay the Navy's recognition of the nuclear submarine's true value. The General Board agreed with all of Rickover's recommendations. Adapting the existing hull design for diesel-electric boats, the world's first nuclear submarine, a new attack sub with six torpedo tubes, was added to the 1952 shipbuilding program as a war-fighting fleet boat (given the long timeline for boat design, construction, and completion, new Navy vessels were added on lists for approval to commence work two years out). A second nuclear sub would follow on the next year's list.

In June 1950, US forces sent the first of its military into what became the Korean War. Soviet- and Chinese-backed North Korean forces quickly drove the Americans down the Korean Peninsula. In the White House, a beleaguered President Truman feared that nuclear war was on the horizon. On August 8, 1950, without any public fanfare, President Truman signed the bill authorizing the design and construction of the world's first nuclear-powered submarine. That unnoticed moment happened to fall on the anniversary of the day five years earlier when the United States dropped a second atomic bomb on Japan, devastating the city of Nagasaki. At a White House press conference two days later, a reporter asked Truman, "in the light of the past five years, [do] you have any comment on the future of atomic energy?" The president replied pointedly, "No comment."[51]

4

‹•◆•›

Rickover Made Us Do It

RICKOVER NEVER LEARNED to drive. A colleague would pick him up early each morning outside his apartment building on Connecticut Avenue and drop him off at Tempo 3. His office day began with breakfast at his desk and often continued past midnight. At first Rickover could not be bothered about gaining clearances for afterhours work. The doors to Tempo 3 were locked at night, so he found a window through which to exit. But after the night watch arrested him at gunpoint, he finally got a pass.[1]

Throughout 1950 and beyond, he traveled incessantly. He regularly left on Sunday night, often flying first from Washington to Chicago and Argonne. From there he would take a train to Pittsburgh for meetings at Bettis. Later in the week, he flew, went by rail, or would be driven to Knolls in West Milton or Electric Boat in Groton. He frequently returned by overnight train or flight in time to get to his Naval Reactors office first thing in the morning. Saturday was a regular workday for all NR staff. Wherever Rickover went, he arrived with a sense of urgency that bowled over every person and organization he encountered. He mustered all the engineering tools, political weapons, and sheer cussedness he could to drive contractors to meet his sub-reactor deadlines.

Rickover brought his wartime experience at the Electrical Section to bear at his new Naval Reactors offices, breaking down the engineering "problem" of nuclear propulsion into its systems and components—from radiation, cooling, shielding, and heat transfer to chemistry and metallurgy; from training, budgeting, and contracts to materials, construction, laboratory, and shipyard inspection; and so on—and then assigned trusted, experienced engineers, a mix of civilian and naval personnel, to head up each subsection. He could point to the responsible person if something went wrong, but in the end *he* would be held responsible if *his* reactor failed. That was his expectation for himself. As such he faced the endless job of pushing for perfection in every project that Naval Reactors personnel and vendors undertook. He brooked no excuses from subordinates, company executives, or officers in training, permitted no distractions or lapses.

To keep all of his dawning empire in hand, nights and on Sundays and while on the road, he read through the pinks. He marked them up and followed up as needed. Rickover kept two telephones on his desk that rang constantly. He answered calls without greeting, moved brusquely through the business at hand, and ended with an abrupt hang-up, no good-bye. He ate at his desk. He yelled out the door to his four secretarial and administrative assistants or shouted down the hall for a staff member to drop whatever he or she (in later years) was doing and come running. When he walked, he moved briskly while others struggled to keep up.

Nothing Rickover touched was ever free from follow-up inspection, scrutiny, and ongoing audit, testing, and evaluation. He kept in daily touch with the branch's technical specialists in the field, who regularly visited contractors' labs and yards; some lived on-site, where they observed the contractors' projects and inspected work unannounced. He made sure that laboratory, shipyard, and equipment contractors' employees reported any developing concerns to his site representatives. "The devil is in the details," Rickover repeated to them; "so is salvation." He would not allow his site representatives to fraternize with contractors' managers or workers. They were not to be "good guys" who understood the "difficulties" the company faced. They were there only to find fault and deviations from standards, never to do the contractors' job for them by suggesting corrective measures. He expected immediate reports on any matter that could affect production schedules. "Don't tell me what's going right," he told his field representatives. "I only want to know what's going wrong." Rickover said that his field staff's hands-off yet all-seeing responsibility took "God-like qualities." He eventually had seventeen field offices; the largest at Bettis employed sixty-one civilians and seven naval officers on-site. Contractors loathed them. From his NR desk, like Stalin in Moscow—to whom Rickover was sometimes, not kindly, compared—he seemed to have eyes everywhere and know everything going on. "We were," remarked one of his field agents, "simply his spies."[2] Yards were tense places, with agents ready to pounce. Rickover's operatives knew about developing problems often well before local managers did, which, if they failed to correct the issue swiftly, brought a dreaded Rickover call. Once, while on a call with Rickover in Washington, a shipyard agent happened to see smoke billow from a dock workshop. Rickover quickly telephoned the yard's general director in his office, warning him about the fire before an alarm had even sounded.

Critical matters that could not get resolved locally went to Rickover. He would telephone a supplier's executives, even the presidents of large corporations that may have had hundreds of government contracts, demanding that they give his problem immediate and undivided attention. Late-night calls were common. A Sunday-morning call from Rickover supposedly forced an executive vacationing in Miami Beach out of the surf.[3] After one such call from Rickover, they would rather have wrapped themselves in barbed wire than endure a second lashing from his tongue. One official of a big industrial concern remarked to a reporter, "Now, don't misunderstand me. I don't dislike Rickover. I hate him."[4] But, as Rickover wanted, they made sure their managers gave his programs priority. If a petulant, high-voiced call did not unknot a conflict, he insisted on flying out Saturday night for a meeting first thing Sunday morning, even on holidays. According to Westinghouse's Simpson, he deliberately held meetings during off-hours in violation of company policy as a show of force.[5] Once Rickover got the answer he wanted, he would get back to his desk by morning.

A brushup with Rickover stung. He rarely spoke to newer personnel, but as a staff member showed worth, rewards came in the form of *more* criticism. "The longer you stay here and the better I like you," Rickover explained, "the more you will get told off. In this way you will learn quickly. I never start to like a man until I tell him off three or four times a day. If you don't agree with what I tell you, you are always free to argue and fight back."[6] At technical presentations, he probed without end. Nothing drew his ire faster than when an engineer fumbled an answer to a question that demanded certainty. In watching him closely over the years, Simpson observed, "One of the secrets of his phenomenal success was his temerity and tenacity to ask the second question whatever the circumstances. He took absolutely nothing for granted and no one on faith." But he added, "More than once, we could have cheerfully murdered him."[7]

NR had an open-door policy. Staff could walk unbidden into any office to raise an issue. The revolutionary nature of the undertaking and the need to weigh frequent design alternatives led to stormy ad hoc meetings almost daily in Rickover's office and conference rooms. When Rickover presided, he demanded everyone at the table contribute his viewpoint. As a result of the continuous state of crisis as the team scrambled to make determinative decisions for the future submarine reactor, the daily rounds of meetings in which a junior civilian could stand up to a senior engineer or a lower-ranking officer to his superior sometimes devolved into shouting matches. Rickover said in later years that he wanted just such "an atmosphere unembarrassed by any suggestion of authority or even respect."[8] In the end, Rickover considered what he heard, polled those who were present, and made the most consequential decisions himself—sometimes after ignoring the consensus in the room.

Simpson sat through countless such meetings, in Washington and at Westinghouse sites. Rickover, he said, was "a good intuitive engineer. He believed in keeping things simple and never cutting corners." Rickover's "worst trait," Simpson thought, was his absolute confidence in his ability to judge others. He would make an almost instantaneous decision "based on a single incident rather than on overall performance," Simpson observed. Many highly qualified people lost their jobs at industrial labs after Rickover's snap judgment of their character and fitness for technical work. He asked leading questions, sometimes deliberately seeking to throw the other person off balance, and when he did not get the answers he sought or believed someone was trying to play him, he tossed them out of his office with a curse and withering glare. "He was the ultimate inquisitor as well as a masterfully Machiavellian politician," Simpson said.[9]

Rickover was ruthless, more than willing to inflict personal and career harm to advance his program. Not long after one high-ranking Bettis engineering director started to work on the reactor program, Rickover invited him to his Washington office. He was supposedly there, Rickover told him, to "learn how the Navy operates." In a private memoir, the engineer wrote, "I soon found out that his real purpose was to convince me of the necessity of taking all orders directly from him, bypassing my superiors at Westinghouse, both in receiving and relaying information to him." He quickly gathered that Rickover "would use whatever means were necessary without regard to morals or ethics to accomplish his purpose . . . [and] to maintain his absolute dictatorial power over the project and all concerned." At one point, the man confronted Rickover over a move he considered devilishly underhanded. He asked whether "morals and ethics and the impugning of personnel didn't enter the picture [when accomplishing things]." Rickover answered, "Not if it interfered with getting the job done."[10]

Although Simpson believed that only Rickover could have accomplished what he did at the time, the two former Oak Ridge housemates butted heads many times over the course of nearly a decade's close association. Rickover never let their collegial past override his goals. Sometimes that meant twisting Simpson's arm until he too broke. After a meeting at Argonne, Rickover and Simpson took a train together to Pittsburgh. Rickover asked Simpson to meet in his roomette. Rickover told him that he wanted Simpson "to get rid of" Bettis's ranking technical director. "He's my boss. I couldn't do that even if I wanted to," Simpson replied.

"If you threaten to quit unless they remove [him], it will be done," Rickover said, knowing how much senior management valued Simpson.

"You can't ask me to do that," Simpson protested.

Rickover looked at him grimly. "If you don't do it," he said, "I'll have you fired. And I can do it." He meant it. Simpson went to division head Weaver to tell him what had transpired.

Before long, Weaver transferred the Bettis technical director to another division. "But," said Simpson, "to be a Rickover reject became a badge of honor" at Westinghouse.[11]

As Naval Reactors expanded, Rickover attracted technically adept, young, and also experienced engineers eager to work at the forefront of a new technology and willing to devote backbreaking hours to their jobs in return for serious responsibility. Many came from private industry and academia, often taking big pay cuts—one dropping from a $16,000-a-year salary to $7,500—for the chance to work six, and sometimes seven, days a week, twelve hours or more a day, under Rickover's gimlet eye.[12] Civilians who were not comfortable with Rickover's demands left quickly. Whatever their hours of toil, Rickover worked harder than any of them.

Early on, Rickover made education a foundation for his program. He decided that all who worked on a boat's power plant must fully understand it, from theory to materials, operations to crisis response. He even instituted afterhours courses for the secretarial and clerical staff and dispatched some of them to observe at various sites. He preferred to hire young people who were not yet "spoiled" by the Navy or private industry. He sent most of them for a year's study at the new School of Reactor Technology, which he helped set up at Oak Ridge's Clinton Laboratory, or MIT's advanced nuclear engineering program, which he also helped to establish.

Rickover even expected shipyard workers to understand why they had to take previously-unheard-of steps to ensure workplace safety, cleanliness, and precision standards. On EB's ways in Groton, they were building a sub with a power plant unlike any the yard had previously constructed. Rickover instituted training in nuclear power for dock workers and managers alike. Their learning curve was steep.

* * *

The Navy's Bureau of Personnel (BuPers) typically handled all sub-force staffing decisions in coordination with the Atlantic submarine-force commander (who held personnel responsibility for the entire sub fleet). But for the first atomic submarines, CNO Admiral Arleigh Burke gave Rickover control over officer selection, training, and assignments.[13] BuPers sent Rickover a series of candidates eager to win the prestigious nuclear-officer billets. Rickover interviewed and rejected *all* of them. After finishing with one candidate who proved particularly dull despite coming strongly recommended based on twenty years' sea duty, Rickover telephoned the admiral who had made the recommendation. "Why don't you send me a deck winch?" he snapped. "Some of those have had as much as thirty years' sea duty."[14] In these early days at the frontiers of nuclear engineering and science, he wanted experienced operational officers who were also mentally equipped to handle an unprecedented machine and, given the public interest in the program, able to project the right image. Few diesel-sub operators fit the bill, and fewer still could bear up under the scrutiny, perfectionist demands, and fiery temperament of Rickover the man. He expected prospective officers to have a personal relationship with him. In rejecting so many candidates, he also made clear to the Navy that he alone would determine which officers would operate his submarines.

In effect, he relieved BuPers of its duty. The first group of officers he selected went to Bettis to observe the reactor's construction. He left nothing about their future handling of the power plant to chance. They would know its particularities, machinery, systems, and components down to the bolts, nuts, and piping. Many of these Navy officers held advanced degrees in scientific fields; he now required them to pass a welder's qualification test. They in turn gave real-world insights into seagoing realities to Bettis's engineers building the reactor.

The first sub's commanding officer was the most important choice. Rickover knew early on the one he wanted, a World War II submarine engineering officer and postwar commander, Captain (and future vice admiral) Eugene "Dennis" Wilkinson. On the surface, Wilkinson seemed as different as could be from Rickover. At around six feet three inches tall, Wilkinson stood nearly a head taller than his boss. Wilkinson was a submariner's submariner—athletic, dashing, genial, a poker player who cleaned out other officers in wardroom games and supplemented his pay with outside games despite the Navy's prohibitions against gambling. He had also proved his physical bravery in World War II in winning decorations aboard one of the most successful subs in the very dangerous hunt for Japanese ships. Wilkinson could handle the pressure of the role. But what mattered most to Rickover was that Wilkinson was smart—very smart. While stationed in San Diego, he had pursued a PhD in nuclear physics in his spare time. Rickover sought out Wilkinson early on, convincing him to go to Oak Ridge in 1948 to study reactor engineering and operation. While there, Wilkinson did computational work on the new reactor. And Wilkinson ticked off another column for Rickover: he had not gone to the Naval Academy. He was an independent thinker, outside naval orthodoxy.

In 1953, Rickover wrote Wilkinson, by then captain of a diesel sub, a brief letter telling Wilkinson that he had, in effect, been chosen to serve as the inaugural commander of the *Nautilus*. The two men must have understood each other well. Rickover congratulated Wilkinson with his usual sarcasm: "For Christ's sake," he wrote, "don't be as lazy as you always are; *act* on this *at once*. Of course, it is also at a great personal sacrifice that I will have to put up with you for another period of time but I will do this 'for the cause'!!!!"[15] He *liked* Wilkinson.

Rickover's choice of Wilkinson amounted to a slap in the face of the many, justly proud wartime commanding officers.

Some complained that Wilkinson's selection was due solely to his having been "trained as a scientist" and based on the "technical view" he represented. Newspaper articles quoted officers who said that a nuclear power plant was "just a steam plant" like any other and complained that Wilkinson's engineer's perspective was all wrong for a skipper. Some scoffed at "Captain Nemo" and said, "You can't command a submarine if you've got your mind in the engine room."[16]

Many among the Navy brass had instead favored Edward Beach, Rickover's brilliant, respected onetime ally inside BuShips. Beach's background made him an outwardly ideal candidate. But despite having risked career backlash in helping Rickover in his "orthodontic" days of trying to push nuclear propulsion ahead, Beach was a career naval officer. The son of a noted Navy captain, he had graduated second in his Naval Academy class and was a highly decorated veteran of multiple combat tours. He was politically connected enough to have served on the CNO's staff and was presently naval aide to General Omar Bradley, chairman of the Joint Chiefs of Staff. He would shortly become President Eisenhower's naval aide. And Beach wanted a nuclear command. But Rickover viewed all such presumed qualifications as demerits.

In putting Wilkinson at the head of the vanguard of the nuclear Navy, Rickover let the wider Navy know that among his prerogatives was making the final decision about every officer he and his staff would train to operate and command his nuclear ships. Before a single atomic-powered sub had been launched, his grip on the nuclear Navy was already tightening.

The months that Rickover and the Naval Group spent at Oak Ridge had jump-started engineering a submarine thermal reactor. In simplest form, a steam thermal reactor is a fission stove used to boil up steam, like heating a gigantic tea kettle. The reactor typically operates in a relatively straightforward way: Nuclear fuel sitting inside the reactor core begins and sustains a neutron-driven chain reaction, known as "going critical," when the neutron-absorbing control rods that pass through the core are lifted far enough out to allow the radio-active fuel's neutrons to collide. More collisions generate more heat, lots of it. A continuously flowing coolant, or moderator, such as pressurized water or a molten metal such as sodium, circulates through passageways in the reactor's core, taking up its thermal energy. That high-temperature heat energy then gets transferred, using a heat exchanger, in essence a metal plate, to a separate, secondary, nonradioactive circulating-water system that boils water into steam. That steam shoots directly into two pairs of turbines—one that produces electrical power and another that, through a reduction gear, turns the ship's propeller shaft. To stop the chain reaction and its energy production, the control rods are lowered back into place in the reactor's core, blocking the neutrons and halting the fission process.

But making that giant stove and tea kettle required major engineering advances. Rickover and his staff faced numerous, crucial decisions. In many ways, they were more complex than those facing the atomic-bomb builders during the war. A bomb had to go off just once; a sub reactor must not fail to function— ever. Little existing knowledge from the production of atomic-bomb material could explain how to design a nuclear thermal power plant that was highly efficient and simple to operate, monitor, and repair. And the reactor could never release radiation yet had to fit inside a slender sub's hull and operate when tossed about at sea and while enduring the shocks of combat.

The Navy statement authorizing the program did not specify which type of nuclear reactor would go into the sub because nobody knew which of the two most advanced coolant systems would work better, Bettis's pressurized water or Knolls's molten sodium. Each had its advantages and disadvantages in heat production, chemistry, fluid dynamics, and operational safety. Also, nobody knew how much enriched-uranium fuel would be needed for efficient, sustained powered operations or how many control rods would be needed to make the power plant responsive to the throttle. In fact, nobody knew what material would hold together the structurally weak, flaky, and fiery U-235 fuel to energize the chain reaction, and nobody knew what corrosive effects ultrahot radioactive water or molten sodium would have on various metals being considered for the reactor core and cooling system.

Shielding the crew from radiation inside a hull was an entirely unexplored domain. The engineers had to figure out how to encase and shield a reactor sufficiently to keep the crew safe inside the sub without making the reactor too bulky and heavy for a submarine to handle the weight. At the same time, nobody knew what effect seawater outside the sub hull reflecting back (back-scattering) radiation would have on crew exposure levels. And what would the profound squeeze of deep-sea operation do to the reactor and its components?

Once the reactor was designed, industry would have to cast an immense cylindrical reactor vessel and bolt and weld its cover in a structurally sound, leak-proof manner—yet give it the precision of a Swiss watch. Moreover, the engineers were learning how to craft and test coolant channels, valves, pumps, motors, thermometers, and pressure gauges that would prove durable enough to sit inside a radioactive reactor vessel and coolant circulator without breaking down even after months underwater. Repairing highly radioactive machine parts at sea was simply unthinkable.

Several times Rickover's engineers proposed installing newly developed, lighter-weight materials for the turbine motors and other nonnuclear components to reduce overall power-plant weight and size, giving more wiggle room for the reactor itself. Each time Rickover "hit the roof," recalled his deputy

James Dunford. Rickover told them, Dunford said, "Didn't we understand that nothing unproven was going into that ship unless demanded by the nuclear plant itself?"[17] Nothing except the nuclear power plant would innovate within the standard diesel-submarine hull.

Nonetheless, Rickover would have to engineer a miracle if he wanted to launch the world's first nuclear sub in early 1955. Few expected the new organization to succeed in its revolutionary aim. "Everybody knew it was going to fail," Rickover would quip a few years later, "so they left us completely alone so we were able to do the job."[18]

One of the first and most essential engineering decisions Rickover faced was the choice of metals for encasing the fuel and constructing the control-rod assembly and the reactor-vessel shielding. Rickover's first hints that led to his eventual choice of materials came in 1947 at Oak Ridge. A Manhattan District metallurgist showed Rickover a small bar of silvery-gray, ultradense zirconium. It was an eye-opener. Zirconium, Rickover learned, possesses a unique combination of strength and transparency to thermal neutrons. At the same time, circulating superheated radioactive water did not heavily corrode it. Those qualities made zirconium potentially uniquely right for encasing the reactor's enriched-uranium fuel rods. Zirconium's special properties led Rickover to the chemically similar and geologically twinned element, hafnium. Hafnium is almost always found in small quantities naturally bonded to zirconium, but unlike zirconium, hafnium absorbs and blocks neutrons. Hafnium's properties made it a good candidate for the control rods used to stop the chain reaction.

But Rickover faced a daunting barrier: the two metals were exceedingly rare. Just eighty-six pounds of pure zirconium, a bit more than enough to fill a shoebox, were refined in 1948. Each pound cost nearly $300—equivalent to around $3,000 today. And Rickover needed tons, not pounds—about fifteen tons of zirconium for a single reactor. And he was building four.

Unable to source enough zirconium, he asked the Atomic Energy Commissioners to let him manage metals production for the reactors. After they gave him the go-ahead, he awarded Bettis the contract to build a factory in Pittsburgh that could turn out three thousand pounds of refined zirconium a month, along with enough hafnium for reactor control rods. Seeing such an enormous investment in an exotic metal, skeptical metallurgists scratched their heads about "Mr. Zirconium," worrying, "Was it gonna work?" Nobody would know until the reactor was operational.[19]

Before the end of fall 1950, Bettis was meeting its quota and had successfully lowered the price of zirconium to about five dollars per pound. Bettis metallurgists kept experimenting with ways to improve zirconium's natural characteristics for reactor use. Eventually they came up with an alloy that combined zirconium with tiny amounts of tin, chromium, nickel, and other impurities, which paradoxically improved zirconium's resistance to corrosion.[20] Zircaloy-2, as it was labeled, would remain the standard nuclear-fuel cladding for several decades to come, as would hafnium alloys in control rods. In 1952, a congressional committee asked Secretary of the Navy Dan Kimball how the production of zirconium and hafnium had gone from virtually nil to tons practically overnight. He testified that industry leaders told him, "Rickover made us do it."[21] Seventy years later, virtually all reactors' fuel cladding still derives from "Mr. Zirconium."[22]

With enough zirconium and hafnium in hand, the race was on. "Nothing was fast enough for Rickover," recalled Simpson.[23] With an eye on the January 1955 deadline, Rickover made a controversial decision to speed things up. In developing big,

innovative technologies, engineers most often arrange proto-
typed components in a flattened format, a schematic layout
known as a "breadboard." Breadboards make it easy to test, access, tinker with, and improve parts one by one. From that experimental process, an iterative rework of the breadboard eventually evolves into a full-scale prototype in the project's actual
architecture. At that stage, engineers can make final refinements to the system before going into production. But the submarine thermal-reactor power plant had to be ready by May 1,
1952, if it was going to get installed in the sub hull in time to
launch as scheduled. Rickover ordered Bettis and GE to skip
the breadboard stage and go straight to the final prototype.

The prototype would have a home far from the sea. The
AEC had opened the National Reactor Testing Station in August
1950, on a nine-hundred-square-mile former naval artillery-
testing range in the high desert barrens of Idaho. That was
about eighty miles northwest of Pocatello and sixty miles west
of Idaho Falls and more than twenty-four hundred miles from
the Groton, Connecticut, site where the sub hull was to be constructed. The station would eventually house the largest collection of reactors in the world, each dedicated to testing various
nuclear fuels, breeding nuclear materials, and training nuclear
engineers. Rickover contracted with Bettis to engineer the
Mark I, a full-scale prototype pressurized-water-reactor plant
at Arco, as the Idaho testing station was called for the tiny near-
est town. The reactor would sit inside one compartment of a
submarine hull, shielded from a compartment housing a control
room and another compartment containing the steam power
plant. The hull would lie partially submerged within a giant
seawater bathtub—a land submarine designated Mark I Submarine Thermal Reactor (STR). Bettis subcontracted Electric
Boat to build the Arco land sub. EB had already begun construction in Groton of the first nuclear-powered submarine,
USSN-571, later named USS *Nautilus*.

The engineers would design the prototype at a pace barely ahead of the real engine for the *Nautilus*. "Mark I," Rickover declared, "equals Mark II," the real power plant.[24] Problems discovered in Mark I at Arco would get corrected on land instead of at sea. Everything that happened in Arco was relayed to the Pittsburgh labs for further engineering, always with an eye toward improving the safety and simplicity of Mark II. But success or failure of Mark I would, Rickover wrote in February 1952, "determine the extent of the support we receive from the Atomic Energy Commission and the Navy."[25]

Mark I was for now the only hope for getting the *Nautilus* to sea on schedule. GE's Knolls laboratory scientists seemed unable to figure out how to handle liquid salt's complex chemistry for use as a reactor moderator for the second sub. The entire program would thus steam ahead or sink based on Mark I. It was a big gamble since every previous power reactor had sunk. As an engineering and scientific feat, Mark I was unprecedented, and, if less showy than the actual future submarine, it would, if successful, represent the true breakthrough in the invention of atomic power.

Rickover's naval critics scoffed at what they called the "impossible project." But Westinghouse put its top engineers on it, and EB sent craftsmen for weeks at a time to Arco, where they gained experience to apply in building the real sub. Rickover sat in his office in Washington always imagining a catastrophe more than two thousand miles away at Arco. Increasingly uneasy as the months went by, he set up a three-person group, including two of his most senior engineers and Simpson, to act as his "alter ego" when he was not there himself—though he was frequently. Each of the engineering leaders had to approve any variation from plans. With work and testing going on around the clock, the three and Rickover, often in three different time zones, spent many late-night hours on the telephone discussing changes.

Back at the Bettis facility, engineers also built yet another identical reactor, except minus the core. Engineers tested every component with the same hot water temperatures and pressure ratings they anticipated for the real thing. At the same time, Rickover had EB construct a full-scale mock-up of the submarine's power plant, with the secondary circulatory system and machinery on a dock at Groton, just down from where the real hull would soon take shape. Shipyard workers would use it to train for the day when they would install the real thing. Rickover also spent hours crawling about the mock-up's tangle of equipment and pipes. He imagined the future sub's possible problems at sea, jotting down notes for changes to the design, always with an eye to making it easier to carry out both routine maintenance and emergency repairs.

Thomas R. Weschler, then a lieutenant commander and later promoted to vice admiral, accompanied Rickover on a car ride to the Pittsburgh airport in late 1955. Rickover explained to Weschler his design philosophy for the reactor. "Really," he said, "I have a very simple rule. I say to myself: 'I have a son. I love my son. I want everything that I do to be so safe that I would be happy to have my son operating it.' That's my fundamental rule."[26]

With Arco's land sub under construction and preparations nearly complete at EB for construction of the new sub, Rickover met with President Truman in the White House on February 9, 1952. This was Rickover's first visit to the Oval Office, though he would return many times in years to come. He brought visual aids with him, including a cutaway model of a nuclear submarine and a weighty, small bar of refined zirconium. He explained to Truman the power plant's inner workings and the revolutionary advantages it would give a sub or other warship. The president was eager to see atomic power applied to constructive purposes—and a rethinking of his atomic legacy from his order to drop the A-bombs on Japan. Rickover knew how to impress important people, and, handing Truman the dense zirconium slug, he joked that it represented enough investment to pay off the Democratic Party's debt.

Seeing Truman's eagerness for the *Nautilus*'s success, Rickover thought up a way to boost its public standing and to keep the AEC and Navy fully committed. The traditional keel-laying ceremony for the sub—in reality, placement of the first steel hull section since a sub does not have a keel—was scheduled for late spring at the Electric Boat shipyard. Normally, such ceremonies were brief, relatively simple affairs, with the ship's sponsor—sometimes a naval officer, sometimes an officer's or Pentagon official's spouse—receiving the honor of declaring the ship's keel "well and truly laid," marking the formal start of construction. Rickover saw an opportunity to transform the event into a public-relations spectacle. Through his strong supporter, the gravely ill Senator McMahon, Rickover took the unprecedented step of inviting a sitting president to lay the *Nautilus*'s keel.

On June 14, 1952, a crowd of some ten thousand spectators looked on from the Electric Boat docks and ways along the Thames River while a smaller press of government, naval, and business officials stood behind Truman on a platform set up next to the hull section. The Navy had determined long beforehand which dignitaries would share the stand with the president. In an obvious snub, Rickover had been left off the list altogether. Learning that the captain was not invited, his representatives at EB protested. After initially expressing reluctance to intervene in a matter of naval protocol, company head O. P. Robinson made sure Rickover would stand next to Truman.

Attired pointedly in a business suit, not his captain's uniform, Rickover watched stone-faced as the president delivered an effusive speech highlighting the *Nautilus* as a harbinger of peace and progress and "something new in the world." Truman's language echoed his speech seven years earlier announcing to the world the dropping of the atom bomb on Hiroshima.[27] This time, Truman wanted attention on fission's transformation into energy for humankind. "Today, we stand on the threshold of a new age of power," the president said. Clearly Rickover had helped to craft his speech. Truman noted that in engineering the sub, "new metals had to be produced. Wholly new processes for refining and using these metals had to be invented, tested, and put into production." He pointed out that fabricating the reactor "required specifications more rigid than anything ever attempted by American industry before." He listed the complexities of fitting the nuclear power plant inside the hull, shielding the crew from radiation, and operating the reactor "instantly by the flick of a switch. And all this intricate mechanism had to be rugged enough to withstand combat shock from depth charges and from other attacks." Without naming Rickover, he celebrated the speed at which *Nautilus* came to pass: "When it was started four years ago, most people thought it would take at least ten years, if it could be done at all. But one tough problem after another has been conquered in a fashion that seems almost miraculous, and the work has forged ahead."[28]

The day was a triumph for Rickover. AEC Chairman Gordon Dean singled out "Captain H. G. Rickover, . . . whose energy, drive, and technical competence have played such a large part in making this project possible." With Rickover looking on, Truman signed his initials on the steel hull section, and a welder permanently inscribed them into *Nautilus*. Standing nearby, Rickover's wife, Ruth, and son, Robert, watched proudly.[29]

* * *

Nine months later, the miracle of thermal nuclear power became a reality. On March 30, 1953, at 11:17 p.m.—March 31 in the Eastern time zone—Mark I went critical, its first chain reaction. The power produced was rated at one-hundredth of a horsepower, enough to boil up just a few pounds of steam pressure, still plenty to begin generating physics data, radioactivity measurements, and shielding results. This was the first time in history that a dedicated thermal reactor had produced a significant, albeit minor, quantity of energy. (Two years earlier, Zinn and Argonne scientists had used waste heat from an experimental gas-cooled breeder reactor at Arco to power a string of four lightbulbs for a few seconds.)[30] After this initial run, some eighty different safety circuits shut down—or scrammed—the reactor so frequently that engineers feared rapid changes in neutron levels were at fault, potentially a grave flaw. The engineers eventually pinpointed the cause in the measuring instruments' sensitivity, so exquisitely primed that they picked up bumps from crew members walking through the reactor compartment, radioactivity increases from radium on a wristwatch, bolts of lightning striking a power line some three hundred miles off in Montana, and other minor electrical noise in the circuitry.[31] Eventually the scrams were subdued to an acceptable rate.

Around the clock over the next two months, the Arco team built up power ratings in small increments. Each step up carried its risks. However, the machine proved remarkably stable, despite the inexperience of the operators. The engineers surmised that the Mark I appeared unlikely to become an atomic bomb. The shield designers were delighted to learn that radiation levels were less than half those that their projections had calculated, meaning the future submarine could easily carry its radiation-shield load. Fuel consumption appeared lower than expected as well, greatly increasing the reactor's forecasted life. At this point, Simpson, who oversaw the operation with Rickover, was confident in their handiwork's success. "The value of Rickover's decision to make Mark I a true prototype of the *Nautilus* was proven again and again," remarked Simpson.[32]

Rickover was less certain, but he thought that the bar was low. "If the *Nautilus* makes two knots on nuclear propulsion," he said, "she will be a success."[33] However, he knew that only a true operations-worthy warship would ever silence his many critics and doubters. Nobody knew yet whether sustained full power would cause the fuel elements to overheat and destroy themselves, spewing radioactivity throughout the plant. The many moving parts of the reactor were lubricated by super-hot, radioactive water, not oil. Again, this was something untried, and nobody could say whether they would warp in fully powered operation or for how long they could continue to function.

Engineers at GE Knolls Laboratory were following progress at Arco as they worked on Mark A, the prototype liquid-sodium reactor. Their troubles continued. In principle, molten salt's far-greater heat reserve compared to water would make the Mark A significantly more efficient than the Mark I. A sub utilizing Mark A's technology would thus need a smaller, lighter engine than the Mark I. The reactor also used magnetic conduction to circulate the coolant, reducing pump noise—important for avoiding sonar detection at sea. However, molten metal was dangerous: even a droplet that hit water would explode, and leaks were proving difficult to prevent. Given the added complexity and danger, the project required much more study. Still Knolls pushed ahead, and the real engine, known as the Submarine Intermediate Reactor, was slated to go into the nation's second nuclear submarine, *Seawolf*, USSN-575. A month after Truman's *Nautilus* keel-laying speech at the EB shipyard, the Navy signed off on a contract for the company to begin the *Seawolf*'s construction, with a launch date set for late in 1957.

Along with the two subs, Rickover and Naval Reactors had several other early-stage development projects on the blackboards. Even before ground was broken at Arco in February 1950, Bettis and Knolls began studies of new, more powerful, smaller, longer-lived reactor designs for a future fleet of submarines—a standardized power plant known as the Submarine Fleet Reactor, SFR. Watching the Air Force gain backing for its strategic bomber and missile force, in the summer of 1949 the Navy also asked Naval Reactors to study construction of an atomic power plant for a large aircraft carrier.[34] Going from the prototype sub-reactor designs to a power plant for a gargantuan surface warship was not simply a matter of expanding the underwater atomic engine's size. The ship would require vastly more horsepower than a submarine and an engineering compartment designed to house one extremely large or multiple reactors. The additional physics involved in a greatly enlarged reactor core loaded with far more nuclear fuel or in a multireactor configuration kept many engineers busy.

The push to move reactor technology ahead went beyond its obvious if unproved benefits for naval ships. In fact, few among the Navy brass believed a reactor would ever drive their boats. But more was at play in the global game. Since the world war ended, Soviet industry had begun catching up with the United States'. The Soviets were also developing their nuclear arsenal. Advancing scientific and technological frontiers had emerged as a new field of competition between the two superpowers. Long regarded as backward, Russian scientists were now surpassing the United States in some technological arenas, especially rocketry. The US government worried that support might grow for communism in a war-ravaged

Europe and among nations of Africa and Asia moving toward independence, especially after the 1949 communist victory in China. The outbreak of the Korean War added to the importance Americans attached to outpacing the Soviet Union on the ideological battlefield. The Air Force's costly and dangerous atomic-jet program thankfully remained grounded while US rocketry was misfiring. Thus, Rickover and his submarine stood out as the country's most advanced application of atomic power at the dawn of a new technologically fired era.

While the Navy and the AEC kept a tight lid on atomic secrets, the public's and Congress's awareness and admiration for Rickover's efforts grew. Newspapers, radio, *Life*, *Time*, and the *New York Times Sunday Magazine* featured laudatory stories about the atomic submarine under construction, the land-sub reactor being tested in the Idaho barrens, and what the *Times* article called "the much disputed figure in Washington . . . [who] fights without stint for whatever he wants for his projects."[35] Three weeks after the *Nautilus*'s presidential keel-laying ceremony, Secretary of the Navy Kimball awarded Rickover a Legion of Merit medal, his second, following one he had earned for his wartime Electrical Section achievements. Acknowledging the "discouraging frustration and opposition" Rickover had encountered, Kimball said, "Rickover had accomplished the most important piece of development work in the history of the Navy."[36] He pinned the medal to Rickover's suit jacket. Even for this high naval honor, he eschewed uniform.

As Rickover's fame, responsibilities, and power grew, he steadfastly refused to bend a knee to the wider defense forces' interests should they conflict with his program. He made that clear when the Pentagon came looking for high-temperature stainless steel to build more jet fighters during the Korean War. Rickover had soaked up every bit of stainless on the market—some six hundred tons for his reactor vessels, piping, and instruments. Someone from the secretary of defense's office warned Louis Roddis, the Oak Ridge Naval Group associate now a high Rickover staffer, that the Pentagon wanted NR to hand over some of its stockpile. Roddis asked Rickover what to do. His response was blunt: "Well, I'm not going to do it." He continued, "Some staffer thinks it would be easier to get the stainless steel from me than to do what I did and go out and find it. Well, he's going to find it's easier for him to get a shovel and dig it out of the ground than to get it from me." He was not done. He explained to Roddis that his notoriously obstreperous predisposition toward the Defense Department's requests was conscious strategy. "You guys are always telling me I should be more reasonable," he said. "Well, I don't see any advantage to the Naval Reactors program of being reasonable. Suppose they start talking about cutting back the Reactor Development Division budget. Everybody is supposed to be reasonable and absorb part of the loss. Do you think anybody'll say, 'Let's talk to Rickover, he'll be reasonable?' Hell, no. They'll do anything they have to, to keep from talking with me about it. They'd rather take the cuts themselves. So tell me: Is my attitude beneficial to the project, or not? I'm not asking, what's the best way to have lots of friends and get invited to parties. I'm asking, what's good for the project."[37] He was purposely being vicious and antisocial because it helped in getting *his* reactors and subs built at a pace nobody believed possible. That was all that mattered.

5

Another Dreyfus Case?

THE DAY AFTER Navy Secretary Kimball pinned that gold star for Rickover's second Legion of Merit medal on his suit jacket, a nine-member committee of flag (admiral) rank officers known as a Selection Board met to consider senior captains for promotion to rear admiral. Although Rickover was the most senior candidate and winning national plaudits, his fate was anything but certain. A year earlier, he had already failed to win promotion. Under the military's up-or-out formula, if he were passed over a second time, he could remain in the Navy for just another year but then must retire. By tradition, Selection Boards met in secret with no record of their deliberations and with no appeal of their decisions. "Of course, you don't expect to make admiral," a bureau chief said offhandedly to Rickover before his second-round Selection Board convened. Considering his thirty-one-year career record, the fifty-three-year-old

Rickover *was* expecting to make admiral. "Jesus," he fumed over the remark, "I was so God-damned mad."[1]

Rickover determined on making it as hard as possible for the Navy to fire him. He would become irreplaceable by making sure no replacements were waiting in the wings ready to assume his post. Soon after Naval Reactors opened its offices in 1949, he brought Captain Robert L. Moore Jr., a trusted deputy at the Electrical Section, onto his staff. Rickover had expected he would win promotion at the time and move to a higher-status billet for an engineering duty officer, thinking eventually he would rise to chief of the Bureau of Ships. He groomed Moore as his handpicked successor, sending him for a year to MIT before formally recommending him as NR's next commander. But now instead of a successor, after Moore came back to the NR offices, he was a rival. Rickover froze him out. "From the first day," Moore said, "he took no action to recognize my status or in any way to prepare me for relieving him. In fact, he did everything he could to make my life miserable, my work assignments almost impossible, and in every way to show me I was no longer wanted." Moore found that there was "no place in the inn" for him.[2] He transferred to supervise shipbuilding for BuShips at Electric Boat. He would eventually make admiral and became assistant chief of BuShips, requiring him to deal constantly with Rickover. Their undisguised hostility became legendary.

After Moore's abrupt banishment from NR, Rickover refused to consider or train anyone as a potential relief.

But the Navy ran on the principle that any well-rounded line officer, with training, could relieve any other officer of comparable rank in *any* billet. To that end, the Navy rotated officers among billets every year to two years. Rickover hated the practice, at least in engineering disciplines. He believed failing to keep an officer at his post wasted hard-won expertise and foreordained that individuals responsible for initiating projects, which might last for years before coming to fruition, were out of the picture by the time problems surfaced. This left nobody responsible for the project's ultimate failure or success.

Theodore Rockwell, a civilian chemical engineer who had worked on the Manhattan Project in radiation shielding, joined Naval Reactors in 1949. He now directed its Nuclear Technology Division. Around the time the second Selection Board was about to convene, he bumped into an admiral, who quipped that "there are lots of people over at the Pentagon who would like to see a destroyer named after Rickover." Only *dead* naval heroes had ships named for them.[3] On July 19, 1952, the Selection Board announced that the Navy would promote thirty-nine captains to rear admiral. Rickover was not on the list. No officer who had twice failed to gain promotion in the nearly forty-year history of the Selection Board promotion-review system had avoided forced retirement. A two-time loser, Rickover would have to leave the Navy on June 30, 1953.

Rockwell and others among Rickover's senior staff refused to accept the Navy's decision as final. They considered him irreplaceable at this critical stage of the *Nautilus* project. Raymond Dick, one of the original Naval Group at Oak Ridge and since the formation of Naval Reactors a top engineer within the organization, reached out to a naval-affairs reporter, Clay Blair Jr. The twenty-five-year-old Blair, a writer for *Time* and *Life* magazines, had done two submarine tours as a sailor during the war and had followed the atomic-sub story since it became a real program. His 1951 *Time* article was among the first to give national coverage to it and the "hard-driving" engineering officer who had "declared war on naval indifference." The story did much to cement Rickover's public image and appeal.[4]

Three weeks after the second Selection Board passed over Rickover, Blair wrote a story about his pending forced retirement, in the August 4, 1952, issue of *Time*. Under the provocative headline "Brazen Prejudice," the article explicitly pointed to the Navy brass's unified opposition to Rickover, but only as part of their broader distrust of technical specialists—despite the Selection Board having promoted four Engineering Duty Only officers to rear admiral. Blair did not mention that Rickover was Jewish. But the headline hinted that something sinister lay behind Rickover's failure to win a deserved promotion. Suspicions spread that antisemitism had forced Rickover out.[5]

Certainly, the US Navy, like the rest of the military at the time, had a deserved reputation for antisemitism, though since the war, many of the worst offenders had kept their thoughts about Jews private.[6] Still, when the Rickover aide and Navy commander John Crawford Jr. told another officer he worked for Rickover, the officer offhandedly remarked, "Oh, Hymie," a name nobody used for him except derogatorily.[7] Rickover's 1922 Annapolis classmate E. Ruthven Libby, who rose to the rank of vice admiral, refers to him at least twice in an oral history interview as "Hymie." As a vice admiral, Libby reportedly said, "I know Hyman, too. When they circumcised him they threw the wrong end away." But Libby insisted that Blair drummed up interest in Rickover's fate by turning his promotion failure into "another Dreyfus case."[8] He was referring to the notorious trial of Alfred Dreyfus, a French Jewish officer unjustly accused of treason by antisemites in the late nineteenth century. As the Rickover controversy boiled up, some people smeared Blair, a Catholic, for being part of a "Jewish cabal" working on Rickover's behalf and referred to him contemptuously as "Rabbi Blair." Various publications picked up the story that antisemitism lay behind the Rickover case. One magazine wrote, "The real charge against Dreyfus was his religion. And it was because of his religion that Rickover was black-listed by the Navy he had served so well."[9]

The Navy's decision to end Rickover's career incensed his backers in Congress. A small number among them were Jews;

mostly they were non-Jews. The Rickover supporter Carl Durham, a representative from North Carolina who had followed the late Senator McMahon in chairing the Joint Committee on Atomic Energy, protested to Secretary of the Navy Kimball that he did not know anyone in the Navy "who could carry on the job just as effectively." Kimball at a press conference admitted that he would elect for Rickover to stay on the job but refused to intervene: fellow officers judged their own.

The Navy moved to blunt the swelling protests by demonstrating that Rickover was just a spoke in the naval wheel. Chief of BuShips Rear Admiral Homer N. Wallin wrote "the complete, authoritative story" of the *Nautilus* for the popular *Collier's* magazine. He did not bother mentioning Rickover even once.[10] With the Mark I and *Nautilus* consuming Rickover's every waking hour, he was slated to retire on June 30, 1953.

A month before that fateful day, in the afternoon of May 31, the first true test, powered operation of the Mark I, was set to begin at Arco. Rickover; Thomas Murray, the AEC's chief; Simpson; Rickover's project officer in charge of the Mark I, Commander E. E. Kintner; and a few others crowded into the small maneuvering room, the power-plant operations compartment, inside the land sub half immersed in its green seawater pool. They stood behind three nuclear-trained engineering officers seated at three consoles against the curved steel pressure hull. To the left was the reactor control and monitoring panel; next to it were the steam controls and throttle; and to the right was the electrical-system console. The simplicity and compactness of the maneuvering room bore no comparison to the sprawling control rooms used to operate the massive atomic piles scattered at points several miles distant around the National Reactor Testing Station. A steady hum came from the coolant circulators continuously pumping water through the reactor vessel beyond the steel bulkhead wall.

ADMIRAL HYMAN RICKOVER

Rickover looked to Simpson a final time. "Are you sure?" he asked. Several engineers had asked him for a remote start-up in case the reactor became an atomic bomb. Simpson assured him. "OK. Let's go."

Worried that Murray would manhandle the throttle, Kintner had not wanted Murray to open it, but Rickover insisted, knowing the political value of giving a big supporter of the program the honor. Under Rickover's watchful eyes and with Kintner ready to reach over to scram the reactor on the instant, Murray opened the throttle. An angry whining as the reduction gears spun up pierced the room so fast that the men were startled. The power transferred immediately to the propeller shaft, which started slowly turning. Outside the land-sub hull, the water brake, acting as a propeller, churned. Nothing changed, but of course everything had. "This," remarked Simpson, "was the Kitty Hawk of the Atomic Age."[11] The age of controlled atomic power was born.

The throttle was steadily opened further. When the Mark I reached a few thousand horsepower, Rickover and Murray climbed out of the hull and down the seawater bath's wooden staircase to the concrete floor. They walked around in awed silence. The screech of the reduction gear sounded through the cavernous test-station shed. Watching the propeller shaft and water brake rotate, the fifty-three-year-old Rickover experienced pure elation for just the second time since learning he would go to Annapolis.[12]

Step by step over the next month, the power was raised until full power, more than thirteen thousand horsepower, was reached on June 23.[13] In less than a month, the world's first nuclear power plant had reached its maximum specifications—and continued to run smoothly. It had not become an atomic bomb. In fact, no radioactivity above its surrounding environment had yet been detected within the hull.

* * *

114

At the time when the Mark I STR generated the world's first practical atomic power, Rickover seemed to have reached the limits of his personal power. After he was passed over by the Selection Board, the AEC offered to hire him as the civilian head of Naval Reactors, and the Navy suggested the possibility of extending his present duty for an unspecified period until his relief could be identified. Rickover rejected the offers, refusing to stick around as a lame duck while being rotated out of the program he had created. He and Ruth began to think about what they might do next.

But unknown to him, his top associates at Naval Reactors still hoped somehow to alter his fate. Rockwell, Robert Panoff, and Harry Mandil, his top civilian engineers, began lobbying Congress on his behalf. They met first with Representative Sidney R. Yates, who had been elected the year before to succeed Adolph Sabath, Rickover's old benefactor and Chicago's "Jewish congressman." Yates proved crucial to the future of this now-famous son of Chicago. Separately, another group of senior Navy officers on the NR staff, Roddis, Dunford, and Robert Laney, went to Capitol Hill. Rear Admiral Wallin warned them not to: "Your careers in the Navy will be finished if you do," he said.[14] They went anyway.

Hearing out Rickover's staffers, Yates was distressed. But what could a freshman congressman do? He knew somebody who might help. Yates arranged for Panoff, Rockwell, and Mandil to meet with Scoop Jackson. Now a senator, Jackson still served on the Joint Committee on Atomic Energy; he also held a seat on the powerful Senate Armed Services Committee, which had the pro forma duty of signing off on thousands of military promotions annually. The senator in turn set up meetings for the four staffers with the Armed Services Committee's powerful chairman, Massachusetts's Leverett Saltonstall. Although sympathetic, Saltonstall balked at helping out a lone captain, especially one from outside his home state.

Rockwell figured he had little to lose at that point by going public. He tracked down a reporter he knew from a small-town newspaper and explained the situation. The reporter wrote a three-part series of articles criticizing the Navy's shortsightedness, under the headline "Intraservice Row May Imperil Immediate Future of America's First Atomic Powered Submarine." It happened that a Boston paper picked up the story. Saltonstall now had local cause to react to Rickover's imminent retirement. Adding fuel to the fire, Clay Blair, the author of the "Brazen Prejudice" article in *Time*, wrote another lengthy article for the magazine about the submarine program and the promotion controversy. Before it ran, his editors submitted it voluntarily to the Navy for security review. Upon reading it, Wallin called it "a scurrilous and uninformed emotional appeal to sympathy for a supposed underdog." The Navy now understood that Rickover was not simply going to leave. "Traditionally, the integrity of our selection boards," a confidential Bureau of Personnel memo fretted, "has never been challenged by individuals who were selected or not."[15]

Wallin told a congressional committee in March 1953, "The nuclear power billet in the Bureau of Ships is presently a captain's billet, and we now have on hand a number of Engineering Duty captains who are well qualified for the post."[16] Rickover was replaceable.

But powerful forces loudly embraced Rickover's cause. Yates sent out a bulletin, drawing wide press coverage, demanding that the Armed Services Committee probe the Selection Board decision.[17] In a lengthy March 2 speech in the House, Yates called the failure to promote Rickover a "flagrant injustice" and declared, "the success story of the atomic project is one almost entirely of individual achievement — the vision and devotion of a single man." He condemned the secretive Selection Board process: "Only God and the nine admirals on the board know why Rickover was passed over."[18]

Yates knew how to scare the Navy brass; he submitted a bill proposing major reforms of their promotion procedures. The proposals included reconstituting the standard makeup of a Selection Board to include more Engineering Duty Only officers, opening deliberations to public scrutiny and executive-branch intervention, and setting special standards to encourage advancement of technical specialists, not just line officers. Yates then sent a public note to Saltonstall asking him to take the unprecedented step of withholding endorsement of July's Selection Board appointees. The Armed Services Committee then did something unheard of: out of 5,887 promotions at all grades, the senators held back 39 Navy captains appointed rear admiral. The Navy was terrified that it was on the verge of losing control over its own promotion system.

Newspapers and magazines around the country began to pile on. "Without his leadership," wrote *Look* magazine, "the atom sub would still be a dream. Captain Rickover's reward for this service to the nation is . . . that he must retire from the Navy next June, with his work half done, at the age of 53."[19] The decision not to promote him blew up into national controversy and now threatened to scuttle the Navy's command structure.

Rickover still kept his distance from his staffers' efforts. However, even his wife, Ruth, joined the fight. Using her legal research background, she studied the laws and procedures manuals governing Navy promotions. Nothing, she learned, prevented the Navy from convening yet a third board or an interim one. Perhaps here was a path to an exit from the controversy. She suggested the idea to Rickover's associates, who shared it with the Navy secretary's office.

Recently arrived at the White House, President Dwight D. Eisenhower viewed the promotion controversy with dismay. He wanted it resolved quickly. Secretary of the Navy Robert B. Anderson proposed in a March 6, 1953, letter to Saltonstall that the Navy convene a special Selection Board to recommend retention of a single EDO officer experienced in atomic power for ships for the period of one year. That way Rickover would not be forced to retire on June 30, 1953, and he would remain eligible for promotion review at the next regularly scheduled Selection Board in July. The secretary would then require that the board select one EDO with experience in atomic power for ships for promotion to rear admiral. After learning of Anderson's plan, Rickover said to Rockwell, "The Secretary of the Navy . . . didn't actually say they had to promote a one hundred-twenty-five-pound Jew, but he came as close as he could."[20]

By mid-May, it was clear that, regardless of what the Navy wanted, Rickover was going to get promoted.[21] But some officers still refused to accept the finality of the secretary's message to the Navy. When the July board met, rather than admit Rickover into their ranks, all three of the EDO flag officers on it refused to select him. The six line admirals on the board cast their votes unanimously for Rickover to avoid a congressional takeover of the Navy's promotion system.[22] He made admiral.

In the final trophy head carried off from Rickover's complete triumph, the CNO ordered Admiral Wallin rotated out of his BuShips chief's post a year and a half earlier than scheduled. The Navy dispatched him to the other side of the land, placing him in charge of its Puget Sound shipyard at Bremerton, Washington.[23]

A year and a half later, after the promotion controversy had been resolved, Blair's admiring book, *The Atomic Submarine and Admiral Rickover*, came out. Blair blamed Rickover's initial rejection on antisemitism in the Navy. However, some people in and out of the Navy disputed the charge. "There wasn't that bias against Rickover," insisted Albert Mumma, after Rickover's former BuShips nuclear-program rival had retired as a rear admiral. "That wasn't the problem," he claimed. "Rickover was a vertical specialist, and he hadn't broadened."[24] Others, such as New York representative and later senator Jacob Javits, a Jew, expressed the view that Rickover's unbridled push for adaption of a modern technology clashed with the conservative service branch. "It's more a Billy Mitchell case than a Dreyfus case," he said, referring to the Navy aviation pioneer, court-martialed in 1925 for his overly vociferous advocacy of aerial warfare.[25] The authors of an official AEC history of the first decades of the nuclear Navy surveyed many of the participants in the controversy and concluded, "Religious prejudice was in our opinion a reinforcing but not a controlling factor in Ricko-ver's unpopularity in the Navy."[26]

Rickover was not the victim of—and ultimately victor over—an antisemitic inquisition. Rather, what is clear is that he was obstinate, egotistical, and abrasive, a specialized engi-neer indifferent to and sometimes actively in rebellion against the Navy's chain of command, protocols, and culture. By push-ing the Navy into technology frontiers, his nuclear-power pro-gram proved alien to existing thinking. He was unwilling to bend to authority and unwavering in his insistence that his pro-gram receive absolute priority. And he would fight to the death for his principles. He was also a Jew, even if no longer practic-ing and reputedly a convert to his wife's Episcopalian faith. The combination proved toxic to the many fellow Navy officers he had frustrated, infuriated, or bruised over the years.

The freshly promoted rear admiral's victory over the Navy was trumpeted across the land when he appeared on the cover of *Time* magazine the following January. He even wore his Navy uniform in public, for perhaps the first time in five years, for the *Time* photographer. The story was coordinated with the publication of Blair's laudatory book, which he wrote in part at the Naval Reactor offices and with the cooperation of Rickover and his staff and with editorial help from Ruth. Rickover, Blair wrote, was "convinced that nuclear submarines will save the Navy from near-complete elimination as a fighting arm of the nation."[27] He intended to "save" a Navy that did not want him to save it and despised him for trying.

6

———◆◆◆◆———

Underway on Nuclear Power

WHEN THE MARK I reached its full power rating on June 23, plans called for shutting down the reactor after forty-eight hours. However, the first twenty-four hours went so smoothly that the team decided to stop at that point to review physics data rather than risk more strain on the power plant. Also, they were concerned about the possibility that the reactor's fuel would build up a poorly understood, scaly black material known as "Chalk River Unidentified Deposit" or by its acronym, CRUD, from which the now-common term derives. CRUD had caused a costly earlier meltdown at a Canadian water-cooled pile. Should accumulated CRUD block up coolant channels inside the Mark I reactor core, a partial meltdown would scuttle the entire nuclear-propulsion program.

But Rickover looked not just at the technical aspects of the powered run. Faced with Eisenhower's desire to reduce post–Korean War military budgets, the Pentagon had recently halted the aircraft-carrier reactor program and had not yet authorized the SFR — submarine fleet reactor — to go into production. Progress on the molten-salt reactor, the Mark A, at Knolls still lagged. Mark I was the only operating nuclear engine that Rickover had, and the Navy still doubted that his power plants would ever drive a warship. Over the objections of several engineers, Rickover ordered the trial run to continue. He knew it would be the ultimate demonstration if the power plant held up during a long-duration, high-powered run. He upped the ante and ordered a full-power run to simulate a real Atlantic crossing, the equivalent of a Nova Scotia to Ireland underwater transit. No sub in history had traveled more than about forty miles underwater at top speeds before having to resurface. A successful, simulated, twenty-five-hundred-mile trans-Atlantic crossing would take about one hundred hours. Rickover said to the naysayers among his staff, "This run will show people that this thing is real. It's not a toy."[1] Once again Rickover risked everything to show the "Navy bastards" that he was overturning their world.[2]

Rickover rolled out a chart of the Atlantic Ocean outside the hull. As each hour ticked by, he plotted out the approximate distances the simulated *Nautilus* had traveled. The land sub churned away without incident until, a little short of three days into the run, strange noises started coming from a circulation pump. Then sparks flew out of the generator. Readings from some of the nuclear instruments grew erratic. The engineers assessed the malfunctions; they decided the sub should steam on. Early on the fourth day, a condenser tube in the steam plant developed a leak, and water and power levels dropped. Rickover's staff called on him to end the run rather than put everything at risk. What happened next is in dispute. According to his project officer, E. E. Kintner, Rickover was adamant that the run must continue. "If the plant has a limitation so serious," he said, "now is the time to find out. I accept full responsibility for any casualty," a Navy term for a damaging incident. But according to Simpson, Bettis's technical director, Rickover told his staff to get in touch with Simpson. "He's in charge," Rickover said. At that moment, Simpson was at his wife's Pittsburgh hospital bedside, where she had just delivered their child. An engineer at Arco called asking him what to do. He wondered later whether, by shifting the decision to him, Rickover was not setting him up as the "fall-guy" if something catastrophic occurred. With the Arco engineers waiting nearly two thousand miles away, Simpson weighed the possibilities: "An accident on this test run," he figured, "could have made the project politically impossible. On the other hand, since there were many in the Navy who thought that the nuclear submarine was just too complex to be practical, not being able to make the submerged crossing could have jeopardized the program." He said to keep going.[3]

After ninety-six hours, the sub "passed" Fastnet Rock, Ireland, on the chart. Excess steam was dumped into the holding ponds outside the building, the reactor control rods were lowered, the power plant shut down. The men on hand clapped and breathed a sigh of relief. During the simulated crossing, the Mark I's crew had throttled back below full power for barely over three hours in total. No sub engine in history had come close to running for that duration at high speed. At one point in the historic run, an experienced naval power engineer watched the propeller shaft turning and turning. "So much comes out back here," he said, and then gesturing toward the power plant that ran and ran without refueling, "and nothing goes in up there!"[4]

Nautilus's first skipper, Dennis Wilkinson, and his future team of officers studying the reactor were among those following the simulated run closely. After this, they stood two eight-hour watches per day operating the Mark I for six months.

While they did, NR staffers deliberately scrammed the reactor, shut off the pumps, messed with the water chemistry, induced leaks, and otherwise initiated real and simulated emergencies. After each watch, the officers studied the power-plant manuals, submitted to demanding examinations, then drove or bused the sixty miles to the town of Arco, the only local housing, where they slept a few hours before returning to stand watch again. (On real subs, watches ran four hours on and four off, but the living situation at Arco made this impossible.) As at sea on a long cruise, the crew's exhaustion, their upset internal clocks, their continuous cups of coffee, their overtaxed brains, constant worry about a nuclear accident, everything except the possibility of military action, were real. And actual anomalies and unexpected problems did occur. Before the nuclear trainees went to sea, they responded to nearly every sort of malfunction, unpredicted fluctuation, and emergency they might have to face in the real sub.[5] When problems arose, the officers on hand and engineers reviewed the incident together and, based on their determinations of causes and solutions, made recommendations for changes to the Mark II being assembled in Pittsburgh. Many bugs were ironed out; nothing was left to chance.

As EB built out the *Nautilus*, Wilkinson and his crew, having completed their training on the Mark I, were sent to Groton, where they participated in its construction. The Navy had never done anything like this before—usually sending officers and crew to the new ship only after its formal handoff to the Navy.[6] The *Nautilus*'s future sailors watched, learned, and advised the shipbuilders. This would become standard procedure for all future vessels. Before the nuclear submariners ever went to sea, they knew their ship inside and out. Rickover's NR team worked with the early officers to revise operational procedures and codify them into the shipboard manuals and procedure books that still fill Maneuvering Room shelves aboard naval vessels.[7]

"No machinery has ever been tested more than the components and systems for the Mark I and *Nautilus*," Simpson commented.[8]

Mark I endured at Arco. The prototype would operate as a reactor testing and training center for more than thirty-six years, burning through several reactor cores. At one point, the reactor ran sixteen hundred hours straight, almost seventy days, at full power—enough to circle the Earth twice.[9] Thousands of officers were trained on it before the Mark I was decommissioned on October 17, 1989. The prototype would outlive Rickover.

With the *Nautilus* still a hull under construction on the EB ways and *Seawolf* soon to begin, Rickover signed an agreement, on November 19, 1953, with BuShips that designated Naval Reactors permanently responsible for all naval reactors regardless of their stage of development and operation. Perhaps there would never be another nuclear ship after *Nautilus* and *Seawolf*, but from this point on, any change at any point in a ship reactor's life cycle would require Rickover's formal approval. He understood very well the special powers he had acquired. Many people within the Navy still considered a nuclear fleet a pipe dream; regardless, every future nuclear-powered ship would need the consent of the director of Naval Reactors before going to sea. A midlevel bureau chief within BuShips could, in effect, overrule operational orders and hold back any nuclear ship that he considered unsafe. "No one could foresee," wrote Captain Edward Beach, "that the energy of the atom would become so important that whoever controlled it would in time become the most important man in the Navy."[10] Before a nuclear vessel existed, Rickover had placed himself at the throttle of the United States' nuclear Navy of the future—and he would damn well make sure there would be a future nuclear Navy for him to control.

In the summer of 1953, the Mark II reactor went into *Nautilus* on the ways at EB. That milestone came just eighteen months after the prototype started up at Arco. Even BuShips was coming around to the idea that a nuclear sub was truly on its way. The new chief of BuShips, Rickover rival Rear Admiral Albert Mumma, elevated the nuclear-power division to report to him. However, that put the two engineers directly at odds. Mumma attempted to wrest Rickover's domain loose from his grip. Mumma publicly criticized his fellow officer in a newspaper interview. "Rickover," he said, "works like a dog himself, but he's not a happy, pleasant individual. People feel rebuffed by someone exceptionally tough, and Rickover makes a fetish of that."[11]

Despite the backbiting, Rickover kept pushing to meet his incredibly short timeline. In retrospect, the federal regulatory review and approval process for this brand-new and dangerous technology seems laughably superficial. A lone safeguards committee of outside experts held a series of review meetings, with Edward Teller, father of the hydrogen bomb, as its chair, concluding with a session in a private dining room at Electric Boat. With Rickover and the leadership of Naval Reactors, Bettis, and EB eager to please, Teller noted that the last time he was in New London, the train was delayed by a hurricane that had scattered and overturned boats onto the track. He asked what would happen to the reactor's control rods should the *Nautilus* roll at such an extreme angle. Rickover and his technical staff had in fact put Mark I through just such a test. The pressurized coolant system could operate upside down. Teller shortly sent the gathered officials on their way.[12] The *Nautilus* was set to launch on January 21, 1954.

* * *

However, the Navy still was not through with its attempts to downplay the significance of the atomic submarine's advent—nor to poke one last finger into Rickover's eye. With the launch approaching, President Eisenhower told the Navy and Electric Boat that he wanted his wife, Mamie Eisenhower, to christen this revolutionary new warship. The First Lady's participation in the launch would spotlight both the United States' technological prowess and the wider promise of atomic power. Even if nuclear energy was first going into a warship, the *Nautilus* was a harbinger of peaceful civilian applications for it, which the president was eager to play up. News about Mamie Eisenhower's planned presence at the big event stirred broad public anticipation.

With just weeks to go, the influential military affairs analyst and reporter John Finney met with two Navy public-information officers to learn more about the sub. Finney wondered about the extravagant claims being made for the *Nautilus*. No friend of Rickover's, the press officer Commander Slade Cutter, a decorated World War II sub veteran, had prepared a fact sheet for Finney comparing the new $55 million (amounting to more than $500 million today) atomic submarine to the capabilities of World War II's most powerful subs—which had cost on average about $3 million (less than $30 million today) to build.[13] Despite *Nautilus*'s vastly higher price tag, it by contrast seemed a warship with less firepower. Cutter told Finney that the *Nautilus* was, in truth, an experimental vessel that would never join the operational fleet. With a little more than two weeks until its launch, the January 4, 1954, *Washington Post* headlined a front-page article, "A-Submarine Held Unfit for Battle Now." Other newspapers picked up the story, asserting that the Navy's latest technological marvel was "already obsolete" before it went to sea. *Time* magazine quoted Cutter that the *Nautilus* was "strictly a test vehicle": "I doubt if she will ever fire a shot in anger."[14]

President Eisenhower read the stories and, furious, called Secretary of Defense Charles Wilson at seven in the morning: "What do you mean by asking my wife to sponsor this test vehicle?" he growled. Caught flatfooted, Wilson quickly assembled several AEC and Defense Department officials, including Cutter. They discussed canceling the public launch event altogether. Then the fact sheet that had served as a backgrounder for the denigrating stories circulated at the table. Cutter's animosity behind what *Time* called "a deliberate leak" emerged. A sense developed that an anti-Rickover vendetta fed into the negative stories. Wilson reassured the president: this submarine merited the hype. The launch would go ahead as planned.

January 21 dawned foggy, wet, and cold.[15] Despite the weather, some twelve thousand spectators, the *New York Times* reported in front-page coverage the following day—twenty thousand exclaimed the newsreels, *thirty thousand* insisted a General Dynamics postevent brochure—overflowed the stands and crowded the docks, riverbanks, and boats on the Thames River.[16] A special nine-car train rolled Mamie Eisenhower and other dignitaries from Washington to dockside, where they climbed a temporary platform. They sat and stood before the sub's flag-bunting-festooned prow, with the gigantic hull, black below the water line, olive green above, looming up before them on its ways. The skipper-to-be, Wilkinson, paced nervously on the dock below while the rest of *Nautilus*'s future officers and crew stood on its deck beneath a line of colorful pennants stretched fore and aft from its sail (sometimes referred to as the "conning tower"). Shortly before the scheduled eleven o'clock christening, a brilliant sun pierced the fog and shone down on the gathering. Mamie Eisenhower raised a bottle of champagne. "Hit it good and hard, Mrs. Eisenhower!" someone shouted.

With the president's naval aide, Captain Edward Beach, counseling Mrs. Eisenhower as the prow started to move— "Here we go—hit it!"—the First Lady, in a mink coat, pink gloves, and a flowered straw bonnet, smashed the bottle against the steel prow and declared, "I christen thee *Nautilus.*" Glass shattered and champagne sprayed. Cheers exploded, horns blared, camera bulbs flashed while the *Nautilus* slid slowly back. It picked up speed on its launching cradle until it splashed into the water. Foam trailed as it glided back. When it was finally at rest, four tugboats gathered along its sides, nudging it to the pier.

Rickover stood unsmiling within a tight clutch of on-lookers, two rows behind and to the side of Mrs. Eisenhower on the christening platform. In the speeches prior to the launch, Rickover was the lone military officer mentioned by name by CNO Admiral Robert Carney and AEC Chief Lewis L. Strauss. Photographs, films, and stories covering the first atomic sub-marine's launch went worldwide.

Workers scrambled around the clock to ready the *Nautilus* for its first sea trials before the end of the year. Rickover wanted them to take place *ahead* of schedule. Then the unthinkable happened: on September 16, pressurized steam pumped in from shore burst an engine-room pipe. An inspection team found that Electric Boat had installed a length of pipe that was not intended to handle high-pressure steam. The impli-cations were devastating; no records or test equipment could determine whether *thousands* of feet of comparable-dimension piping running throughout the power plant and hull met their design specifications. EB had installed the same size pipes at Arco and on both the GE West Milton Mark A liquid-sodium prototype and Knolls' Submarine Intermediate Reactor power plant being readied for USS *Seawolf* (SSN-575) on the EB ways downriver. Rickover could have accepted that the rest of the pipes were the correct ones based on the design specs. But he ordered, "Rip it all out and replace it. Every damn inch . . . however long it takes. We're not going to sea with faulty piping."[17] He also ordered checkoffs to ensure that all future pipes were the right ones before their installation. The 'round-the-clock repair work inside the cramped *Nautilus* delayed its completion by three months.

At the end of 1949, when Naval Reactors did not yet exist and not a single contract had been drafted, Rickover claimed that he would have a nuclear-powered sub ready to go to sea by January 1955. On December 30, 1954, the crewman at the reactor control panel aboard the *Nautilus* slowly turned the throttle. Shortly before midnight, a chain reaction set in on a shipboard reactor for the first time. The fission energy heated the water. But *Nautilus* had yet to steam up. Against the advice of shipyard personnel worried about the heavy stationary forces on the engine, on January 3, 1955, Rickover ordered the reactor brought to full power and the throttle opened. The sub strained against the mooring lines. The new power plant performed flawlessly.[18]

At eight on a frigid January 17 morning under bright blue skies, Rickover boarded the boat. Electric Boat's general manager, Carlton Shugg, came aboard shortly after that. Rickover insisted that shipyard executives sail aboard the *Nautilus* for its sea trials, as he would for every new boat after it. If something went wrong, they would experience it in the flesh. With eleven officers, eighty-five enlisted crew members, and sixty civilian executives, engineers, and technicians packed on board, at eleven that morning, *Nautilus*'s sailors cast off the mooring lines. Short and tall, Rickover and Wilkinson stood side by side on the bridge of the sail, where the officer of the deck called out course and speed changes to the helmsman. The sub's twin propellers frothed the greenish water. Slowly the dark, mostly submerged warship pulled back from the dock into the Thames

River. Rickover had hoped for a quiet departure because he knew sea trials rarely went without hitches. But the Navy announced to the press that the *Nautilus* would leave port that morning. When the ship inched back, a crowd numbering in the thousands let out a roar along the riverbank, while, on the piers, almost as many yard workers and crew members' family waved and shouted to the sailors and officers standing at attention on the deck and bridge. A Navy tender carrying news reporters and photographers waited in the middle of the river. An Air Force helicopter hung overhead. *Nautilus* made ready to pull back and turn out into the ship channel.

Then a heart-sinking call came from the engine room to the bridge. One of the two reduction gearboxes was making an ear-splitting, metal-on-metal screeching noise; engineers shut down the turbine.

Wilkinson wanted to return to dock, but Rickover, unwilling to accept such an embarrassment, suggested—as an EDO, he could not order Wilkinson, the ship's commander—that he continue with just the one working turbine and an auxiliary electric motor. An anxious Rickover raced below to help figure out the cause of the problem while the crew members on the slow-moving boat's deck smiled uneasily back at the curious onlookers. The rear admiral donned coveralls and handed tools to the machinist mate working to discover the source of the noise.[19] Finally, he figured out that a bolt had worked itself loose enough to rub against the reduction-gear casing. The problem was corrected. It took a full half hour for the *Nautilus* to back out and make a half-circle turn into the ship channel before it headed down the Thames River. Seeing no diesel exhaust, a disbelieving World War II submariner on the dock insisted, "I think she's running on batteries."[20]

Just before exiting into the Long Island Sound, Wilkinson sent a brief, soon-to-be-famous message to the commander of the Atlantic Submarine Force: "Underway on nuclear power."

Those words announced the beginning of the age of nuclear propulsion.

A front-page article with a big photograph of the new sub on its way down the Thames River channel appeared in the *New York Times*. The reporter noted the presence of Rickover on board, the admiral "who fought against strong Navy opposition for the revolutionary submarine."

Over the next two days, *Nautilus* steamed for several hours on the surface before returning to port in the afternoon. Upon the sub's reaching the North Atlantic on the first day, twelve-foot seas sent its unstable reverse-teardrop-shaped hull rolling thirty-five degrees. Waves ripped away teak decking. A quarter of those who were on board got sick. Some urged postponing further trials pending calmer seas. Rickover ordered the trials to continue. The reactor handled the pitching and rolling without a hitch. At last, on January 20, a log entry recorded, "First dive ever made on nuclear power," at 1:32 in the afternoon.

The crew and visitors took turns exploring the *Nautilus*'s underwater performance and characteristics. A few small saltwater and oil leaks developed, and two quickly smothered electrical fires flared up—not atypical for a sea trial. Its pumps roared, and at high speeds, loud noises and hull vibrations echoed through the boat. But it reached its top speed of twenty-three knots, about twenty-six miles per hour, and sustained it for hours. At speed and with its advanced control systems, *Nautilus* maneuvered more abruptly than previous subs. A surprised cook could not stop a huge pot from sliding off the range. Spaghetti and meatballs intended for 160 hungry people splattered across the galley.

With less space needed for enormous batteries and diesel engines, living quarters and other spaces in the nearly block-long ship were luxurious compared to the "pig boats" of World War II—although with so many people on board for the trials, many had to double bunk and spread out to sleep in the torpedo room. Rickover recalled the misery of life on the hot, smelly, crowded S-48. He insisted on better for the first nuclear vessel's crew. With a berth for each sailor, future crews would no longer have to "hot bunk," or alternate in a berth; powerful air conditioners maintained a steady temperature and humidity; the mess hall could seat thirty-six at a time, fifty when used as a movie theater. There were film and reading libraries, washer-dryer machines, soft-ice-cream dispensers, and a jukebox.

To dive a diesel-electric boat required shutting off air intakes and closing hatches in an orchestrated scramble just prior to going under. *Nautilus* moved seamlessly between air and water, diving and surfacing like a dolphin, fifty-two times in all that day, the first of many submarine records it would establish. Rickover took the helm for the forty-first dive. On the *Nautilus*'s first four-hour submerged high-speed run, Rickover ordered a crashback, a full-astern emergency stop, one of the most taxing stresses on a sub's power plant. *Nautilus* performed without a hitch. Barely a flicker of emotion crossed Rickover's face, even when he took the dive controls, but Wilkinson said to a friend, "When nobody is looking, I've caught him smiling." Rickover radioed birthday greetings to Ruth "from the *Nautilus* at sea."[21] The sub performed beyond its engineers' highest expectations.

Rickover was careful about keeping his congressional backers informed and impressed, and at his invitation, the congressional Joint Committee on Atomic Energy met aboard the *Nautilus*, in underwater session on March 20, another historical first. The twelve congressmen and four staffers recorded in the published minutes their quorum "beyond the Continental Shelf at a depth in excess of three hundred feet" under the Atlantic Ocean. They were so impressed that following the underwater meeting, they issued a joint statement declaring, "we deeply believe her success marks the beginning of a new approach to naval warfare, and, indeed, of the ultimate replacement of conventionally fueled submarines and surface ships by ones driven by atomic energy." Their statement applauded Rickover, "to whom more than any other person the success of the *Nautilus* is due." During his underwater testimony, Rickover suggested that the committee minutes record the fact that "during the course of the Committee meeting, the *Nautilus* had operated longer at high speeds submerged than any other operating submarine," surely a thumbed nose at the rest of the Navy's fleet. Two days later, speaking on the Senate floor, one of the committee members joked that although it was a meeting of the full committee, "I think it might be correct to say it was a meeting of the 'sub' committee," eliciting gales of laughter.[22] Congress now viewed the nuclear Navy as Rickover's Navy. And Rickover understood what he owed his Capitol Hill backers in turn; he would unabashedly declare in congressional testimony a decade later, "I am a creature of Congress because, had it not been for Congress, I would not be here today."[23]

Nautilus was formally commissioned into the Navy's Atlantic Fleet on April 22, 1955. In May, Wilkinson took it on a shakedown cruise of thirteen hundred submerged miles in eighty-four hours to Puerto Rico, averaging sixteen knots for the 1,381-mile run, a distance tenfold longer beneath the sea than any previous submarine in history. Many more firsts lay ahead.

There was a before and after. Even doubters in the Navy now understood that in the *Nautilus* the submarine service possessed the most powerfully versatile naval warship ever built—precursor to an entire fleet of such vessels. Like its science-fiction namesake, it could dive and stay submerged, going anywhere in secret. It could sneak up on an enemy's surface warships, attack undetected, and outrace pursuers. One day nuclear subs would have the potential to patrol within range of an enemy's strategic targets carrying cruise and ballistic missiles designed for underwater launch. No present power on Earth could defend against such an unprecedented, mobile weapon hidden deep in the oceans. A Navy that seemed to have lost its bearings in the postwar Atomic Age now possessed the most invulnerable force in the Cold War arsenal. The Navy and Congress also had an invention that dazzled minds. They intended to exploit the nation's newly won advantage to its fullest. But Rickover intended to hold the inaugural subs on a short leash and keep them and all future nuclear ships there.

Problems in early reactor technology opened doors for Rickover, the shore-bound admiral, to extend his reach out to sea. Multiple issues remained unresolved in the liquid-metal reactor, the Submarine Intermediate Reactor, at General Electric's Knolls Laboratory. In theory, molten sodium's far greater heat reserve—850 degrees Fahrenheit versus the 500 degrees of the *Nautilus*'s STR—could produce hotter pressurized steam and thus more power, permitting a smaller, lighter, and longer-lasting reactor core, taking up 40 percent less space. But the superheated liquid metal posed serious hazards: for one, it caught fire when exposed to air, and for another, even a small leak into water, never far off inside a sub, would explode with lethal force. Less dangerous but complicating, sodium froze at 200 degrees Fahrenheit and had to be kept warm even after the reactor was shut down, making maintenance time-consuming, complex, and costly.

At the time when the AEC's regulatory Safeguards Committee greenlighted the *Nautilus*'s STR power plant, the influential Edward Teller had already voiced concerns about the future *Seawolf*'s SIR. The committee consented to its production on the condition that Rickover circumscribe the *Seawolf*'s port and sea operations. The Navy would have to ask Rickover before operating *Seawolf* outside those limits. Never before had a "beached" officer exercised authority over a warship's operations. Rickover's technical director, Ted Rockwell, said, "The Navy's operation people [understood these rules] as a raw power play. And indeed they were."[24] When the *Seawolf* finally went to sea with relatively little fanfare in February 1957, it remained within Rickover's designated sphere of operations.

However, bristling at the new restraints, the Atlantic sub fleet's commanders tried to send the *Seawolf* out on an extended mission without first getting Rickover's permission. In the ensuing struggle over operational control, Rickover overruled the Navy's claims of "military necessity" and finally, humiliating the Navy, forced the sub back to base. At a congressional hearing, he testified, "They [line officers] finally realized they must not move these ships around the way they were accustomed to move conventional ships." Rickover deadpanned, "This new system was irksome to the submarine operators," who "never [before] had to discuss with anyone how to operate their ships."[25] In fact nothing seemed more maddening to the proud, independent line officers than to have their orders countermanded by an EDO who had never captained a sub or capital ship. They would have to get used to it.

Rickover soon instituted similar rules that gave NR the authority to stop any nuclear vessel that failed inspection from sailing. His inspection teams visited nuclear vessels "without anybody's permission or any notice," recalled Admiral Charles Duncan, who served as commander in chief of the Navy's Atlantic Fleet from 1970 to 1972. The inspection teams had more authority than anyone, even the CNO, to hold a ship in port. Admiral Duncan recalled, "The tight control that he held on the nuclear Navy . . . I've never seen anything like it in my life. Just absolutely unbelievable."[26] Eugene Tissot, one of the early commanding officers of the first nuclear aircraft carrier, *Enterprise*, said, "When we were in port, his representatives were on board all the time." At the end of a regular review, Rickover himself would arrive and go through the engineering spaces. "I spent many an hour looking at the back of his neck," Tissot said. "He'd only berate me in no uncertain terms for what was wrong. Only perfection was acceptable to him."[27] From Rickover's desk in Tempo 3, his power extended over his Navy wherever it steamed.

Despite Rickover's breathing down the neck of the sub's captain, the *Seawolf* still managed to set a record by remaining submerged from August 7 until October 6, 1957. It traveled nearly sixty thousand underwater miles in all before its unwieldy reactor was switched out for the new, more advanced pressurized-water Submarine Fleet Reactor (SFR).

Naval Reactors designed the SFR, also known as S5W (the fifth-generation submarine reactor built by Westinghouse), to power smaller and more economical subs, with a core engineered to last far longer without refueling. Eventually, NR intended to engineer a reactor that would last a ship's lifetime. The SFR was standardized for quicker, more affordable production for the numerous boats the Navy expected to build over the coming decade. The first SFR would go into the new Skate class of smaller, fast-attack subs. The Navy wanted its own yards to develop nuclear construction capabilities. Over Rickover's initial objections to government yards that he could not compel to meet his standards, the Navy assigned its Mare Island, California, yard to build two of the new class of subs and its Portsmouth shipyard two more. Electric Boat would build the class's namesake boat. The *Skate*'s keel was laid just six months after the *Nautilus*'s early-1955 launch and went to sea just two years later.

After the dazzling success of the first few subs, more and then yet more would follow; additional shipyards would open, as would other prototypes and training centers. The training program would turn out the hundreds and then thousands of fresh "nukes"—or "nucs"—young officers and mates schooled in Rickover's unwavering standards of perfection in operating a nuclear-propelled vessel. All of them in the end would report to Rickover. As the nuclear Navy grew and took shape, Rickover's imprint was everywhere upon it. Over the coming years, Rickover's imprint would stamp itself onto the whole Navy.

7

---◆┃◆┃◆---

Atoms for Peace

ALONG WITH RICKOVER'S submarine engine, the Navy tasked Naval Reactors with designing surface-ship power plants. While engineering his first reactors and building the *Nautilus*, Rickover had started work with Argonne and Bettis on the so-called Large Ship Reactor (LSR). The massive LSR was engineered to produce enough power to drive a massive aircraft carrier. But the costly program had barely begun when the Department of Defense, saddled with post-Korean War budget cutbacks—and committed to growing the Air Force's portion of the budget pie—canceled it. He tried to save the LSR but failed. Even then, after an initial reluctance to get involved in civilian programs, Rickover saw an opportunity in the abandoned LSR project. In his inimitable way, an apparent setback proved a boon for Naval Reactors and the nation.

After nearly a decade of the Atomic Age, the United States had given little more than lip service to developing peaceful uses for atomic power. In the Cold War race to keep well ahead of the Soviets militarily, the new Atomic Energy Commission was focused on producing more and bigger nuclear bombs. At the same time, the Soviets, along with their atomic-weapons programs, had embarked on civilian electricity-generation projects and construction of a nuclear-powered icebreaker. The USSR had also begun sharing its nuclear know-how with Warsaw Pact lands and, in a diplomatic coup, even some non-aligned nations.[1] Despite the United States' investment in technology leadership, it had little to show its people or share with its allies except an expanding nuclear-arsenal umbrella. The new Eisenhower administration and the AEC began to search for ways to move beyond the United States' bellicose, bomb-stockpiling image by developing civilian uses for this mighty technology. Eisenhower pushed for a fleet of nuclear-powered merchant "peace ships." But just one demonstration project, the NS *Savannah*, was built, by private firms using a Rickover reactor design, and commissioned in 1959. Rickover fought against building any more merchant ships when a Naval Reactors review of commercial shipping records showed that cargo vessels were in collisions on average about once every twenty years. Putting multiple nuclear ships into crowded urban ports would run a mounting risk of collision, with the potential for release of radioactivity into a city. The economics of nuclear propulsion for commercial ships also fell short. After *Savannah*, the merchant-ship concept died.[2] Meantime, Rickover had a partially engineered LSR stowed at Bettis. But he saw in it a safer and faster way to put atomic power into civilian service.

He spoke to the AEC and the Joint Committee on Atomic Energy. "We have the technology in hand," he told them, "and the organization to handle the project, and timing is politically perfect."[3] Moreover, Rickover promised he would have a civilian power station built and running quickly. Some AEC staff members objected to putting a naval officer in charge of a civilian program. And the Navy considered it a distraction. But, on July 1, 1953, the commission authorized him to begin preliminary studies. By October, Thomas Murray, the same AEC head who had turned the throttle on the Mark I in May, announced to the world that the United States would construct the first entirely civilian electric power plant. Rickover would be in charge. The Soviets were readying a small reactor, which connected to the power grid in June 1954, and the British had also begun constructing a power reactor at Calder Hall, England; but both were designed primarily for weapons-fuel production, with electricity as a by-product. Rickover's power reactor would be the first solely devoted to civilian purposes.

Wanting to make a splash on the global stage, President Eisenhower went to the United Nations on December 8, 1953, to announce what he called the Atoms for Peace program. The United States would, he declared, make US atomic expertise and even nuclear materials and machinery available to allied nations for peaceful uses.[4] Eisenhower told the gathering that "this greatest of destructive forces [could] be developed into a great constructive force for all mankind."[5] Soon the United States began to ship nuclear materials to universities in Europe. But as a first step in developing peaceful uses for atomic power, through the AEC, Rickover contracted with Westinghouse to reengineer the beached LSR project for installation in a central station power plant.

Converting a ship reactor to utility purposes was not a simple task. Bettis had to produce a new type of only slightly enriched uranium-dioxide fuel—as opposed to scarce highly enriched uranium used in naval reactors—as well as to engineer various mechanical innovations and an entirely different style control system. The stationary reactor would, for safety reasons, sit inside a partially buried bunker within a multilayer concrete-and-steel containment structure. Then there was the reactor itself. Its pressure vessel—five times larger than the Mark II—would, in the end, stand thirty-two feet tall and twelve feet across inside with eight-inch-thick outer steel walls; the reactor would require 264 tons of carbon and stainless steel in all. No metal structure that large had ever been cast before— and it would take two and a half years by itself to fabricate.[6]

The ambitions and scale were daunting, but nine utility companies bid for the prestigious project. A Pittsburgh regional power supplier, Duquesne Light, won the bidding, at more than $23 million.[7] That would cover the cost of the site and electricity-generating portion of the power station; the AEC would pick up the far greater tab for the nuclear reactor. The power station would go up in Shippingport, fittingly on former coal fields on the banks of the Ohio River about twenty-five miles upriver from Pittsburgh.

Rickover knew the value of a publicity stunt. On September 9, 1954, some fourteen hundred people gathered at the Shippingport site to watch Eisenhower, who was recovering from a heart attack in Denver, via a closed-circuit television hookup. As if performing magic, the president waved a neutron-radiating wand over a neutron counter that sent a signal to an unmanned bulldozer at the site. The earthmover roared to life and dug into the soil in a sort of futuristic automated groundbreaking. The crowd cheered. The press ate it up.[8]

Rickover vowed to have the plant online by mid-March 1957. He posted a motto for the project at NR and contractors' offices: "Full Power in Fifty-Seven." Nobody thought this was realistic. But Rickover cajoled, threatened, bullied, and squeezed the necks of his contractors. "Nothing was ever being done well enough or fast enough to suit Rickover," recalled Simpson, who oversaw Bettis's work at Shippingport. When delays started cropping up, Rickover went to see the president of the construction firm responsible for building the facility at his office. After a particularly rough Rickover harangue, the executive committed to speeding up work. Rickover took a crayon off the man's desk and wrote out the agreed-on schedule on his office wall. "I want it to stay there until you have met your commitment," Rickover snapped and then left.[9]

His tirades made managers shake with fear. Some broke down in tears, but when he pushed too hard, construction foremen and workers simply sat down or walked off the job. Labor troubles and steel-production delays slowed progress, so that despite huge cost overruns, Rickover could not get the project done early, which he had intended. But he did meet his deadline.

On the evening of December 23, 1957, the CBS newsman Walter Cronkite stood on a hill with the lights of Pittsburgh glittering behind him. He announced to the nation and the world that the new Shippingport Atomic Power Station's sixty-eight thousand kilowatts of electricity helped energize those lights. (A new reactor core in development would boost output to one hundred thousand kilowatts.) With atoms generating power, few people cared that a highly critical federal General Accounting Office report blamed the AEC, thus Naval Reactors, for weak cost controls—including heavy use of overtime labor—leading to huge overruns to build the power plant. In the end, Shippingport cost a then phenomenal sum of nearly $116 million (more than $1 billion today). While later refinements and increased reactor output would greatly reduce its price per kilowatt, the station's electrical output cost eight times that of a typical coal-fired plant.[10]

But in the bright light of bringing peaceful atomic power to the people, only the accountants cared about the inordinate cost. As Eisenhower wanted, news about Shippingport's "atoms for peace" carried around the world. At a repeat dedicatory wand-waving performance from the White House in late May, this time throwing a symbolic switch at the plant, the president declared, "This plant . . . represents the hope of our people that the power of the atom will be able to open up a vast new world of peaceful development."[11] At the president's behest, Rickover declassified most of Shippingport's technology. The plant became a university for the utility industry, as private companies in the United States, Europe, and Japan began building their own atomic power stations. A stream of American and foreign engineers and leaders visited Shippingport. Rickover personally toured a Greek princess, British energy ministers, and even the Soviet first deputy premier, Frol Kozlov, through the plant.

But despite Rickover's lobbying to oversee civilian atomic-energy development within the AEC, Naval Reactors received no role in future atomic utility projects. With a mandate to encourage free enterprise, the AEC opted for civilian authority and self-policing by the utility industry. Rickover never lost his worry that business executives would fail to keep their reactors safe. He forced the Navy to give him the individuals he wanted for his ship-reactor operators. He trained them and then re-tested them and ran frequent inspections throughout their time at sea, countermanding operational orders if a ship failed an inspection. Who would be the utilities' Rickover? He worried out loud at a hearing of the Joint Committee on Atomic Energy about weak industry oversight. People, he said, had the false idea that reactors were "much further advanced than they are." He warned, "The whole reactor game hangs on a much more slender thread than most people are aware. There are a lot of things that can go wrong and it requires eternal vigilance. All we have to have is one good accident in the United States and it might set the whole game back for a generation." Only, he admonished, "ability and intelligence among the engineers" and "a high order of watchfulness" could safeguard against disaster.[12] He did not see that happening when industry put profit first with such a sophisticated and potentially dangerous new technology.

"Management," he lamented, "thinks operators are stupid and unmotivated, and so it selects and trains them on that basis. And what do they get? Stupid and unmotivated operators."[13]

Over Duquesne Power's objections, he did insert an NR inspector into Shippingport. The staffer held the authority to shut down the plant if he considered conditions unsafe—which only happened twice over its twenty-five-year life.[14] But Rickover and NR could not apply their standards anywhere else in the civilian atomic-power industry. Another generation would pass before disaster finally struck, but when it did, on March 28, 1979, at the Three Mile Island Power Station, just as Rickover predicted, that accident permanently darkened US attitudes toward nuclear power.

But before then, private companies and foreign governments built many utility reactors, most modeled on Shippingport's pressurized-water reactor technology. It remains the reactor coolant in widest use today, comprising about 65 percent of the world's 450 nuclear power plants.[15] And from *Nautilus* to Shippingport, Rickover's fame as the father of the nuclear Navy *and* the civilian atomic-power industry reached worldwide.

Around the same time that Shippingport came online, three other technological milestones solidified Rickover's hold on the nuclear Navy and moved him a long way toward winning the "genius" label and support from Congress that would place him outside the Navy brass's control. Soon after becoming CNO in August 1955, Admiral Burke, a strong backer of atomic innovation, put a nuclear-propelled surface ship back into the shipbuilding program. At the same time, he revived the earlier LSR program with the goal of building a nuclear supercarrier. In early December 1957, the keel was laid for the *Long Beach*, a missile cruiser to be powered by dual reactors, at the Bethlehem Steel shipyard in Quincy, Massachusetts. The ship's inaugural commanding officer, Eugene Wilkinson of *Nautilus* fame, would take it to sea in September 1961.

At about the same time that the *Long Beach* keel was laid

down, the Navy put in an order for what would be, at 1,123 feet, the longest and heaviest ship ever to go to sea and the largest and most complex piece of hardware ever conceived by humanity. Construction began in 1958 on the future *Enterprise* aircraft carrier at the Newport News Shipyard in Virginia. The enormous ship promised major advancements over previous carriers. Although far more expensive to build than a conventional carrier, the new warship would have no need for the massive fuel bunkers found on other capital ships. With the extra space, it could carry more aircraft squadrons and stockpile more weapons and aviation fuel, decreasing overall operational costs for force projection.

Just two months after *Long Beach* went to sea, "Big E" joined it in November 1961. Less than a year later, a second guided-missile nuclear cruiser (known then as a frigate), *Bainbridge*, completed the world's first all-nuclear task force.

The Navy wanted to show the world what those three ships meant for its global mission. In a first since President Teddy Roosevelt's coal-burning Great White Fleet made its famous demonstration journey around the world from December 1907 to February 1909, the Navy sent out a task force to circumnavigate the globe. The three nuclear ships sailed on July 31, 1964. They steamed 30,565 miles in sixty-five days—fifty-seven at sea—without refueling. Global dignitaries were flown aboard for tours, and the ships welcomed locals at ports of call. As the three nuclear ships cruised their final leg into the US East Coast, *Enterprise* sailors lined up on its dark-gray flight deck in their whites to spell out "$E = mc^2$" for photographers and film crews flying overhead. Images of the great ships splashed across newspapers and on television news reports everywhere they went.[16] Rickover's reactors were once again the talk of the world.

But ahead lay a previously impossible maritime milestone for Rickover's Navy to conquer.

8

Nautilus 90 North

WITH THE LAUNCH OF THE *Nautilus* and *Seawolf*, the Navy, which had been foundering since the end of the war, discovered a new and potentially enduring mission. *Nautilus* and other nuclear submarines quickly demonstrated their world-changing capabilities, breaking one underwater record after another and participating in NATO exercises that proved their war-fighting value. The advent of the nuclear submarine scared the daylights even out of allies: conventional warships lacked the means to detect *Nautilus* before it attacked or even to react fast enough to counterattack. Pentagon planners expected that the Soviets would one day build an atomic-sub fleet of their own, and this prospect dictated the US Navy's development of antisubmarine technologies and tactics completely different from previous underseas-warfare doctrine. The two subs gave the United States and its allies a head start on innovating anti-submarine warfare tactics for the age of nuclear propulsion.[1]

The bigger revolution came with the convergence of missile technology with the new nuclear submarines. Not long after the *Nautilus* demonstrated the value of underwater nuclear propulsion, the first conventionally powered cruise-missile-loaded submarines came off the ways. The world's first submersible-ballistic-missile-carrying nuclear-propelled submarine, the *George Washington*, put to sea at the end of 1959. A year later, the Navy armed the sub with sixteen of the new Polaris nuclear ballistic missiles. Its capacity to remain submerged in the ocean for as long as the crew's provisions lasted made it a potent deterrent to any Soviet threat to invade western Europe or launch atomic-warhead-loaded missiles at the United States.

Seeing the value of subs as the third arm of the nuclear triad of ground-, air-, and sea-launched strategic weapons, President Eisenhower and the Navy wanted more subs and wanted them fast. Four nuclear subs were added onto the 1955 shipbuilding program along with *Seawolf*. In 1956, the Navy included yet four more subs (along with the frigate *Long Beach*) in the nuclear portion of the program. Rickover intended one of them, the *Triton*, at nearly 450 feet more than 100 feet longer than any previous US submarine, to serve as a test platform for the high-horsepower reactors needed for surface ships. The innovative fast-attack submarine *Skipjack* was also part of the program. It would marry nuclear propulsion with the soon-to-be-standard teardrop-shaped hull. The whale-like hull formation increased underwater speed—to more than thirty knots (nearly thirty-five miles per hour) submerged, fast enough to outrace most large surface vessels—while improving the sub's maneuverability and reducing drag and noise. It was thus far less vulnerable to sonar detection, making the stealthy *Skipjack* the Navy's first true underwater hunter-killer.

The Navy's willingness to stake its future on a nuclear force owed much to Admiral Arleigh Burke. In summer 1955,

President Eisenhower had jumped Burke over ninety-two more senior officers to chief of naval operations. Just fifty-three years old, Burke held an advanced degree in chemical engineering. In World War II's Pacific Theater, he won fame as a combat commander and staff officer known for his risk-taking leadership. He had both insights into technology and a broad strategic grasp. Burke advocated nuclear propulsion as early as 1948 and now strongly supported building more nuclear ships for the Cold War fleet and arming them with the most advanced strategic weapons then in development. But fully half of the US defense budget was by now going to the Air Force in support of its atomic-bomb-carrying aircraft and silo-launched missiles that, because of their vulnerability to sudden attack, dictated a terrifying "use it or lose it," first-strike strategy to "win" a general nuclear war.

In working papers and in the Navy budget, Burke advocated replacing that doomsday strategy with strong deterrent forces designed to check others from attacking the United States and its allies. He believed that staving off war would protect the country and its allies more effectively against its enemies while waiting out what he predicted would be an eventual Soviet decline and collapse. Through the Navy's nuclear force, and submarines in particular, it could field a "deterrent force so carefully dispersed yet strategically concentrated that initiation of war will be Russia's suicide," he wrote.[2]

Burke had gone to sea aboard the *Nautilus* even before he was named CNO. Shortly afterward, he told the House Armed Services Committee that nuclear propulsion was "not only warranted but mandatory" for the Navy's future. As CNO, he ordered that all planned submarines, including some already under construction, go nuclear and that the Navy increasingly shift surface-ship programs away from diesel to nuclear power. To grow the nuclear Navy, Burke greatly increased Rickover's responsibilities—and powers. Over the objections of many others in the Navy, especially in the Bureau of Personnel, which previously controlled all assignments, in January 1958 Burke granted Rickover almost complete authority over selection, training, and assignment of atomic-sub fleet officers.[3] But he did not want Rickover amassing total control over the Navy's nuclear programming. He placed the strategic Polaris submarine-launched ballistic-missile program under a newly created director of special projects at the Bureau of Weapons. To protect the person in the new position from Rickover, Burke had the director report directly to him, but in any case, Rickover's Navy would still field those missiles. And no matter what a nuclear ship's mission, every aspect of its design went through Rickover's shop.

With subs and surface ships under construction at several Navy and private yards on both coasts, Rickover's nuclear fiefdom was becoming an empire. Nonetheless, while he remained the autocratic ruler of Naval Reactors, he had yet to establish permanency—a concept at odds with all Navy traditions and rules. And his time for mandatory retirement in 1960 was now approaching.

As a rear admiral, Rickover was slated for automatic retirement at the end of the decade—unless he was promoted. The Navy brass had grudgingly accepted that his nuclear-reactor power plants had saved their service. They hated the man and respected his Navy. Burke's powerful voice for the atomic force belied Rickover's frequent criticism of a backward-facing Navy, but with the nuclear revolution now well under way, the brass happily anticipated seeing him retired out. His fate in the last years of the 1950s remained in limbo, even as his achievements proved their worth again and again.

Well before relieving Eugene Wilkinson as commander of the *Nautilus*, William Anderson, another smart, ambitious, and daring officer, envisioned transiting the North Pole beneath the ice cap. The existence of the first nuclear-powered submarine cried out for the attempt; Cold War military interests also dictated a demonstration of *Nautilus*'s ability to penetrate beneath the ice pack to steam undetected within range of open waters that were normally accessible only to warships of the Soviet Union—even within Soviet territorial waters. Rickover adamantly opposed the idea.

In the summer of 1957, Anderson made the first extended probe under the polar ice from the North Atlantic. He steamed within two hundred miles of the North Pole before navigational troubles due to the pole's complex magnetic forces led him to back out. After word of the exploratory voyage got out, in October 1957 the Navy openly declared it "one of the most incredible adventures in naval history."[4]

Rickover, always conservative with his vessels, feared that the *Nautilus*'s one reactor might fail at a point where its electrical motor lacked sufficient battery reserves to reach open water, possibly stranding the ship and crew beyond rescue. The strategic risk equation changed when a major technological breakthrough blazed across the world's headlines, but it was not a US triumph this time. On October 4, 1957, the Soviet Union launched the satellite *Sputnik* into close-Earth orbit.

The *Sputnik* launch, Rickover observed, was "in matters of the intellect" a national-security shock equal to the Japanese attack on Pearl Harbor and a Soviet propaganda coup of the highest order.[5] To date almost all of the United States' many attempts to launch rockets free of the Earth's gravitational pull had ended in fiery and embarrassing failure. The Soviet triumph brought visions of intercontinental ballistic missiles raining down on the United States. *Sputnik* in orbit pierced the nation's image as the dominant global technology and military power. A secret US Information Agency (USIA) report warned President Eisenhower that "Soviet claims of scientific and technological superiority over the West and especially the

US have won greatly widened acceptance." *Sputnik* alarmed even friendly countries "that the balance of military power has shifted or may soon shift in favor of the USSR."[6]

Eisenhower wanted something dramatic to reestablish confidence in US scientific and technological prowess. When Eisenhower's naval aide suggested that transiting the North Pole under the ice might serve as an answer to *Sputnik*, the president quickly embraced the idea.

The mission remained dangerous, even foolhardy, despite improving navigational and overhead-ice depth-detection equipment. *Nautilus* could easily get trapped between the hundreds of feet of irregular polar ice and the sea floor. Along with the loss of the great sub and its crew, a tragic outcome would have terrible consequences for national prestige and the president's public standing. Eisenhower wanted no public leaks about the mission this time around. Eisenhower told Anderson and Navy top officials, "I want no one—I mean no one—to announce the success or failure of this attempt until I, personally, indicate where and when the announcement will be made." Nobody outside a tight White House and Navy circle knew of Anderson and the *Nautilus*'s true mission over the next several months of intense preparations. Anderson made several secret flights over the polar ice, and the *Nautilus* announced a fabricated itinerary for upcoming operations.[7]

Rickover was never formally notified of the plan, but he learned of it and remained opposed. But even he could not stop a mission ordered by the president. On the day before the June 9 scheduled start to the voyage, Rickover made a surprise inspection of the *Nautilus*, which was tied up in Seattle. He did not let on that he knew anything about the impending mission. After a two-hour inspection, he joined Anderson in his state room. The two did not discuss the *Nautilus*'s announced operations or its true destination. But as Rickover rose to leave, he handed Anderson a scrap of paper from his pocket. On it he had written out permission for the *Nautilus*'s skipper to reduce pressure in the main coolant loop in case of an emergency such as a water leak. That would allow the vessel to continue to operate the reactor on lower power. This was an indication from Rickover that he had built into the system a sufficient safety margin for the normally prohibited move; the submarine would have far-greater range should it encounter a serious problem without a way to surface through the ice pack to radio for help. Anderson understood: "Rather than coming right out and saying, 'You have my blessing, Anderson,' or wishing me good luck beneath the ice, he did the same thing in his own inimitable way." The skipper found the gesture "deeply inspiring."[8]

After months of planning, reconnoitering, and rejiggering navigational and depth-finding instruments, plus one more false start, the *Nautilus* headed out through the North Pacific into the Bering Sea. After crossing the fifty-one-mile-wide Bering Strait shoal without Soviet detection, the sub sped through the floating ice of the Chukchi Sea. Off Point Barrow, Alaska, *Nautilus* submerged a final time. It headed due north beneath the formidable, milky-gray Arctic ice floes and polar pack, speeding through the half-light of the translucent ice cover hanging like a bank of clouds over the Beaufort Sea. Finally it penetrated into the Arctic Ocean. As the sub progressed, it both recorded continuous measurements of the little-known ocean bottom and tracked ever-changing ice depth overhead as it churned through the ocean ice cave. No radio transmission from the sub could reach receivers while below the ice. Eisenhower waited anxiously for word from the mission.

On August 3, 1958, shortly before midnight, the *Nautilus*, making twenty knots at four hundred feet below the ice, approached the geographic North Pole. After Anderson counted down the seconds to the crossing for his crew over the loudspeakers, he offered a brief tribute to the polar explorers who had come before them. He noted their predecessors' bravery in facing icy hardship and death to accomplish what the *Nautilus* had just achieved in climate-controlled comfort. (Press reports later noted that the crew shared a celebratory white-icing "North Pole" cake.) Then, switching the jukebox back on, country and western music played while *Nautilus* set a due-south heading.[9]

Two days later, the submarine resurfaced in the open waters of the Greenland Sea. Its 1,830-mile voyage under the entire polar ice cap took just four days. Only then did Anderson send to Washington his top-secret, soon-to-be-famous radio dispatch, "Nautilus 90 North," signal for successful completion of the polar transit. A day later, off Greenland, a Navy helicopter whisked Anderson from the boat. Shortly after, he was on his way to Washington, DC.

On Friday afternoon, August 8, more than one hundred reporters and photographers crammed into the White House press-briefing room, enticed by the promise of a "showcase presentation." A small group of dignitaries—Admiral James Russell, the acting chief of naval operations (Burke was out of town), the secretary of the Navy, the AEC's current and former chairmen, and Commander and Mrs. Anderson—entered the briefing room through a side door. President Eisenhower followed and announced the successful polar voyage. He pinned a medal on Anderson and then left the others to answer questions. An easel displayed a large map of the top of the world, with a line showing the course the *Nautilus* had made. National radio outlets broadcast the event live.

News of the voyage electrified the world. Although the White House touted the opening of an underwater Northwest Passage as a possible route for cargo submarines, *Time* magazine knew better: this was about "the contest called the Cold War," the magazine wrote; the voyage "increased the power of the US deterrent by laying bare the Communist empire's northern shores to the future Polaris-missile-toting nuclear submarines." Tributes poured in from around the world. London's *Telegraph* called the voyage "America's answer to the Soviet Sputnik." Many accounts celebrated the atomic submarine that accomplished a previously only dreamed-of feat. "The great subsurface polar crossing was," asserted *Life* magazine, "essentially a triumph of machinery and of diverse intellects of the men who had invented it. *Nautilus* herself was the star of the show." The *New York Times* wrote, "once under the ice cap the men of the Nautilus were simply servants of their wonderful machine."[10]

Yet the man who more than any other bore credit for the invention of the *Nautilus* was not there.

Where was Rickover at the moment of triumph for his Navy? the press asked. The White House and Navy said that the crowded room was simply too small to include him. But years later, the acting CNO Russell admitted that he had deliberately left Rickover off the list. Russell had not forgotten a brushup he had had as a young officer with Rickover. He had vowed at the time, "If I ever meet that guy in a black [*sic*] alley I'm really going to let him have it."[11] Here was that alley.

The Navy brass was not finished with spiting Rickover. They led him to understand that his wife, Ruth, had been designated to christen the gargantuan *Triton* at Electric Boat on August 19. Ruth never received the invitation for the honor. Outraged at this further slight, Rickover skipped the launch of his latest and largest nuclear submarine, telling reporters, "I am too busy." Not mincing words and acting like anything but the reserved naval wife, Ruth told the *New York Post*, "The stupid windbags who run [the Navy], they are really out to hurt my husband. . . . Doesn't it frighten you that such dumb people have our fate in their hands?" She would never attend another Navy event except those held to honor her husband.[12]

Rickover's "battle fleet" struck back. Commentators condemned the Navy for "forgetting" Rickover. A caption for a nationally syndicated cartoon showing Rickover standing outside the White House looking in read, "No room at the inn." Another cartoon, by the *Washington Post*'s widely syndicated Herblock, depicted the *Nautilus*'s sail next to a dock where a pompous-looking figure labeled "Administration" stands in front of a Navy admiral while holding up a medal, with a caption declaring, "This splendid achievement made possible by a man whose name I forget." A piece of paper with Rickover's name on it lies crumpled in a trashcan.[13]

Congress quickly got into the act. On the Senate floor, Senator Clinton Anderson of New Mexico ridiculed the Navy for its failure to include "the little man who wasn't there," who had made the polar transit feasible. Senator Hubert Humphrey of Minnesota said he had never heard a "lamer excuse" than the lack of room at the press briefing. Then Congress acted. Rickover had been a rear admiral since 1953. If he were not promoted, in two years he would again face mandatory retirement. Senator Anderson admonished the Navy against forcing out "a man who is, and has been, outspoken in his criticisms of old, outmoded Navy concepts." He introduced a resolution awarding Rickover a Gold Medal, Congress's highest honor, which Congress approved unanimously.[14]

Stung by the backlash, the White House needed to save face. Eisenhower deputized Rickover as his personal representative to greet the world-famous *Nautilus* when it steamed into New York Harbor to a hero's welcome on August 27, 1958. A quarter million people lined Broadway's Canyon of Heroes as confetti streamers showered down on Rickover, skipper Anderson, and 116 *Nautilus* crewmen, who rode in a train of open cars and jeeps, while accompanying Army, Navy, and Marine Corps bands played "Anchors Aweigh." As Rickover passed, onlookers pointed and shouted out, "Attaboy, Ricky!" The *New*

York Times ran a front-page photo of the admiral and Anderson in bright Navy whites with Mayor Robert F. Wagner Jr. between them holding their arms aloft like champion boxers for the cheering crowd.[15]

The next day, President Eisenhower announced that as of October 23 Rickover would receive his third star and promotion to vice admiral. At that rank, he would not face mandatory retirement until age sixty-two, another four years. With his promotion, the chief of a fourth-echelon bureau outranked his boss's boss, the chief of the Bureau of Ships.

The Navy brass despised Rickover but understood that he had produced an entirely new dimension in naval warfare — and a strategic future for the Navy. As submarine, reactor, and missile technology coalesced into a silent satellite loaded with unstoppable atomic-tipped rockets, the Navy ratcheted up the sub-building program even further. In 1958, Navy plans called for Naval Reactors to engineer the power plants of eighteen more nuclear subs.

A sailor who had never fired a gun in anger, an Engineering Duty Only officer barred from seagoing command, a three-star admiral reviled by most of his fellow admirals, Rickover was the world's most famous naval officer. He intended to exploit his status and the power that came with it to the fullest, "Navy bastards" be damned.

9

Education and Freedom

Following the *Nautilus* polar-transit festivities and the Navy's public flogging, reverence for Rickover outside the Navy overflowed. Politicians solicited his views on nuclear technology and broader naval questions. His highly anticipated annual Atomic Energy and Armed Services committee briefings, which came to be known as "Rickover lectures," ranged far and wide; he covered naval, governmental, industrial, and civilian affairs, whatever was on his and the committee members' minds. Congress and the nation also solicited his thoughts on the state of health care, religion, the family, schools, and education, even the books he recommended. His constant reading and the scores of notebooks he filled over the decades with thoughts and quotes provided the basis for dazzling displays of historical, philosophical, and cultural knowledge. Rickover's unique brand of insult humor, in particular his flagrant goring of his fellow admirals and Defense Department bureaucrats, his fiery contempt for inept, profiteering contractors, and his fierce defense of taxpayers against government waste enthralled Congress and won him fans everywhere outside the Pentagon and corporate offices. His frequent—equally abrasive—public talks to university and civic groups, engineering associations, and other professional organizations and his published articles kept him in the headlines. He rarely gave interviews yet was as much a public figure as any statesman of the day. It was no surprise when, in July 1959, Rickover's lack of restraint again made national headlines, this time for his freewheeling intrusion into Cold War diplomacy.

As part of a post-Stalin thaw in Soviet-US relations, the two nations set up a highly anticipated goodwill exchange of trade fairs and top official visits. In early July, the first deputy premier of the Soviet Union, Frol Kozlov, at the time the Kremlin's second-most-powerful official, considered a likely successor to Premier Nikita Khrushchev, visited various sites in the United States. Toward the end of his tour, Kozlov stopped at the Shippingport atomic power plant, where he met Rickover. With a scrum of reporters surrounding them, even Rickover feared he might have overstepped a line when he patted Kozlov's portly stomach and remarked that he looked like the stereotype of a capitalist, while he, the wiry admiral, had the appearance, Rickover said, of a "hardworking man." The vice premier laughed it off. In the spirit of the moment, Kozlov then suggested that an exchange of nuclear experts might improve their nations' relations. Rickover immediately agreed.

He invited Kozlov and his entourage to tour the plant with the press in tow. When Kozlov asked where they should leave their cameras, Rickover told him to bring them along, that nothing inside was classified. Rickover then remarked, "Just like your atomic-powered icebreaker ship, the *Lenin*. Isn't that right, Mr. Kozlov?" The *Lenin*, the Soviet's first nuclear ship, was under construction at the Leningrad (Saint Petersburg)

shipyard. Rickover had him pinned down. A sputtering Kozlov was forced to agree. As the two men moved through the
power plant, Rickover explained the systems they were seeing. Never one to shy from a chance to insult anyone's intelligence, even the second-most-powerful leader of the United
States' principal adversary, he asked Kozlov, "Are you smart
enough to understand everything I am explaining to you?" But
when they exited the generating station, their banter turned
tart. Kozlov said, "Isn't it fine we've been able to spend so much
time together talking about peace?" Rickover snapped, "It's all
right to talk about peace. Now you go home and do something
about it!"[1]

Vice President Richard Nixon's reciprocal trip to the Soviet
Union would begin two weeks later. After Kozlov's remarks
about the *Lenin* being open to visitors, Nixon added the Leningrad shipyard to his itinerary. He asked that the AEC suggest a
nuclear expert to accompany him. They gave him the names of
two academics and Rickover. He had never met Rickover but of
course knew his reputation. Nixon immediately picked him—
despite the Navy's warnings about the admiral's brashness and a
purported desire to send a "better looking" officer in his stead.[2]

CIA director Allen Dulles came to meet with Rickover at
Naval Reactors in Tempo 3 before he left for Moscow. Dulles
could not help but remark that Rickover's dilapidated "quarters
live up to their reputation." Rickover, Dulles agreed, should
take the visit's opportunity to look as deeply as he could into the
little-known state of Soviet nuclear technology and to promote
further atomic scientific exchanges. Dulles and Nixon, apparently without presidential or State Department concurrence,
encouraged Rickover to offer the Soviets complete access to
US land-based reactors, even those producing weapons-grade
plutonium—though excluding classified ship reactors. Rickover could even offer to train Soviet personnel at Shippingport.[3]

On July 24, the Jewish émigré from a shtetl in tsarist Poland accompanied the US vice president to Moscow, seat of the vast Soviet empire. Rickover encountered Premier Khrushchev for the first time at the US trade-fair exhibition. The bluff Soviet leader said to him, "You must be the admiral who has been making warlike speeches against the Soviet Union." Rickover snapped, "No. Are you the Khrushchev who has been making speeches against the United States?"[4]

The next day, Rickover and Nixon went alone (except for an interpreter) to the Kremlin, where they met with Kozlov and two other Soviet officials (and their interpreters).[5] During the meeting, Rickover made the offer of carte blanche entrée into all US nuclear reactor facilities except Navy reactors as part of a trust-building scientific exchange. Kozlov promised an answer soon. Over lunch Rickover goaded a Soviet official to respond quickly to the proposal, claiming he had the authority "to make these arrangements. Can't Russia act as fast as the United States?" But no reply ever came. That is particularly unfortunate considering the many Soviet nuclear accidents over the coming decades.

On July 27, Nixon and Rickover went to Leningrad, where they were scheduled to tour the *Lenin*, as Kozlov had promised. After a walk around the shipyard and a cursory visit inside the icebreaker, still in final buildout, their guides escorted them to the ship's wardroom, where they were shown a film about construction of the icebreaker. Then their minders said it was time to leave. Furious, Rickover refused to budge. He demanded his promised tour of the ship's power plant. The guides claimed that they did not have keys to the engineering-compartment doors. "This is nonsense," Rickover sputtered. He barked, "Get me Comrade Kozlov on the telephone. Now!" The keys magically appeared. While Nixon walked about the yard and mingled with workers, Rickover crawled through the power plant and took copious notes for the next two hours.[6]

He was not impressed. The propulsion system looked

rugged—though of course he could not peer inside the core. He could see poorly planned housing for the *Lenin*'s three reactors, which were packed together in a single compartment; any radiation leak from one reactor would contaminate all three. He also thought that the combined steam and electric propulsion system looked overly complex and difficult to maintain and probably prone to break down.

On the way back to Washington, the vice president's party stopped over briefly in Poland. Almost fifty-four years after Rickover had left, this was his first, and would remain his only, visit to the land of his birth. Nixon wrote two years later that he wanted to get across "to the Polish people the way of life in America." He introduced Rickover wherever they went as a Polish émigré who grew up to become an American hero. Nixon observed about Rickover that the tumultuous reception he received moved him deeply, though he did not betray his feelings.[7]

Back home, Rickover went to Chicago. While there, he visited his parents and sisters. He told them about having sat in the tsar's box at the ballet in Leningrad. They marveled at the notion that their son, whose Jewish family had fled the blows of the tsar's Cossacks, returned to Russia like a tsarist prince.[8]

Rickover returned from Russia deeply troubled at the failings the trip spotlighted in the United States. In a briefing before a Senate Armed Services subcommittee after his return, he told members that the Soviet leadership remained intent on "world domination": "We must never forget that their objective is conquest."[9] But along with the military threat, another one disturbed him to the point of obsession: education, especially science and technology education. "Today," he told the committee, "education is indispensable for survival and progress" and is "the nation's first line of defense." The poor quality of US schools showed that society was not taking the Soviet threat seriously.[10]

During the Russian visit, Rickover met with officials from the Soviet education ministry. He claimed to have toured schools and universities, though there is no evidence that he ever actually stepped inside a classroom. But he was already certain that Soviet schools and students were outstripping their US counterparts—speeding the Soviet Union's technological progress. Despite being a backward country that "unquestionably" lagged the United States in most areas, "as far as the rate of technological progress is concerned, they are ahead," he said. That was a shocking assertion given US postwar leadership in almost every field except rocketry. Staying ahead in technology was critical, Rickover asserted, to US survival. But in the face of a concerted Soviet effort to overtake the United States through technical and scientific education, "only the massive upgrading of the scholastic standards of our schools will guarantee the future prosperity and freedom of the Republic."[11]

Rickover's day job of course remained focused on naval engineering matters, but he took the opportunity of his newfound fame to campaign for US school reforms.[12] Among his many public statements on the subject, he testified eleven times to Congress, spoke to audiences around the country, and published articles in journals and popular periodicals. He even deviated from his general rule of avoiding the press when the topic was education, appearing to speak about it, for instance, three times on the television interview program hosted by the famous journalist Edward R. Murrow.

Rickover warned that US schools were not educating enough capable people in math and science to fill the ranks that his and other technical programs needed. "Good men aren't available; good men already have good jobs," he said. Instead, he was forced to recruit "the best youngsters from the best schools in the country," smart people with potential, and then devote tremendous resources to making nuclear engineers out of them. Even then he was falling short in finding promising candidates.[13] Meantime, Soviet schools were populating Soviet labs, military, and industries with engineers, mathematicians, and scientists.

Many educators and pundits questioned an admiral's qualifications for reforming education or how someone with his life story and career could criticize a system that produced such world-beaters. Rickover pointed to his experiences at Naval Reactors to justify his concerns: "For as long as I have worked in the atomic-energy field I have been absorbed in educational problems," he said. "Indeed, I found the two so intertwined that I would have had to be unobservant not to have gotten myself involved with American education."[14]

Educators contended that US schools were the best in the world. Rickover and Ruth, who knew European schools and universities well from her own education, worked together to compile data and compare US schools to their European and Soviet counterparts. They found that the United States came up consistently short. "The first thing we must do is to recognize that our schools are not the best in the world," Rickover declared. "Best in what?" he asked and answered, "Certainly not in basic education, not in scholastic achievements, not in the amount of education we get for each dollar we spend, not in the intellectual and educational qualifications of teachers—not, as compared to Europe. Someone once remembered that we are 'best' in everything that has nothing to do with genuine education: playgrounds, athletic fields, workshops, social entertainment, fun and games."[15] Weak schools and poor-performing students jeopardized democratic society, squandering the nation's tremendous advantages—geographic isolation, wealth of natural resources, and postwar economic prosperity—in failing to develop brain power to maintain those advantages. He warned that "unless we solve our educational problem, we will not be able to solve any of our national problems."

He was not shy about asserting the need to put more national resources into education—and tweaking the Pentagon's nose while saying so. On NBC's widely watched *Meet the Press* on January 24, 1960, he suggested that slashing the Pentagon's budget by 20 to 30 percent would actually improve national defense by reducing administrative intrusions on his and others' military programs, especially were the money redirected into education.[16] At the same time, he insisted that more dollars going to education would not by themselves overcome US schools' shortcomings: "We have yet to learn that education is one thing that money alone cannot purchase. The only acceptable coin which buys an education is hard intellectual effort."[17] That effort was not getting made.

Rickover scolded American parents who "by their own lazy habits" set a "bad example" for their teens to have "a lot of fun." Students in the Soviet Union did not enjoy such luxuries. "Russian youngsters," he said, "simply study harder because they fully realize what education will mean to their future."[18] In an impoverished land, Soviets underscored the importance of education by giving their best students free university tuition and better food and housing, while holding out the possibility of membership in the Communist Party, key to a career offering material rewards and societal advancement in an otherwise poor country.

But above all, he claimed that the Soviets—and western European lands—fostered a climate that encouraged their young people to value and pursue education. The children in the Soviet Union, he declared, "are imbued with a love of intellectual adventure through books in which the hero is a scientist or engineer who does valiant deeds that will benefit the country—not, as in so many of our books, and even more on radio and television, a cowboy or space cadet."[19] Why were American children not growing up reading about such heroes? Of course, many were, including in books about Rickover himself, but he ignored them. He railed against American students and schools for wasting time on fun and games and failing to meet the nation's future challenges. He said of the schools he claimed to have visited in his travels with Nixon, "I searched far and wide in Russia and Poland and could not find a single drum majorette. Nor did I hear of a single school where the principal was an ex-athletic coach."[20]

With Ruth's assistance, Rickover edited his talks and articles on education into three books laying out his case.[21] In them he charged progressive educators with raising "a generation of Americans who expect to obtain all good things without effort and who acquire a wholly false notion of their own importance because they never had an opportunity at school to compare their own true accomplishments with those of others."[22] He wanted schools to redirect their students to serious academic subjects and to test their performance on the basis of national and international standards. That was a heretical notion in a nation that prized local control of education. "We have standards for railroad transportation," he scoffed; "we have standards for airplane travel, for lipstick colors, for the size of socks, but we have no standards for education." Only testing could reveal shortcomings and make room for improvements. "Education," he contended, "has not been improved anywhere else in the world without first setting up standards."[23]

And he wanted performance expectations raised for all schools, "so that every child in every school is working as hard as he can." He saw no value in "trivial, recreational and vocational subjects. . . . Even for the average pupils, these subjects are not mentally stimulating—they barely touch his mind." Schools should also separate out their brightest students, "to recognize and nurture superior intelligence."[24]

Finally, Rickover wanted an end to school-based extra-curricular activities—"it is with the mind that the school must solely concern itself." He saw no purpose in schoolboy athlet-ics, which "is done more for the entertainment of the parents than it is for the children themselves," apostasy for a sports-obsessed nation. He maintained that children's noneducational needs were better taken care of at home, in church, or by the community. "But," his tone dripping with sarcasm in congres-sional testimony, "the educationists"—his derogatory catch-all for sociologists, psychologists, and other progressive school advocates—"will say, 'They will have to work too hard. It will be bad for their health.'"[25] Schools were for teaching and learn-ing academic subjects; anything else wasted precious public re-sources and students' time.

As Rickover intended, his school-improvement campaign stirred up a brawl. Pundits lauded his criticisms of US schools. But most educators and their professional associations roundly condemned Rickover's views. Many called him naïve, dogmatic, or worse. He was, wrote one critic, "a resident of the ivory conning tower" who had never actually spent any time in US or foreign classrooms (probably true) and who possessed "a nurs-ery school-level . . . knowledge about comparative education" (not true). Some charged Rickover with ignoring the broader physical, emotional, and aesthetic needs of the "whole child," in the interest of raising little "egg heads." Others claimed that he wanted "to educate the best and shoot the rest."

Rickover slapped back, defending his reform ideas as a basis for all young people, whatever their family background or intellectual ability, to grow into responsible, productive citizens of a democracy. He contended that schools that sepa-rated students by ability would better ready *all* students for the future. "A school system that insists on the same instruction for the talented, average and below average child," he told an audi-ence of educators, "may prevent as many children from growing intellectually as would a system that excludes children because of social, political or economic status of parents. Neither system is democratic."[26]

Ultimately, he wanted to ennoble the individual mind. Whether a student was bound for advanced studies or vocational training, he believed a quality education amounted to a lifelong intellectual inheritance that made everything worthwhile possible. "Nothing we bestow upon our children in the way of material advantages can compare with the gift of a good education," he wrote in his 1959 book *Education and Freedom*. "We must know how to dig up our own facts—how to discover truth for ourselves." Education freed the mind: "The person who has learned to trust only proven facts, who knows how to find and recognize truth, and who has been trained to decide all issues on the basis of truth and reason—he and he alone is a free man."[27] Without quality education, freedom would die.

Rickover's words fell mostly on deaf ears—at least in the government. Nobody from the Eisenhower administration, he told Congress, asked him to consult on education.[28] But he eventually found more favor in the executive branch. President John F. Kennedy invited Rickover to meet with him in the White House on February 11, 1963. Education was among the topics Kennedy wanted to discuss. Rickover recalled his surprise at learning that the president had read two of his books: "so he knew my views on the subject." Kennedy and Rickover talked about their very different upbringings' shared emphasis on applying themselves at school. The president was also interested in the admiral's idea "to have a national education standard . . . as a yardstick by which parents and local communities could measure the performance of their schools." Soon after their meeting, the president tasked the commissioner of education "to get into the matter," recalled Rickover. Kennedy was not merely paying lip service to Rickover; he began having internal "Progress Reports for Admiral Rickover" forwarded to the admiral. "I am convinced that had he lived something would have been done in this matter," Rickover lamented.[29]

Rickover's influence on public education would fall short until Jimmy Carter, a Rickover submarine trainee and acolyte, entered the White House in 1977. Carter read Rickover's books and other writings and shared his belief in the need for national support and standards for schools. He established the Department of Education as a full-standing cabinet post. Over the decades that followed, Rickover's ideas for improving school performance worked their way into the US educational mainstream. As happened in so many domains, as Edward R. Murrow wrote in a preface to Rickover's *Education and Freedom*, Rickover alienated the established hierarchy but acted as "a prophet and a leader."[30]

In the Navy, though, Rickover's push for educational reform carried far more weight. As in other areas, he made more enemies than friends, overturned some of the service branch's longest-standing traditions, and put his imprint on every officer.

10

◆◦◆◦◆

A Different Kind of Man

On the morning of July 25, 1961, Rickover walked down the corridor to his office at Naval Reactors with Navy commander John Crawford Jr., among his longest-serving naval staffers. The admiral mentioned to Crawford that even in the Washington summer heat his hands felt painfully cold. Concerned, Crawford insisted that the resisting Rickover lie down in his office. Later that day at the Bethesda Naval Hospital, tests showed he had suffered a major heart attack. The stress of long hours and an irascible temperament had taken its toll. He spent the next two months recuperating but hardly relaxing. The first day at the hospital, he ordered the daily "pinks" delivered to him. He set up a makeshift office in his room and soon began leaving the hospital for a few hours each day on NR matters.[1]

One afternoon, a pretty, young day nurse assigned to him, Lieutenant Eleonore Bednowicz, straightened papers he had left strewn about his room while he was testifying on Capitol Hill. When he returned, he snapped at her for disturbing his materials. She answered back, "Admiral, this is my ship." The three-star admiral realized, "She was tough."

She was also smart and had a sharp sense of humor. Rickover appreciated her devout Catholic faith. She welcomed Ruth into the hospital room so that she and her husband could have lunch together regularly. Rickover enjoyed when the nurse checked in on him. He gave her flowers and some other small gifts that were sent to his room. One of his first gifts to her was a copy of the Milton sonnet "On His Blindness," a favorite since he memorized it in high school.

By late September, Rickover was back in his office on his regular work schedule. He did add four miles of brisk walking daily. He had not forgotten Lieutenant Bednowicz. He sent her letters from time to time after her Navy postings took her to distant bases and visited with her in Guam while on business there.

In 1962, President Kennedy was keen to avoid disruptions in the fast-growing nuclear Navy. He used his presidential powers to extend Rickover's active-duty status for two more years beyond the Navy's obligatory retirement age. By law, once he turned sixty-four, in January 1964, his active-duty status could no longer be renewed. Many within the Navy held their breath, ready to stomach two more years until the admiral, who was in his forty-fourth year of active duty, would finally have to retire.

Rickover was not done by any means in putting his stamp on the Navy. As the nuclear Navy grew, he needed more naval nuclear-engineering specialists and officers ready to learn nuclear propulsion's intricacies. These nucs under his tutelage also formed the vanguard of an emerging naval leadership ready to meet the demands of the new technologies overtaking the service branch.

Rickover wanted the Navy to recognize the revolutionary transformations that powerful new technologies were causing, whether the service branch accepted the changes or not. Sophisticated new technologies took expertise to engineer and operate, and they could cause grave harm if mishandled. To utilize their advantages required reshaping organizations, even society itself, and granting engineers and scientists greater authority over them. Society would come to rely increasingly, he wrote, on "men who can handle the intricate mysteries of complex scientific and engineering projects" and "on whose judgment, concentrated attention, and responsibility may depend the functioning of some new and gigantic piece of engineering." He of course meant his own ships first, the most complex and gigantic machines ever built. But Rickover also intended his Naval Reactors program to show the way for the rest of society. He wanted the Navy to educate and promote "the man of the future on whom we shall depend more and more[,] . . . the technical expert."[2] Technocracy would take command.

The risks of ignoring specialized expertise were growing. In congressional testimony in April 1960, Rickover admonished, "You cannot entrust a nuclear plant to people who do not have the mental capacity to absorb such training because sure as shooting you are going to have an accident."[3] Nothing would derail nuclear power's development faster. Thus, he insisted time and again that his most important job was "to select and train the technical people working for him—not to issue orders and directives."[4] But the Navy was not producing enough of the type of officers he wanted in command. The Navy's line officers were traditionally the "verbal men," as he called them, the men of broad command abilities with limited technical expertise who were, he declared, "on the way out." He needed to identify and train "a different kind of man . . . who will run the atomic navy."

As he so often did, Rickover saw in the search for those

officers and crew another lever with which to shove the whole Navy in the direction he wanted it to go. The steps he took to place the technical expert who formerly stood at the bottom of the naval hierarchy on top provided a sourcebook for countless Rickover legends.

By the time Rickover and Kennedy sat down at the White House in early 1963, submarines were coming off the ways in an almost assembly-line fashion; the building program would accelerate from there—less so surface ships. While the carrier *Enterprise* and its escorts *Long Beach* and *Bainbridge* steamed around the world, the Navy chieftains, Congress, and the White House became increasingly concerned about the cost of building nuclear surface vessels, which could cost up to five times more than the equivalent-sized conventionally powered ships. It would take almost seven years of debate and political battles from the late-1961 commissioning of the *Enterprise* until the next keel was laid for a nuclear carrier, the *Nimitz*, in June 1968, with another seven years on the ways before it was commissioned.

Rickover's fleet of attack and missile subs continued to astonish the world. Voyages under the ice cap, even surfacing through the polar ice in the dead of winter, became increasingly routine. In another demonstration of the atomic submarine's prowess, the gargantuan *Triton* under the command of Rickover's onetime "boy" in the chief of naval operations office, Captain Edward Beach, submerged on February 16, 1960, and did not resurface for nearly three months, until May 10, at the end of a thirty-six-thousand-mile global circumnavigation— another Cold War coup. Not a single navy patrol detected *Triton* during its voyage, further proof of the nuclear submarine's tremendous operational advantages.[5]

In the 1960 presidential election, the admiral did not express a preference between Nixon and Kennedy, though he had returned from his trip to Russia impressed by Nixon.[6] But after Kennedy hammered Eisenhower's administration during the campaign for permitting a supposed "missile gap" to open with the Soviets—a contrived threat, a subsequent Defense Department study showed—the nuclear sub became the hidden and most invulnerable arm in the nation's strategic deterrence triad of air-, sea-, and ground-launched nuclear weapons. The new president made speeding up the nuclear-sub construction program his top defense priority.[7] On November 16, 1963, less than a week before his assassination, Kennedy witnessed a Polaris missile launch from aboard the submarine USS *Andrew Jackson*. Afterward he wrote Pete Galantin, the rear admiral in charge of the Polaris program, "Once one has seen a Polaris firing, the efficacy of this weapons system as a deterrent is not debatable."[8]

When Kennedy took office, fourteen atomic submarines were at sea, but only three carried Polaris ballistic missiles. He authorized building twenty-three more of the costly Polaris submarines and at a breakneck pace. They were part of the "Forty-One for Freedom" Fleet Ballistic Missile nuclear-submarine (SSBN) construction program, which led to production of several new classes of submarines to carry the succeeding generations of Polaris and, early in the 1970s, the first of the more advanced Poseidon missiles. The Soviets were now investing heavily in growing their own submarine fleet. The Navy's construction program added new, highly advanced hunter-killer subs (SSN) to track the new entries in the Soviet nuclear-submarine fleet. In 1961, the peak year of the atomic-shipbuilding boom, thirty-seven nuclear surface and underseas vessels were under construction. A first since World War II, two subs were commissioned in a single month in 1963. By 1965, under President Lyndon Johnson, 102 nuclear vessels were operational, under construction or authorized for the Navy to build. Each month through the middle of the decade, the Navy commissioned a new Rickover boat.[9]

Rickover named each new ballistic-missile sub for prominent figures in US history, from George Washington and
Ethan Allen to Will Rogers and Henry Stimson. During sea
trials aboard the first of the new "Forty-One for Freedom"
boats, Rickover wrote a letter to his teenage son, Robert, in-
corporating a brief biographical sketch of the person for whom
the sub was named. That began a regular practice: Rickover
sent letters to Robert after that from each of his 126 sea trials,
111 in submarines and 15 on surface ships. After the first few, he
started preparing longer biographies of the ships' namesakes,
which he included within the letters he mailed from on board
the ships. He also sent them to congressional backers, important military officials, staffers, and industry executives, a list of
recipients that grew to six hundred names—another way for
Rickover to keep support for his program.

According to Robert, those biographies were researched
and written "for the most part" by Ruth. Rickover eventually
expanded and collected the forty-one Polaris-sub biographies
into a small book, which he published in 1972. *Eminent Americans: Namesakes of the Polaris Submarine Fleet* would prove to be
the last project Ruth and Hyman would undertake together.[10]

Every submariner knew that before the admiral came
aboard for sea trials or inspections, the ship should make ready
a "rig-for-Rickover" list of items for him. His requirements included taking over the ship's executive officer's stateroom and
having his meals prepared for him to eat alone in the wardroom.
He expected fresh khakis were to be laid out, foul-weather gear
hanging with his name on it, thirty pounds of fresh fish and
fruit stocked in the mess, and lemon drops, newspapers, magazines, and hardback books from the *New York Times* best-seller
list waiting for him. His business suit was to be dry-cleaned and
ready for him upon return to shore. The shipyards supplied
typists for the hundreds of letters that he sent, along with com-

memorative postage and stationery embossed with the ship's logo.[11]

He also took home hundreds of small commemorative items from contractors that included tie clips, plates and goblets, and models of the vessels and ordered others made up specially for him. After sea trials, he distributed these items to his staff and some of his prominent backers in Congress. These tokens, trinkets, special services, and, over time, more lavish gifts would one day tarnish his legacy.

Each time a new vessel went to sea, Rickover needed an additional cadre of nuclear-trained officers and specialists ready to operate it. Nuclear subs took significantly more officers than diesel subs. Depending on size and mission, a ballistic-missile submarine needed as many as 150 crew members, though most carried around 120 to 125, including about a dozen officers. But that was still almost double a typical diesel boat crew of 60 to 70. What is more, given submariners' two-month deployments, two full complements of officers and mates rotated aboard the missile-toting boats. Designated Blue and Gold crews, each contingent alternated two months operating deep in thousands of square miles of sea, followed by the same period ashore. The boats themselves endured hard duty at sea about 240 days a year. The remainder of the year was spent dockside for maintenance and restocking—always under the care of officers and crew. With so many subs now shuttling in and out of port, coming up with enough capable officers and mates and training them for nuclear operations consumed a big chunk of every month for Rickover and his staff.

Admiral Burke had granted Rickover authority to choose the officers and engineers he wanted; the AEC gave him responsibility for certifying the ongoing safety of naval nuclear reactors. After the *Nautilus* and the *Seawolf* went to sea, the Navy's submarine command tried to pull back its authority over selection and training of nuclear officers, to integrate them into the regular submarine fleet training, with its emphasis on tactical operations and the lore of the submariner and, secondarily, on engineering systems.[12] The Navy also tried to eliminate the costly months of prototype training, seeking to replace the Mark I and other prototypes with simulators. But Rickover won that fight. In January 1956, he opened the Nuclear Power School at the New London subbase, where enlisted men undertook a basic course and officers an advanced course in nuclear engineering. (In 1958, Nuclear Power School moved to Mare Island, California, and eventually another school was opened in Bainbridge, Maryland, both to accommodate more trainees and purportedly to avoid Rickover's officers being exposed to traditional submarine-training programs still operating at the base in New London. Today the nuclear-officer-training program is in Goose Creek, South Carolina.)

Rickover insisted that every nuclear officer train for six months in nuclear physics and engineering and advanced reactor physics and then six months operating the prototypes at Arco or West Milton. (Eventually, NR opened other prototype trainers at different sites.) He alone would make the final determination of who served as officers and nuclear specialists aboard his boats.

A ready pool of available officers with experience at sea already existed; as late as 1960, diesel submarines still outnumbered atomic subs ten to one. Diesel was on its way out, and those diesel-experienced submariners were desperate for nuclear training. Without it, their careers would dead end.[13] But Rickover turned his back on them after the first years of the nuclear program, refusing even to consider most of these veteran officers.

Many, perhaps most, diesel officers lacked the academic aptitude for the advanced math and physics needed to operate a reactor. But large numbers were still young and bright enough, as well as predisposed to study and train hard, for nuclear billets. The Bureau of Personnel regularly sent lists of potential candidates for Rickover's consideration. Throughout the submarine service's previous existence, the BuPers "submarine desk," as it was called, had made all submarine assignments. Proud diesel-sub veterans, many with stellar war-fighting records, ran the desk; now they raged against Rickover's seemingly capricious rejection of the officers they recommended. "They knew about command," said Admiral Charles Duncan, the Bureau of Personnel's chief from 1968 to 1970. But now, an Engineering Duty Only admiral "who had never commanded a submarine [was] telling them who could be in command."[14] In 1960, the bureau's submarine desk identified three hundred experienced officers who had distinguished themselves academically and continued in postgraduate engineering or other relevant studies. Rickover turned down nearly all of them. The submarine desk accused him of deliberately rejecting qualified candidates.

Rickover almost certainly still held a grudge from when the "Navy bastards" refused to grant him the command he thought he had earned. "Rickover hated the line," the Navy's cadre of officers who could eventually rise to a command, said the former diesel commander Vice Admiral James F. Calvert, inaugural skipper of Rickover's third nuclear sub, SSN *Skate*.[15] But more than simple spite was at work; according to Admiral Duncan, Rickover had a "grand plan." He deployed his ability to control the nuclear Navy's officer selection to engineer a power grab over the whole Navy. Duncan said Rickover wanted to use the prestige of a nuclear command to ensure that "no officer would ever go anywhere except through his interview system." In the end, he intended to "control all the personnel and who went where in the Navy."[16]

Rickover may have wanted power over the Navy, but he legitimately wanted to lead a technocratic revolution within a hidebound organization. He did not believe in the old Navy command ethos when the job was to run a sophisticated and dangerous machine. "The operation of modern warships becomes daily more of a technical job," he wrote in 1963. "Even their use in naval combat now requires scientific and engineering skill rather than the skills of a professional naval officer." Exceptional technical abilities were the primary prerequisites for successful officers: "Theoretically, a competent team from GE or Westinghouse could operate a nuclear submarine or launch a missile. . . . These ships are comparable to our most advanced industrial plants. . . . To run them is essentially an engineering rather than a naval job."[17] The existing naval education system, followed by promotion and command, was not producing officers like that. Rickover wanted a different kind of officer in command.

The Navy brass found such ideas preposterous; far more was at stake here for them than who would operate about one hundred nuclear subs and three out of a few hundred surface ships. These were the most advanced warships ever built. Rickover controlled the Navy ships at the frontier that would take the lead in preventing and fighting future wars, and he wanted engineers to command those vessels.

The line officers fought back. An internecine war broke out between the war-tested line and the technical specialist.[18]

In early 1962, the chief of naval operations, Admiral George W. Anderson Jr., *ordered* Rickover to take 117 diesel officers into nuclear training. Rickover grudgingly agreed to interview the candidates; he accepted just 15. Afterward he went to Congress to complain that he was "being constantly harassed with attempts to reduce training, to use people we don't think are qualified, or put people into the program for short periods of time . . . to help their chances of promotion."[19] Anderson and Admiral William Smedberg, chief of naval personnel at the time, in turn pleaded with the secretary of the Navy, Fred Korth, to force Rickover to accept diesel veterans for nuclear training. They claimed that by rejecting so many officers qualified for training, he was causing shortages of nuclear officers, exhausting existing nuclear officers by forcing them to extend their deployments and rotations, and undermining morale. Korth feared that the Navy brass was on the verge of open revolt. He sought to diffuse tensions, arranging a "summit" at his office for Anderson, Smedberg, and Rickover on April 27, 1963. Rickover brought his naval deputy, John Crawford Jr., with him, and they expressed their fear that accepting unqualified diesel-trained officers would compromise safe nuclear operations. "The criteria for acceptance were inflexible," Crawford recounted.[20] Crawford came ready to prove Rickover's case, laying out statistics for acceptance into his program, including educational standing and technical qualifications of those who gained entry. They were appropriately high, higher than those of most of the officers whom Smedberg sent for interviews. Smedberg and Anderson did not have countervailing data about the qualifications of the men they had nominated. Korth agreed that safety should not be compromised, even if it meant extending tours and tapping other sources for candidates to fill the shortages. Anderson backed off.

After that victory, Rickover held nearly unassailable sway over every candidate for commanding officer, executive officer, and engineer in the nuclear Navy. He sidelined the career pathway that governed throughout the rest of the Navy. "Rickover was the one person in the Navy empowered to pick the talent he wanted," recounted Smedberg. "I was the chief of all naval personnel, but at no time did Admiral Rickover ever acknowledge or feel that I had any business saying anything about the people in his program."[21]

Faced with a shortage of qualified officers, Rickover used

his need for more candidates to force the Navy to expand the pools he could draw on. Outside wartime, the Navy had never taken junior officers directly from the Naval Academy and put them through advanced training and from there into senior positions aboard ships. In a radical departure from tradition, starting in the late 1950s, the Naval Academy sent Rickover every senior midshipman with high standing in math, science, and engineering as candidates for nuclear training—even those who had no interest in the submarine service.

Even then, Annapolis did not graduate enough technically minded midshipmen to fill the need—and most candidates did not get through the selection and training process. Rickover wanted the Academy to produce more and more candidates ready to train as nuclear officers. He advocated wholesale changes to the makeup of the student body. To get his way, he turned to his allies in Congress. Rickover teamed up with Korth and Congress to call on the Academy to convene a committee of civilian academics to review the midshipman curriculum and other academic policies. Rickover personally picked Richard G. Folsom, president of Rensselaer Polytechnic Institute, to head the review committee. The Folsom committee first met in May 1959 and issued its final report later that year. The report struck the Navy like a lightning bolt. The committee called for a comprehensive overhaul of the Naval Academy's curriculum, faculty, and admissions process. All midshipmen had previously "majored" in the Navy, sharing in a broad education; that must change. After this, midshipmen would major in specific disciplines with the need for "emphasis in all engineering courses . . . on analytical methods . . . [not] the descriptive approach." Academy graduates should understand the basic science and engineering principles underlying the systems and machines that they would one day operate. The Folsom report also called for recruiting civilian researchers and academics to the faculty, no longer just Navy officers.[22] In effect, the committee proposed a technocratic revolution at the deepest roots of the Navy, in Annapolis.

When the Navy balked at the proposed changes, Rickover scalded the resisting service leaders. He called on Congress to close all the service academies "if drastic steps are not taken immediately to improve them." He condemned the midshipmen at the Naval Academy as "a regimented group being trained for a Navy which no longer exists by officers, many of whom do not know the real needs of today's Navy and who are not aware that they don't know."[23] The Navy brass were stunned.

Reporters asked the new secretary of defense, Robert McNamara, what he thought about Rickover's views. He responded, "Admiral Rickover is one of the world's greatest authorities on nuclear reactors. But I'm not sure I'd place him in that category on education."[24] Yet over virtually universal alumni protest, Secretary of the Navy Korth enacted all the Folsom committee report's recommendations.

Going forward, all midshipmen would take a demanding core of math, science, and engineering courses, no matter what their major—and only a limited percentage of midshipmen could receive permission to major in nontechnical fields. Adjusted admission requirements emphasized high school science and math preparation. At graduation, academic grades were to be weighed more heavily in a midshipman's class standing. And in perhaps the most significant change for the Academy's culture, civilian professors gradually replaced many of the Navy officers who had previously served as academic deans and faculty. In the late 1960s, James Calvert, the former nuclear-submarine skipper then superintending the Academy, declared that his goal was for "Annapolis to take its place among the nation's foremost engineering schools," a naval MIT.[25] And in the early 1970s, the school's civilian academic dean made explicit that Rickover was driving the ship. The Academy's ultimate goal, he said, was to ready "any midshipman, regardless of his major, . . . for selection to the nuclear power program."²⁶ That was a far cry from father of the Navy John Paul Jones's "Qualifications of a Naval Officer" force-fed to every midshipman: "An officer should be a gentleman of liberal education, refined manners, punctilious courtesy, and the nicest sense of personal honor."²⁷ By the mid-1970s, the traditional Academy, the old boys' school that for more than a century had turned out well-rounded officers fit for command across the whole Navy, was largely a thing of the past; a military-polytechnic institute took up residence along the Severn River in Annapolis.

By the mid-1960s, nearly a third of all nuclear-submarine officers came into Rickover's program straight from Annapolis without ever having served in any other naval billet.²⁸ Many never would. But chronic officer shortages persisted. At most Rickover accepted about a third of candidates for the nuclear-training program, and 25 percent of those failed or dropped out along the way. In addition, first-generation nuclear officers were now retiring. Unable to find enough qualified internal candidates, Rickover took another unprecedented step by reaching into the ROTC programs at top universities and Officer Candidate School—further deepening the divide between the regular line officers and the nuclear Navy.

Seeing that many of those ROTC officers also struggled to pass the program, Rickover pushed for educational improvements far outside Annapolis's iron fence. Late one afternoon, he realized that not a single graduate of a large state university's ROTC program managed to complete Nuclear Power School despite having graduated with high marks and class standing. He put in a call to the university's president, but the man had already left for the day. He then called the state's governor. Taking Rickover's unexpected phone call about his state's university, the governor started to express his personal pride in the school. Rickover snapped that the governor should, instead, "shut it down." According to a witness, George Emery, a young officer on Rickover's staff who later rose to vice admiral, Rickover scolded the governor, "The school needs to give them a proper education so the graduates who have high marks can pass Nuclear Power School!"[29]

But the chronic shortages of qualified officers continued.

Rickover's dim views about US education paralleled his concerns with the nation's industrial standards. On October 29, 1962, Rickover delivered a widely reported keynote speech to the annual National Metal Congress meeting in New York City.[30] Speaking to seven hundred engineers and executives from many of the nation's largest industrial concerns, he pulled no punches. He castigated them and their peers for the "failure of American industry to live up to the exacting standards of reactor technology." He condemned the poor quality of equipment that contractors manufactured for his power plants. The tolerances needed to prevent reactor breakdowns seemed beyond current industrial capabilities. As a result, Naval Reactors engineers were left, he said, with "solving ever-recurring problems in the design, materials and workmanship of conventional components." He blamed the ongoing problems on a wider cultural failure to meet the exacting standards of the new technologies exemplified by nuclear reactors. His audience squirmed as he castigated them as managers "satisfied to sit in plush offices, far removed physically and mentally from the design and manufacturing areas, relying on paper reports for information about the status of design and production in the plant itself—the real center of the enterprise." They were endangering lives and the nation's defense. He told his audience to go back and change the lax culture at their firms. "Quality control," he said, "must be recognized as an essential tool to

enable management to meet today's technological imperatives."
Continuous monitoring and testing were paramount.

His talk combined many of the same concerns that ani-
mated his criticisms of US schools. US industry and even the
nation would fail if they did not pay constant, close attention
to detail and meet the higher standards that new technologies
like reactors demanded. "Whenever society advances—be it in
culture and education or science and technology—there is a
rise in the requirements man must meet to function successfully." Failure to do so, he warned, could destroy the benefits
that new technologies brought the nation. "Great undertakings
often founder because of negligence in some small detail, or
because of some minor, obvious and easily corrected mistake."
His words would shortly prove prophetically tragic.

At the time Rickover delivered his speech on quality control, the USS *Thresher*, the most formidable hunter-killer
submarine ever built, sat dockside at the Portsmouth Naval
Shipyard. It was nearing the end of nine months of major maintenance following nearly two years at sea. At a time when the
Soviet navy was embarking on a new and more aggressive stage
of sub development, the US Navy was eager to get *Thresher* back
into regular service. The *Thresher* was the world's first completely modern fast-attack sub, perhaps the most sophisticated
piece of Space Age machinery yet built. Its water-shedding,
shark-shaped hull and low-profile sail were constructed of special high-strength steel able to withstand sea pressure up to
eighty thousand pounds. *Thresher* could operate at a maximum
thirteen-hundred-foot depth, known as its test depth, nearly
double that of any existing sub.[31] Among other advances, its
turbines, motors, and other machinery sat on rubberized raft-
ing mounts that eliminated almost all mechanical vibrations
from translating to the hull. At low power, it ran with the barest

burr of cavitation through the deep. It could enter littorals and stalk notoriously noisy Soviet missile subs out to sea, tracking them without its prey knowing it lurked nearby. Should war come, *Thresher* would prove a swift, sure killer, ready to strike an unperceiving enemy with the latest, most lethal weapons. The *New York Times* declared *Thresher* "the finest product of the shipwright's art and one of the maritime marvels of this Technological Age."[32]

On the ninth of April 1963, *Thresher* left the Portsmouth Naval Yard for its final postmaintenance sea trials. It was so crowded with 12 officers, 96 enlisted men, and 21 civilians from the shipyard and various engineering contractors—129 people in all—that thirty temporary bunks had been set up in the empty torpedo room. The next morning, some 220 miles east of Cape Cod, it began its deep-dive tests. The *Thresher* had made at least forty previous dives to test depth prior to its overhaul. As the sub submerged, it maintained contact via underwater communications equipment with a rescue ship, *Skylark*, positioned overhead a couple of miles away.

After several initial maneuvers, shortly before 9:00 a.m., *Thresher* announced to *Skylark* that it was "proceeding to test depth." It was in waters about eighty-four-hundred feet deep. Voices were garbled and difficult to decipher on the "underwater telephone" coming over the loudspeaker, but at about 9:13, the men on the *Skylark* received *Thresher*'s first distress call. They heard the voice to say, "Experiencing minor difficulties. Have positive up angle. Am attempting to blow. Will keep you informed." The rescue ship picked up three more difficult-to-understand calls from *Thresher*. At 9:18, *Skylark*'s navigator heard a "high energy, low frequency noise disturbance" from far below. It was the sound of the *Thresher* imploding and the deaths of 129 men.

The *Skylark* continued to circle and call to *Thresher*. Other ships, subs, and airplanes arrived to search for it. But no further sign could be heard or found. The United States' most advanced submarine lay in fragments on the bottom of the Atlantic.[33]

No technological disaster would strike the national psyche with such force until the space shuttle *Challenger* exploded twenty-three years later. President Kennedy declared that the *Thresher* "had pioneered a new era in the eternal drama of the sea, diving deeper and going faster than any submarine before it." He compared the men lost to "their forefathers, who led the advance on the frontiers of our civilization."[34]

The next day, the Navy ordered a Court of Inquiry convened to investigate the *Thresher*'s loss. In an attempt to reconstruct the disaster, over the course of fifty-six days, the court collected seventeen hundred pages of testimony from 120 people and much material evidence, including photographs taken by an underwater robotic camera that reached the broken-up sub on the sea floor. (Parts of the testimony remain sealed a half century later.)[35] Congress's Joint Committee on Atomic Energy also held four days of hearings in June and July on the loss.

Both inquiries focused on the possibility that one or more leaks may have occurred.[36] According to the Court of Inquiry, seawater piped through the hull under deep-sea pressure to cool equipment in the engineering spaces may have leaked on electrical components and controls. The spraying water could have shorted them out and caused the reactor to scram. Without power, *Thresher* could not drive itself back to the surface. Another conundrum: based on sound recordings from underwater listening devices, the *Thresher* twice tried to blow water out of its main ballast tanks to float the sub to the surface. Each blow failed for unknown reasons. In the end, the committee's final public report concluded "that the specific cause is not known" for the disaster.[37] But that did not mean that systems and the people behind them were not blamed.

Rickover had gone out on the *Thresher*'s original sea trials and knew all its officers and many men among the crew. He wrote personal condolence letters to all the widows or parents of the 129 men lost in the disaster. Less than a month later, he went into the North Pacific for the initial sea trials of the Polaris submarine *Alexander Hamilton*. As the sub made its way back to port, he sent a letter to his son with the loss of the *Thresher* on his mind. He wrote, "There went down with her many fine young men, fine husbands, fathers, sons—a cross section of the flower of American youth. I knew many of them personally."[38] His grief was genuine and deep. However, to this day, some critics contend that Rickover's concern to keep tight operational control of the boat's reactor may have played a part in its demise.[39]

In fact, Rickover immediately feared that he would be made a scapegoat for the disaster. He called Vice Admiral Ralph K. James, chief of the Bureau of Ships, the evening of April 10, the very day *Thresher* was lost. James recalled that Rickover wanted to remind him "that he was not the submarine ship builder, he was simply the nuclear-plant producer." James said, "Rickover went to great extremes to disassociate any likelihood of failure of the nuclear plant from the *Thresher* incident. I considered this thoroughly dishonest." James believed that Rickover should shoulder blame, he said, for "the inadequate design of the nuclear controls for the power plant," which, if unable to operate with water spraying on them, might have led to a scram at the critical time when power was most needed.[40] Rickover managed to remove any questions raised and recommendations made about reactor-plant operations from the Court of Inquiry's findings.[41]

The two inquiries also considered whether Rickover's personnel practices might have contributed to the sinking, but his allies on the Hill came out fully in his support. The Joint Committee's final report declared, "The Committee reaffirms there should be no relaxation of existing procedures used in the selection, training, and assignment of nuclear propulsion personnel."[42]

The Bureau of Ships, on the other hand, did not get off so lightly.

In Rickover's congressional testimony, he condemned "carelessness, looseness and poor practices" at the Portsmouth shipyard for the disaster.[43] The committee shared Rickover's concern that the construction standards and quality control that went into portions of submarines outside his purview were dangerously unsystematic. The Navy Court of Inquiry considered a variety of possible scenarios behind any leak that may have developed but focused on the brazed joints, a soldering technique that was used to join pipes together and that had led previously to leaks on other subs. The joints held back ocean water under immense deep-sea pressure. During the *Thresher*'s overhaul, the shipyard had tested just 145 of the sub's more than 30,000 brazed joints. Thin or brittle spots had been seen in about 14 percent of the tested joints. Rickover had banned brazing outright in the engineering spaces, opting instead for welded bonds, a more expensive and time-consuming but dependable method.[44]

Still, the *Thresher* should have been able to blow its ballast and float to the surface. An unexpected but plausible explanation emerged for the ballast-system failure. *Thresher*'s sister ship, *Tinosa*, was being readied in the Portsmouth Yard for its sea trials. While it was at dockside, investigators simulated an emergency blow of its ballast transfer system—shooting highly pressurized air to blow seawater out the hull ballast tanks. One of the *Tinosa*'s officers on hand recalled hearing "a huge rush of air noise in the control room, then silence after a few seconds." A second attempt also failed to blow out the big tanks. "We were shocked," said then-Lieutenant Zach T. Pate. The inspection team opened the two ballast blow systems. Inside the blow pipes between the compressors and the ballast tanks, they came across two fine-mesh strainers in each. Nothing in the design specs called for the strainers to be there, but during the overhaul, contractors had fitted them temporarily to collect any construction debris. They never removed them. The pressurized air shooting out from the tanks collapsed the strainers in the pipes. The investigators found that ice from falling air pressure had formed on the strainers—the same thermodynamic process that causes clouds to build up in the sky—quickly blocking the air tubes with each attempt to blow.[45]

Rickover's warning to the National Metal Congress had come to pass. He testified to the Joint Committee, "The real lesson to be learned is that we must change our way of doing business to meet the requirements of present-day technology."[46] Congress and the Court of Inquiry agreed. They called on the shipyard and the Navy to raise their weak quality-control procedures and praised Rickover for "standards of design and construction [that] were more stringent than the rest of the ship."[47]

The Navy could not build and operate Space Age machines using outmoded industrial standards and expect to avoid catastrophes. *Thresher* had gone to sea with two separate standards for quality assurance for the work done inside the hull. If the Navy intended to operate a nuclear fleet, it would have to adapt to the propulsion technology that Rickover "owned," not the other way around.

Resistance to the cultural transformation, the technocratic revolution that Rickover instigated, faded away. The Navy instituted a new, stringent SubSafe program. Modeled on Rickover's continuous shipyard testing system for his reactor compartment, SubSafe mandated strict quality-control procedures for the manufacture, repair, and testing of critical components on submarines. After this, the admiral's consistently demanding standards gradually became norms from stem to stern on every nuclear submarine. SubSafe extended eventually to a programmatic overhaul of safety- and quality-assurance procedures throughout the Navy's conventional-ship construction and maintenance program.

Sadly, however, *Thresher* was not to be the last sub lost: on May 27, 1968, the Navy announced that the SSN *Scorpion* was missing and presumed lost in the Atlantic with its ninety-nine hands. The wreckage was eventually located in deep water south of the Azores. To this day, no definitive cause for the disaster has been found, though several have been suggested.[48]

Despite no finding of fault for Rickover's program for the *Thresher* disaster, he had to face the reality that his officers' unbending training in conservative operating procedures may have played a role in the disaster. Every sub still carries large procedure books filled with documents revised from the originals written by Rickover and his staff. Officers must consult those documents with an ostentatious reading aloud of procedures for emergency restart steps following a scram or any other anomalous event. After that, the officers can make their "risk calls" to diverge from standard operating procedures. But when the *Thresher* went down, start-up procedures following a scram were "hard and fast and rigid," Rear Admiral John H. Mauer, director of the Submarine Warfare Division, testified at the congressional hearings.[49] Rickover disputed the characterization, insisting that officers could improvise in an emergency to save the ship. But in going by the book, the officers at the controls on the *Thresher* may not have had enough time to restart the reactor before it descended to crush depth. Had the operators broken with standing rules, some critics speculate that heat left in the reactor could have propelled it back to the surface. Doing so might have damaged the reactor but saved the *Thresher* and its 129 men.[50]

To Rickover's credit, after the hearings, he and his engineers developed ways to carry out a "fast scram recovery procedure." Recognizing the knowledge gaps that may have contributed to the loss of the *Thresher*, Naval Reactors also conducted a force-wide retraining to improve the engineering officers' ability to restart a shut-down reactor promptly—or utilize its heat reservoir in an emergency.

In the end, though, it was naval culture that had to change, not Rickover. After the *Thresher* findings, submarine officers ceased rotating to new posts every twelve to fifteen months. Tours generally ran 50 percent longer. Also, to find the officers he wanted, Rickover held a service-wide draft, forcing technically adept and academically minded aviation and surface-ship officers to report as candidates for submarine duty. Even if they wanted nothing to do with Rickover and his subs, they were obligated to enter his program if he chose them.[51] He could have any officer he wanted and keep the person as long as he needed him or her. The *Thresher* disaster that threatened to sink Rickover placed him more firmly in command than ever.

In August 1963, with the end of Rickover's final two-year extension of active duty approaching in January 1964, his staff and congressional backers agitated for him to stay on. But by law, the admiral had to go. A special-situation clause could work; the secretary of the Navy had the power to call a retired officer back to active duty for up to two years if no other officer were qualified for a specific post. That is what Secretary Korth decided to do. Korth promised Congress that when Rickover retired in January 1964, he would bring him immediately back on active duty for another two years.

Korth left before then, but the next Navy secretary, Paul

Nitze, followed through and called Rickover back from retirement. But Nitze considered his appointment a temporary arrangement and wanted to create a succession plan. Rickover's longtime chief naval aide, John Crawford Jr., had put in for retirement about this time. Nitze asked whether he would reconsider and instead stay on as Rickover's deputy and successor. Crawford said the idea was "nuts." He told Nitze, "If you think you're getting a deputy who functions as a deputy normally does, forget it." Nitze asked him to talk it over with Rickover. When Crawford went to see Rickover about it, Rickover told him that "he didn't want a deputy": "He'd make my life hell." Rickover joked with him, "Crawford, does the Pope have a deputy?" Crawford recalled, "The whole deal fell through."[52] Rickover, the reactor's representative on Earth, let Crawford and the Navy know that he alone could run Naval Reactors— perhaps until the divine intervened.

But by law, Nitze could not permanently reappoint Rickover. After the Crawford plan blew up, Nitze promised Rickover that he would recall him again in two years. A process began that would recur every two years. About six months before Rickover's next "retirement" date, he or his staff hinted to the secretary of the Navy—whoever held the post—that his friends in Congress were eagerly awaiting word of the admiral's reappointment as head of NR. Upon "retirement," Rickover promptly got a letter asking him to come back out of retirement for a special two-year active-duty term.

Few observers could have envisioned that this temporary arrangement between the Navy and the executive branch would go on for years. But when Rickover met Nitze for that first callback to active duty, he warned the secretary of the Navy that he intended to stay on the job for a long time. As he left Nitze's office, he yelled back through the door, "My parents have both lived to ripe old ages, so don't think you'll get rid of me soon!"[53] And he was right.

11

The Chair with the Short Legs

IF RICKOVER HAD any sort of "grand plan" to take command of the Navy, it began by cutting a couple of inches off the front legs of an old wooden chair in his office.

Through his adroit political maneuverings and Machiavellian manipulations, Rickover did not just own the propulsion systems on his ships: he handpicked, trained, and controlled all the men who ran them. And as the nuclear fleet expanded and matured and his standards integrated into the "regular" Navy, he shaped not just his force but the entire Navy that had tried to expel him and whose traditions he despised. He undertook an intense winnowing process to identify, train, and control his nuclear officers. His methods became legendary, as much a part of his mystique as the complex machines he invented.[1]

"Admiral Rickover snapped off every bright scholar he could," BuPers chief Charles Duncan said. He was "addicted to" those with high standing in math, science, and engineering.[2]

Two or three days each month, busloads of senior midshipmen, tops from their classes, arrived at Naval Reactors' Washington offices. After President Nixon ordered the fifty-plus-year-old "temporary" buildings torn down in the early 1970s, NR moved to a modern office building in Crystal City near the Pentagon in Virginia. The candidates filed into a room where three senior staffers grilled them with technical questions, assessed their ability to think logically, and inquired about their naval career commitment. Then, one at a time, they were led into Rickover's office.[3] They entered a room that was as bland and bare as a police interrogation room—a standard-issue Navy desk and chair, a conference table, metal shelves and file cabinets, a US flag—into which the young men had been thrust to face the third degree for a crime they had yet to realize they had committed.

Often quaking, the midshipmen in uniform sat down in a wooden chair opposite the gnome-like admiral behind his desk in civilian clothing. Eyeing the glowering Rickover, the candidate suddenly noticed that he was sliding off the slick, shiny chair seat. Much to the young officer's consternation and discomfort, the two front legs of the chair were shorter than the rear legs. Rickover explained later that by shortening the two legs, he was forcing the already uneasy young men "to maintain their wits about them while they were asked these questions while they were sliding off the chair."[4]

Then came the unorthodox part.

He almost never asked technical questions.[5] He had already read their school records and heard from his deputies how they had fared in their interviews. Rather, speaking in a deadpan, high-pitched, nasal voice, he questioned them about their parents, plans for a family of their own, their favorite college course, the last ten books they had read. The rapid-fire questions were unpredictable, eccentric, perplexing, intrusively personal. He wanted responses fast and brief. He interrupted interviewees midsentence to curse wrongheaded answers. He would ask them to define religion, how they could pick out the most intelligent person in a room full of people just by looking at them, and if they saw a woman officer who was sloppily dressed, whether they would tell her. Rickover claimed that he did not care what the answers were but how the candidate came up with his responses. "I want to find out whether a man can think straight about a problem he has never considered before," he said, "because that's what he's going to have to do every day of his life here. And whether he'll stand up to me when he's convinced I'm wrong. Too much depends on his decisions to have it otherwise."[6] He wanted clear-thinking problem solvers who had the confidence and agility of mind to make smart choices in tough situations.

His reaction to weak, vacillating, or deceitful answers was scary to behold. Not liking an answer from midshipman William Toti, spittle shot out of the admiral's mouth as he jumped up, slamming his desktop, eyes bulging, and screamed at the top of his lungs, "That's bullshit!" His apoplectic rage seemed genuine after Toti tried to defend a C grade he had received in a philosophy class. "I've heard a lot of bullshit in my day, but I have never, *ever* heard such bullshit before! I want you to know, young man, that you now hold the bullshit record! Get out of here! Get the hell out of my office!"[7] Rickover was "a great actor," said Admiral Duncan.

"Bullshit" was the cardinal sin. The penalty was instant banishment to a janitorial closet, "with brooms and bad smells and a deep sink, . . . nuclear purgatory," Toti recalled. There the penitents sat for hours on end. "I'd give them a chance to think," Rickover said. "I'd put them in there for a couple of hours, three hours, and it gave them plenty of time to think." The time in the broom closet led some to stew in anger and simply wait to be dismissed; others hardened themselves to prove their endurance, and some considered what led them to their predicament. Once released, the candidates faced the same question all over. Rickover sent them away again if their reply was not right, repeating the process until he got the answer he wanted. He ended many interviews by asking, "How would you improve the Navy?" Those with the temerity to answer the admiral frankly often were hired.[8] Without a good-bye, he turned back to his work until the candidate realized his interview was over.

Jack Crawford remembered being kicked out by Rickover for the first time in 1949. He was soon brought back. Eventually as a deputy manager and naval liaison at NR, he participated in vetting hundreds of candidates and sat in on scores of Rickover interviews. "He had ways of getting to the weaknesses of a person that were absolutely superb and absolutely unique," Crawford witnessed. But he added, "I'm not saying whether they were legal, normal, or appropriate." According to Crawford, "He looked for two types of people: intellect, not memorizers, who could think logically and quickly, and he wanted hard workers. Their class standing was unimportant if they didn't work hard. If they start low and go high, that shows they will continue."[9]

What mattered most beyond a candidate's smarts and character was the strength of the relationship that developed with Rickover over the course of as much as two hours together. But the determination of that relationship was entirely one-sided, unfathomable, and often based on Rickover's spot judgment. Sometimes, the outcome seemed arbitrary. According to William Anderson, the officer who captained the *Nautilus* on its first-ever polar voyages, Rickover invited one hapless commanding-officer prospect to lunch. After the admiral watched the interviewee put salt on his corn without bothering to taste it first, he snapped, "I will not have you in my group!

You did not properly assess the situation before you took corrective action." That ended the lunch, the interview, and the would-be candidate's chance for a nuclear command.[10]

Rickover could also prove simply cruel. At times he took malicious glee in hazing interviewees mercilessly with demonstrations of his absolute control over their future lives. "He loved nasty interviews where he called you an idiot," recalled T. R. Reid, who was on Rickover's staff in the early 1960s. "He could cut people to shreds, and he loved it."[11] Hazing by superior officers was as much a part of midshipmen's lives as parade-ground marches. Rickover took it to another level. In his early days building the nuclear Navy, he probed candidates' sex lives, but he backed off on that approach after the Navy brass called him to task.[12] Learning that a midshipman was a member of a chorus, he ordered him to sing a Christmas carol to each of his female administrative assistants; he told others to take off their shirts in front of the women for them to determine if the middies were chubby. The overweight ones had to sign a "fat letter" to be sent to their parents or girlfriends promising to lose weight. He toyed with the midshipmen's machine-like readiness to obey a superior officer's orders to a fault by marching them into walls.[13]

In a few infamous instances, he told young men on the verge of marriage to call their fiancées on the spot and cancel their wedding plans if they truly wanted to join the all-consuming nuclear-training program. "Subs or marriage?" he demanded, pushing his telephone across the desk. After having called the unsuspecting and now-bereft women to end their wedding plans, Rickover rejected the would-be trainees out of hand for their lack of conviction.[14] With others, though, he inquired about their intention to have children, then rejected some of those who said they wanted big families, "nest-building" he called it, which he thought would distract them from their Navy careers.

Complaints flooded the Bureau of Personnel. When questioned, Rickover said that he considered himself an "amateur psychiatrist." He wanted, he explained to Admiral Smedberg at the Bureau of Personnel, "to irk them and see what responses" he got, "see if they're fighters": "This is my method. . . . I want to see what responses I get out of them and in order to do it I have to make them mad."[15] Countless tales grew out of the interviews, some probably apocryphal. Rickover purportedly asked one candidate to make *him* mad. The young officer hesitated and then swept his hand over the admiral's desk, sending papers, lamp, pen, and all flying to the floor; another supposedly grabbed a choice ship model and smashed it to pieces against the wall. Rickover's face reddened, and he screamed at the young men to get out; but they were, again according to legend, accepted into nuclear training. Mounting complaints and seemingly unexplained rejections eventually led Rickover to station a Naval Reactors deputy in his office to document the issues that brought on candidates' rejections.[16]

As Rickover intended, nobody forgot their interview with him. Rickover asked the Navy veteran Elmo Zumwalt Jr. what he thought about his interview shortly before dismissing him. An experienced and widely respected officer already, Zumwalt, a future CNO, was at the time up for command of one of the first nuclear surface ships. After being peppered with questions that made little sense to him, insults, and *four* banishments to "the tank," which left him "so angry" that he "was actually unable to speak," he told the admiral that his interview was "the most fascinating experience" of his life. Zumwalt withdrew from consideration for nuclear training.[17] He and Rickover would bump heads countless times after this.

But many midshipmen considered running the Rickover

gauntlet life altering in a positive way. Midshipman Toti described having sat miserably for nearly two hours "killing time" in the janitorial closet. Then he "had an epiphany." His thoughts strayed to his immigrant family's onetime poverty and his commitment to himself to work as hard as he could to avoid that fate. The admiral asked him when he exited the closet, "Are you ready to tell me the truth?" Toti was. His grade was, in the end, not the real issue, he said; he "could have worked harder" while at the Naval Academy. "By not giving my best effort," he understood, "I betrayed myself, and I betrayed the investment the country was placing in me." The rage leaked away from Rickover eyes. "That's right," he said to Toti. "If you give less than you're able to, you'll let everyone down—me, your ship, your Navy, and your country. I can't use people like that. I can only use people who have the courage and discipline to give all they've got."[18] He got the officers he wanted.

Among those who responded well to Rickover's intensive interview technique was a sharp and solicitous Annapolis graduate and submarine veteran from a peanut farm in Georgia, Lieutenant James "Jimmy" Carter. Rickover interviewed him for two hours in spring 1952, early in the history of the nuclear-submarine program. Rickover asked him about Wagner's opera *Tristan and Isolde*, novels by William Faulkner and Ernest Hemingway that he had read, and especially Herman Wouk's naval novel *The Caine Mutiny*. When Rickover asked Carter about his standing at the Academy, Carter proudly told Rickover that he ranked 59 out of a class of 820. "'Did you do your best?'" Rickover asked. Carter started to answer, "Yes, sir," but then stopped. He recalled "many times at the Academy" when he "could have learned more." He confessed that he had not. Then came "one final question" that Carter said he has "never been able to forget—or to answer." Rickover asked, "Why not?"[19] Without another word, Rickover turned to papers on his desk while Carter sat there for several minutes until he slowly got up and left.

Rickover accepted Carter as a nuclear trainee. Carter went through Nuclear Power School and prototype training to qualify as a nuclear engineering officer. He also helped set up training for the enlisted men being instructed for the USS *Seawolf*, his future boat. Before he went to sea, though, Carter had to resign his commission to help his family run the farm after his father died in 1953. Despite the short time Carter spent under Rickover's command, the impact resonated and endured. He would say more than two decades later that the admiral proved to be the "most influential man" other than his father in his life. With a salute to Rickover's last question in the interview, Carter titled his 1975 autobiography, published in anticipation of his race for the presidency the next year, *Why Not the Best?*[20]

For the one in ten—later rising to one in five and finally one in three—who got tapped to become nucs, their trials were just beginning. Rickover expected everyone around him to work and learn constantly at the highest level, beyond what they had believed they were capable of. In the corridors of all the nuclear power and prototype schools, signs read, "In this school the smartest work as hard as those who must struggle to pass. H. G. Rickover."[21] Slackers fell out quickly.

Nuclear training exemplified a new level of technical rigor and intellectual discipline for the Navy.[22] Rickover wanted anyone who walked into a nuclear power plant to understand the fundamentals of the physics that made it go; even enlisted crewmen, from machinist mates and electricians to welders, attended six months of Nuclear Power School along with prospective nuclear officers. After a six-week preparatory course in math and physics, the enlisted men received the equivalent of an undergraduate-level education in nuclear physics. Nuclear officers in training immersed themselves in a graduate-level nuclear-engineering program. Most trainees had never worked so hard. For six days a week, twelve hours a day, they attended classes and studied mathematics, chemistry, physics, electrical engineering, heat transfer, fluid mechanics, reactor engineering principles, metallurgy, radiological control, and so on.

After Nuclear Power School came six months of training and standing watch at one of the five prototype training sites that NR operated. Hours-long tests and surprise exercises on the prototypes—overseen by experienced nuclear officers and senior technical deputies—determined who passed. Hours off watch went for study and sleep. Trainees could find nothing to distract them in any case. Rickover's sites had no recreational facilities, commissaries, or other stores, just vending machines and the Navy's endless pots of coffee. The men lived in town, reported for their watches, and studied. Few had spare time, even for family.

The tension that came with controlling an operating reactor, the long watches, constant surveillance, arduous testing, lack of social life, and exhaustion drove some in "The Program," as it was known, to the breaking point. About 10 percent of candidates washed out. But all who made it through joined an elite fraternity, the intellectual equivalent to the brutal physical, tactical, and weapons training that the Navy put its special forces such as the SEALs through.

After up to two years of training, the determined, brilliant, disciplined, and indoctrinated officers and enlisted men reported to their submarines, ships, and reactors. They were ready to begin their tours of duty operating on the world's seas, maintaining what Rickover called "eternal vigilance" over their reactors. Never would they escape his vigilance. "The training of our people," he said, "goes on forever."[23]

12

The Crusade

REPEATEDLY DENIED THE opportunity to serve in the new nuclear Navy, veteran line commanders gave way throughout the 1960s and '70s to the fresh generation of warrior-technocrats, officers hand-chosen and trained by Rickover. These ambitious young men, among the most accomplished, smartest, and best educated in the service, demonstrated their operational talents and strategic acumen at sea and on shore. Over the next decade, many of them rose into positions of high command. Among Rickover trainees, four became chiefs of naval operations, and three others whom he *rejected* also made CNO. There were nuclear-trained secretaries of the Navy and finally a president of the United States. At Naval Reactors, many staffers thrived under Rickover. He was not an easy boss, far from it, but they relished the opportunities he gave them and the responsibility they bore at the frontiers of nuclear technology in the nation's service. Many of his engineers stayed with him for years, some returning after retiring from the Navy, forgoing high pay in private industry. Late in his career, a review found that Rickover's hundred most senior people at NR averaged fifteen years, while the heads of his twenty divisions had typically worked with him for twenty.[1]

As a result of NR's increasingly stellar place within the Navy firmament, other parts of the service adopted its cultural and technological model. The other naval platforms—aviation, ships systems, weapons and missiles, even special forces—developed specialty cultures of their own. The old system in which generalist officers rotated to new billets across platforms every twelve to eighteen months increasingly gave way to specialist-commanders who remained for years until they had devoted entire careers to their technical specialty.[2] By the mid-1970s, Rickover's cultural transformation reached into every corner of the Navy, however distant from nuclear propulsion.

Yet his fight for nuclear propulsion never ended. He led the nuclear Navy as if it were a bastion of innovative intelligence, careful engineering, and technocratic elitism besieged by seafaring idiots, leftovers from the era of sail. "Life," he bemoaned during a 1967 Joint Committee on Atomic Energy hearing, "is a constant fight against stupidity."[3] He annually admonished congressional committees, "We have got somehow to drag the Navy into the Twentieth Century. From the beginning the Navy has opposed nuclear power."[4] He and his staff were relentlessly staving off bureaucratic intruders from the Defense Department, uniformed antinuclear backsliders in the Navy, and corner-cutting contractors out to fleece taxpayers. He told his young staffer T. R. Reid, "We'd still be sending out sailing ships today if the Navy brass had its way." Reid, later a distinguished journalist, was a Princeton-educated ROTC ensign who helped Rickover prepare testimony and other documents. He recalled that in the late 1960s and early '70s, when he worked at a desk outside the admiral's office, "We all felt we were in a historic crusade to pull a reluctant Navy into the twentieth century."[5] Little did it matter that by that time, according to Elmo R. Zumwalt Jr., who served as chief of naval operations from 1970 to 1974, "within the Navy there was almost universal support for most of the nuclear propulsion program."[6]

Rickover's crusade was based on his past experiences overcoming the Navy's resistance, but it also served as a leadership technique. Having an enemy beyond the NR citadel inspired drive, fervor, and pride among his civilian and Navy staff members—coupled with the cudgel of his angry screams—that kept them racing to keep up with his unrelenting demands day after day. "I worked my brains out," recalled Reid. And that fight, Rickover said, "to persuade people to do that which common sense alone would dictate to be the right thing," gave him a never-ending David versus Goliath story, one that he repeatedly told Congress and the American public. He stood steadfast as the lonely righteous man who dared to buck a gargantuan, rapacious establishment mired in mediocrity.[7]

Meantime, a real and powerful new enemy had arisen.

When President Kennedy appointed Robert McNamara secretary of defense in 1961, the forty-five-year-old, already an industry giant, was tagged as the best and the brightest in the new administration, which attracted some of the leading minds in the land to Washington. The former president of Ford Motor Company assembled a crack team of "whiz kids" from Ivy League universities and policy think tanks to form the Pentagon's new Office of Systems Analysis. Economists, statisticians, computer programmers, organizational researchers, and operational analysts brought the latest in planning, cost-control systems, and information-management practices to bear on rivers of data flowing from the service branches. As McNamara's right hand on policy questions, they were tasked with applying what McNamara termed "quantitative common sense" to "meet our military requirements . . . at the lowest possible cost."[8] When it came to multimillion-dollar, long-timeline new ship-construction programs for the Navy, the supremely self-confident McNamara had no intention of simply checking off on the admirals' wish lists as other secretaries had most often done. Before the Navy would get another new ship, jet, or missile, his analysts had to run each proposed system through a cost-effectiveness study. Cost-cutters loved him. Republican Barry Goldwater called McNamara "one of the best secretaries ever, an IBM machine with legs."[9]

Rickover detested McNamara. He hated Pentagon bureaucrats who "live in a world of immutable abstractions" and thought their data-driven studies applied a veneer of objectivity—"fog bombs," he called them—to predetermined decisions. He scoffed at their supposed systematizing of the workplace and objective decision-making processes that relieved military professionals of their responsibilities. The bureaucrats were promoting "a sort of new religion, . . . an ism," he told Congress. "One of these days we will have everyone so indoctrinated in cost-effectiveness and systems analyses that a corporal will make a cost-effectiveness analysis before he orders a squad to attack an enemy."[10] He tore up Pentagon requests for additional NR data. Attempts to impose uniform organizational templates on individuals doing real work, he said, amounted to "the lowest common denominator of human behavior, . . . a substitute for rational thought."[11] The data managers did not understand the advanced technologies they were supposed to analyze. The Pentagon was filling up with MBAs under the Harvard Business School graduate McNamara's watch. But Rickover scoffed, "What it takes to do a job, will not be learned from management courses."[12]

He openly mocked the Pentagon's efforts to measure his organization's effectiveness. When a Department of Defense manager asked Naval Reactors to participate in "an experiment in peer rating," he wrote a Groucho Marxian reply: "I do not understand what 'peer rating' is." He pondered the issue in mock wonder: "From my reading, I judge that peer rating is closely related to the 'pecking order' established among pigeons, chickens, and the like. I am aware that some eminent social scientists have advocated training humans by the methods derived from studying pigeons—tossing them a grain of corn when they do well. However, I concluded that this would not work in my office because 'pigeon-trained' people would probably spend too much time worrying about their 'image' in the 'pecking order' and not enough time doing their jobs." Delivering a verbal kick in the pants, he concluded, "For the above reasons and because my laboratories do not operate under the Department of Defense, but under the Atomic Energy Commission, which does not have the money for such experiments, I am returning herewith the IBM cards you sent to me; you will surely be able to use them elsewhere."[13]

Absurdist humor might rebuff some unfortunate bureaucrat, but the Department of Defense controlled the Navy's ship-production budget. Much to Rickover's dismay, McNamara's cost-effectiveness studies led him to conclude that the nation should not buy another nuclear carrier or a new and as-yet-unproved class of fast-attack submarines. The ferocious admiral of the nuclear Navy and the arrogant, thin-skinned secretary of defense were destined for a very public clash.

Since the commissioning of the three nuclear ships comprising the USS *Enterprise* carrier group at the start of the decade, just one additional nuclear surface ship had gone on the building ways, the guided-missile cruiser USS *Truxton*, and it would not set sail until 1967. With growing costs from the escalating Vietnam War and the ongoing operational demands of the Cold War, Pentagon budgets were stretched thin. Inflation, too, was taking a heavy toll; expenses were starting to shoot up.

The *Enterprise* cost $451.3 million ($4 billion today) to build. About a third smaller, the conventionally powered carrier USS *Independence* launched the year before at less than half the price, $182.3 million (about $1.6 billion today). Nuclear- and conventionally powered escort ships had similarly large cost differentials. McNamara's Defense Department analysts objected to paying so much more for a nuclear surface ship over a conventionally fueled one.

But a ship's price tag out of the yard was not true cost accounting, Rickover countered. A 1963 Joint Committee on Atomic Energy study found that an all-nuclear task force, needing no refueling and able to transport and support more airplanes and their crews, ammunition, other firepower, and aviation fuel, would cost just 6 percent more than a conventional oil-fired carrier group over their operational lifetimes. (However, that study failed to account for the high cost of decommissioning a nuclear ship.)[14] That small differential in a ship's total lifetime cost bought nuclear propulsion's decided strategic and tactical advantages to the United States when it needed to project military power across the world. The committee strongly recommended that "the United States adopt a policy of utilizing nuclear propulsion in all future major ships."[15]

The Pentagon would accrue real-world evidence in the early and mid-1960s that nuclear surface ships were a naval-warfare difference-maker. During the 1962 Cuban Missile Crisis, the *Enterprise* remained on station for forty-eight consecutive days while blockading Soviet offensive forces and, after the Soviet forces withdrew from Cuba, overseeing their exit. (The *Nautilus* too patrolled through Cuban waters.) In early December 1965, the *Enterprise*, accompanied by its nuclear escort *Bainbridge*, began its first combat operations, in the Vietnam War. In a year and a half of operations at Yankee Station off the coast of Vietnam and in the Gulf of Tonkin, the carrier launched combat flights on 132 days and set multiple daily carrier records for total numbers of sorties.[16] And the *Bainbridge* never pulled off its station screening the carrier except for resupply and shore relief. (It did rotate away for shore-bombardment duty and to escort conventionally powered carrier groups.) Even those operations did not show a nuclear task force's singular advantage: the ability to steam at sustained flank speed across oceans, without need to put in for refueling, to the crisis spots where a show of force or firepower was needed.

"Of course nuclear-powered ships are better than conventional ships," McNamara acknowledged, "costs not considered. But cost has to be considered because it is a measure of what is being given up elsewhere."[17] He refused to build more nuclear surface ships without first undertaking comprehensive quantitative studies to determine, with numeric clarity, their relative worth. In 1966, he consented to building a second nuclear carrier, the *Nimitz*, which went into the following year's budget. But he waived off buying any additional nuclear escort ships until some unspecified later date.[18] A simmering back-office debate over arcane measures of relative cost-effectiveness exploded into an ugly political boxing match on Capitol Hill and in the press.

Rickover and his two most senior staffers, William Wegner and David Leighton, both retired Navy officers returned as civilian AEC employees, lobbied their congressional supporters to force the Defense Department to use nuclear propulsion in all major surface war ships, as the Joint Committee had insisted back in 1963. Rickover also wanted to build the first in a new class of advanced high-speed submarines to counter the increasing speed of Soviet subs. He also put forward plans to engineer a series of small, deep-submergence vessels, for ocean-floor research, materials testing, and, post-*Thresher*, possible future recovery operations.

Rickover testified numerous times about the strong opposition he faced from Pentagon "nay-sayers" who insisted on study after study to "guarantee exactly what the new item will do"—an impossibility, he contended, without first engineering the technology. "I have fought the red tape jungle for many years," he told the Joint Committee on Atomic Energy, "but it is becoming very difficult to get any new project through the Navy and the Defense Department. You must justify everything eight ways to Sunday."[19] McNamara had his supporters, especially in the Senate, who agreed with his cost-effectiveness arguments. Rickover would not get his new high-speed subs, the Los Angeles class (also known as six-eighty-eights, 688s), until after McNamara resigned in 1968.

Using AEC money, Rickover managed to slip in other defense appropriations to get the thirteen-person, deep-sea research sub *NR-1* built in late 1969. Critics blasted the $100 million submersible, at 148 feet the smallest nuclear vessel ever built, as a Rickover pet project of dubious value. But with a test depth of three thousand feet, the *NR-1* opened portions of the deep to study and mapping and served on multiple recovery missions, though most operational details remain classified.[20]

But Rickover fought on to get nuclear escorts added to the defense budget for the carrier *Nimitz*. Congress had in fact designated funds for two additional nuclear missile cruisers, then known as frigates, the *Truxton* and a second to go with the *Nimitz* program. But McNamara refused to authorize construction of the additional ship. He and his Navy secretary, Paul Nitze, wanted two oil-fired destroyers built instead. What was the point, Rickover and his supporters questioned, of having a nuclear carrier if it could not move at a flank speed to a hot spot without having to dawdle or even stop while its screening warships reoiled? What would happen should world events cut off access in distant ports for refueling?

Rickover was slated to testify on Monday, May 2, 1966, before the House Armed Services Committee. The powerful chairman, Democrat L. Mendel Rivers of South Carolina, strongly backed a fully nuclear Navy. At 11:00 p.m. the night before Rickover's testimony, Paul Nitze telephoned him at home to remind him that the secretary of defense's shipbuilding program called for the two conventional destroyers and *no* nuclear escorts. Rickover told Nitze that the committee invited him to lay out the comparative merits of nuclear ships and that was his plan. An unnerved Nitze exploded. According to Rickover's notes from the call, Nitze said that "*he* was the Secretary of the Navy and was responsible for the welfare of the Navy" and that Rickover "should not take it upon [him]self to mastermind what the Navy or the Secretary of Defense should do." Rickover made it clear that the committee asked for his views, not the Navy's or the Pentagon's, and he intended to give them just that.[21]

Rickover dramatically raised the stakes around the issue when he testified the next day. He did not merely lay out the demonstrated benefits of nuclear power; he depicted the outcome of the ship-propulsion issue as a constitutional crisis. He warned that if Congress did not enforce its power to determine how the people's money was spent, the legislative branch risked ceding its constitutionally stipulated budgetary authority to the executive branch. On May 16, the committee reported to the House of Representatives where its members stood: construction of the two nuclear frigates and *no* conventional escort ships must go forward. The report threw down the gauntlet: "If this language constitutes a test as to whether Congress has the power to so mandate, let the test be made and let this important weapons system be the field of trials."[22] The pugnacious Rivers declared, "We'll do it."[23]

The battle over the ships was not settled by any means, but many observers inside and outside the Navy interpreted this round as a victory for Rickover over McNamara. Rickover's fight for nuclear-powered ships would continue for the rest of the decade and through the next. And it often came down to a power struggle between Rickover and his congressional supporters on the one side and the Defense Department and even the president on the other.

Rickover's insubordination ran him very close to the precipice several times. In 1967, Nitze almost convinced President Lyndon Johnson that Rickover had to go. But after rumors that Johnson was not going to extend the admiral another two-year term reached Rickover's backers on the Hill, the storm of protest quickly convinced Johnson, already embattled over the Vietnam War's increasing carnage, to change his mind.[24] Hoping to reduce internecine tensions, a group of senators brought Rickover and Nitze together for a closed-door meeting to soothe relations. Once caught up in a fight, Rickover never stopped until his opponent was beaten down. With Nitze sitting right beside him, Rickover called him the worst secretary of the Navy in history.[25]

McNamara too faced Rickover's verbal barrages. At Rickover's annual briefing to the House Appropriations Subcommittee on Defense, on May 1, 1967, he went tooth and nail after the secretary of defense and his data-driven regime. He said relying on statistical analysis more than hard-won professional wisdom (ironic given Rickover's own disdain for veteran submariners) was a dangerous way to prepare for war. "The reason our country can stay ahead [of the Soviet military] is because of our technology," he said. "If we do not choose to take advantage of our technology, then we will have to fight wars on the enemy's terms; that is, with numbers of people." Who could argue against the incalculable worth of a service member's life when it came to paying for the best-quality military hardware? This, he declared, was "the most damning thing you can say about cost-effectiveness studies. They don't . . . take account of human life. . . . Human life is not 'quantifiable' in a cost-effectiveness study, and therefore cannot be considered" by the Pentagon's analysts.[26]

Without naming McNamara, all knew whom he meant when he continued, "Our society is threatened by any man who knows method but not meaning, technique but no principle — any man who tries to operate in a professional field in which he is unqualified, any man who depreciates wisdom, experience and intuition." He said that he expected Congress to ignore such a man and his managerial minions. "I don't believe it is Congress that is dense" enough to accept their reasoning, he said. "Maybe the cost analysts are dense." He warned that "by virtue of sheer power and blinded by their own propaganda, those in charge consider themselves competent" to intervene in technical matters and military decisions that they neither understood nor could direct without doing harm. He offered a logical solution: cut the bloated Pentagon bureaucracy back to its pre-McNamara size. "In a homely manner of speaking," he told Congress, "the Defense Department is constipated; it must be purged, or it will become increasingly torpid."[27]

McNamara was outraged by Rickover's rude testimony and obstreperousness. In late 1967, he stormed into Representative Rivers's office. The defense secretary told Rivers that Rickover had gone too far this time; McNamara was going to take disciplinary action against him. He was going to end Rickover's career, even strip him of his rank. But he was speaking to the wrong man. Rivers considered Rickover a unique asset in national service. (He also appreciated that the Charleston Naval Shipyard in his home district handled nuclear refueling and repairs for subs.) According to an account of their meeting, Rivers responded that if the secretary of defense "wanted to give Admiral Rickover a court-martial that was fine, but then he would run into" — he ticked off the names of half a dozen of the most powerful members of the House and Senate — plus, he declared, "the entire House of Representatives, the entire Senate, the Jews, the Catholics, the Protestants, and anyone else you wanted to name." He shrugged that McNamara should "go ahead and do it, but he couldn't imagine why he wanted to do it." McNamara paused. "Thank you," he said and abruptly left.[28]

By the end of 1967, Congress had authorized both the *Nimitz*, first in its class of carriers, and the *California*, first in a new class of missile cruisers, and a second nuclear ship in the same class, though with a longer lead time for construction. No conventional major warships were included in the congressionally authorized Navy budget.

With McNamara gone in 1969 and Rickover's Russia traveling companion Richard Nixon in the White House, Rickover may have thought he would finally get a fully nuclear Navy. But on July 1, 1970, his nemesis, Zumwalt, was sworn in as the new chief of naval operations. Zumwalt was a progressive manager and a thoughtful admiral, with a stellar fighting record dating to the Second World War, as well as outstanding administrative and academic qualifications. But Zumwalt detested Rickover. Following Zumwalt's stormy selection interview with Rickover in 1959 for a position as commanding or executive officer of one of the first two nuclear surface ships, Zumwalt had opted for a conventional-ship command.[29] From there he became executive assistant to Navy secretary Nitze, with whom Rickover had tensely poor relations. But for Rickover most gallingly, Zumwalt next served as the first head of the CNO's own systems-analysis division. He had little technical background, but he got swept up into fights between the Defense Department, Navy, and Rickover. And he believed Rickover was generally in the wrong.

Zumwalt considered Rickover "an archetypical parochialist," without commitment to the "Whole Navy," as he called it.

Rickover, he wrote, "would stop at nothing, bureaucratically speaking, to ensure that nuclear-powered ships received priority over vessels of any other kind." He regarded Naval Reactors as "a totalitarian mini-state whose citizens . . . did what the leader told them to, Navy regulations notwithstanding."[30] He believed that Rickover held onto power solely through fear and force of personality. Rickover was not one to be trifled with, and he did believe he should fight with all he could bring for his program. But Zumwalt did not comprehend why Naval Reactors had succeeded; Rickover motivated his people through his moral and political convictions about the need for continuous, methodical attention to reactor safety, his openness to rational argument and debate, his encouragement of innovative engineering, and the unmatched accomplishments of his organization. These were not values that fit the new CNO's vision of a modern fighting navy. The two admirals were bound to clash.

When Nixon jumped Zumwalt over several more senior officers to make him CNO, among the problems Zumwalt wanted to solve was what he called "the Rickover complication." Zumwalt wrote in his memoirs a few years later that he understood what he faced in the seventy-year-old admiral and was determined to best a man who "brazenly—though seldom openly—challenges the duly constituted authority of every CNO and indeed every Secretary of the Navy, every Secretary of Defense, and every president." He realized "that developing a productive working relationship with Rickover was among the toughest nuts" that he "had been called upon to crack." However, he went to the Pentagon with the belief that he "could do it." In the end, he conceded, "I was wrong."[31]

By 1970, the nuclear fleet had grown to 101 operational ships—among them 46 attack and 41 ballistic-missile submarines, plus the carrier *Enterprise* and three escort ships—along with 2 more surface ships and 22 attack subs under construction and 5 more vessels authorized for future construction.

Almost one-third of all Navy vessels were now nuclear.[32] They were superb, world-beating, enormously expensive ships. Zumwalt recognized their quality, but for operational purposes and cost-effectiveness, the CNO advocated what he called a "High-Low" balanced force, with a small number of major nuclear surface warships coupled with a far larger number of stripped-down conventional vessels designed as a tactical counterweight to the increasingly predominant number of ships the Soviets were sending to sea. He negotiated a quid pro quo arrangement with Rickover to give him more nuclear vessels than Zumwalt felt the Navy budget warranted. In exchange, Rickover supposedly agreed not to oppose the larger number of conventional ships that the CNO viewed as necessary within the Navy budget. Rickover received significant additions to his budget. But, according to Zumwalt, Rickover "did not keep his bargain . . . but continued to work against any and all Low construction programs."[33]

But Rickover, too, felt aggrieved. Although a third and fourth carrier were soon authorized, other surface warships were cut from the budgets. World events seemed to demonstrate the need for reducing dependence on fossil-fueled ships. In late 1973 and continuing well into 1974, war and tensions emanating from the Middle East sparked an Arab-nation embargo of oil shipments to the United States. The resulting severe shortages and skyrocketing fuel prices made earlier cost-effectiveness comparisons between nuclear- and oil-powered ships meaningless. Despite these shocks to national-security planning and the threat to operations, Rickover told the Joint Committee on Atomic Energy on February 20, 1974, the Navy still did not get it. Nuclear power, he said, was "looked upon as something extraneous, as another part of the Navy. . . . They do not consider nuclear power as an inherent part of the Navy." Congress, he suggested, should put a stop to that. He had first called in 1961 for Congress to mandate a "cutoff line" for ships that must steam under nuclear power at eight thousand tons displacement. He renewed the idea now, so that "we will [not] be subject to the foibles of every official that gets into the Navy Department and decides to institute his pet transitory idea."[34]

That summer, as part of the Defense Department authorization act, Congress included—by huge majorities in both chambers—Title VIII, a statement on national nuclear-propulsion policy stipulating that going forward all major new combatant vessels operate on nuclear power.[35] Along with the annual budget, the secretary of defense would have to submit a separate planning document for the nuclear portion of the Navy. Shortly before Nixon resigned as president, he signed the budget bill. But he objected to Title VIII, insisting that he "would recommend nuclear propulsion for ships only when the added cost . . . is fully justified in the national interest."[36]

With Title VIII, Rickover seemed to have achieved his ultimate ambition. National defense policy now mandated that nuclear power drive all major new warships—unless the secretary of defense provided written justification for conventional propulsion. Rickover now projected that the Navy would have four wholly nuclear carrier task forces at sea by 1989 (the third Nimitz-class carrier, the *Carl Vinson*, was scheduled for commissioning in 1980). Each of the nation's four nuclear carriers would have a full escort complement of a nuclear missile cruiser and four nuclear destroyers—plus of course nuclear submarines on the hunt for enemy subs prowling below.

Naval Reactors was making big engineering strides in reactor efficiency and core life, reaching fifteen years of operation before needing refueling in the early 1970s—a tremendous cost savings and reduction in lost operational time. Experimental advances pointed toward reaching the ultimate goal of a single core able to last a ship's entire anticipated life cycle without refueling. (Starting with the Virginia-class attack submarines in the first decade of the twenty-first century, the US Navy began using life-of-the-ship reactor cores.)[37]

But Title VIII never achieved its intentions. Zumwalt's successor as CNO, Admiral James Holloway III, was a former *Enterprise* skipper. Unlike Zumwalt, Holloway admired Rickover. But he concurred with Zumwalt's view that the Navy could not afford it all in an era of tight budgets and rising inflation. He wanted the carriers. In May 1976, he stated in a policy paper that no future nuclear surface ships other than carriers were to be built. Rickover fought back. A cover story in the news magazine *U.S. News and World Report* featured the fiery disagreement between Rickover and Holloway.[38] By then, many of Rickover's supporters on Capitol Hill had retired or died. His effectiveness in drawing Congress into his fights was waning. With rising costs overwhelming shipbuilding programs through the later 1970s, Congress eliminated all but the nuclear carriers under construction and the new generation of Trident-ballistic-missile and the 688 fast-attack subs from the budget. When nuclear-trained President Jimmy Carter took office, even he tried to cut the next carrier. In 1978, Title VIII quietly expired.

Rickover's pace of work and flurry of political fights through those years seems astounding in retrospect. He did not relax, even at home. During the winter and spring of 1972, he and Ruth enjoyed working together on the book of short biographies of the Polaris submarines' namesakes, *Eminent Americans*. But on May 25, 1972, Rickover's life was turned upside down. He arrived home from his office to find Ruth, his wife and steady companion of forty-one years, dead on the floor. She had died of a heart attack. The next day, keeping with Jewish traditions and a desire for privacy, she was buried at Arlington National Cemetery. Only their son, Robert, and Rickover's two most senior NR associates, Leighton and Wegner, and their wives joined him at the graveside. That night, he burned her many letters to him in despair.[39]

He returned to work the next day. But the seventy-two-year-old was stricken. Ruth had opened his eyes to a wider world beyond the Navy. She was his closest, perhaps only, intimate friend, his intellectual equal and continuous support throughout his long, tempestuous career, a singular partner in all things not the Navy. He was determined to complete *Eminent Americans*. When it appeared later that year, he wrote in the preface, "She was at once the most human and intelligent person I ever knew, the greatest influence on my life and work." Those words were followed by a passage in Latin suggested to him by Reid, a college Classics major, from the poet Tibullus. It translates, "You are the solace of my cares, light in the blackest nights and company in lonely places."[40] A few years later, Rickover edited and published Ruth's travelogue from the epic Southeast Asia journeys she made while he was stationed in prewar Cavite.[41]

Work did not end for Rickover. Now, broken in spirit and unable to sleep, according to his biographer Francis Duncan, he seriously considered becoming a night watchman at a local store where he could spend the sleepless hours reading. Once his insomnia nearly got him killed. About two in the morning at the Mare Island, California, naval base, an alarm went off on a sub tied at dock for refueling and repairs. One of the enlisted men on watch ran to the Control Room, his service revolver drawn. He saw a short, gray-haired man in civilian clothing and carrying a cane step off the ladder. The watch called out, "Halt!" He put the muzzle of his .45 to the intruder's forehead. The officer of the deck came screaming into the compartment, "Put the gun down! It's the Admiral!" Ignoring the gun and the fracas he had caused, Rickover barked, "Get the CO [commanding officer] over here now!" Rickover had come aboard unannounced to find out why the sub's routine maintenance was running behind schedule. With a phone call, the skipper, who was staying on base, raced aboard. For ten minutes, Rickover yelled at him, demanding he get the job finished and Rickover's sub back to sea. His point clear, he disappeared back up the ladder and into the early-morning darkness. The work sped up to completion.[42]

The loss of Ruth, lack of sleep, and ceaseless work took a toll on Rickover's health. Early in the morning on November 16, 1972, he flew into Washington's National Airport (today's Reagan National) and then walked the mile to his office. He collapsed shortly after arriving. An initial diagnosis of exhaustion was changed to a second heart attack. Rumors spread that, if he were not already dead, he soon would be.

Three days later, Rickover was in a Bethesda Naval Hospital bed when CNO Admiral Zumwalt walked into his room. Rickover immediately got up and started pulling catheters out of his arms. Zumwalt exclaimed, "What are you doing, Rick? Get back in bed!"

"If you are here," Rickover snapped, "you have figured out a way to screw the submarine force. You only came to make sure I was really dying. I need to get up." Zumwalt and a nurse finally convinced Rickover to get back in bed.[43]

Zumwalt chatted with Rickover for half an hour. But Rickover was right. On the drive back to Washington, Zumwalt, seeing that the admiral would remain hospitalized for a few weeks, decided to move quickly. He had his aide make the calls from the car telephone as they drove back into town. He canceled the appropriation request for the *NR-2*, Rickover's planned second deep-sea sub, which was part of the Navy budget under congressional review. Rickover's pet project was slashed from the bill and never built.

13

Ships and Horse Turds

Rickover recuperated from his heart attack and returned to work. Looking ashen and worn, having lost weight off his already slender frame, his suits bagging out around him, his slender neck and big head with thinning white hair rose like a flower stalk from his oversized shirt collar. After forty-five years of active duty and leadership of a technology revolution, a valedictory feel overtook his tenure. Many people in and out of the Navy expressed the view—privately—that he was approaching the end of his career.

Honors rolled in. On December 3, 1973, Rickover went to the White House. President Richard Nixon met him in the Oval Office, along with Zumwalt, Secretary of the Navy John Warner, his longtime friends Senator Scoop Jackson and Representative Chester "Chet" Holifield, the latter until recently chair of the Joint Committee on Atomic Energy, and a handful of other congressmen and Navy officers. Nixon was already embroiled in the Watergate affair; he would resign half a year later. The president recalled the "very special occasion" when he and Rickover visited Russia and Poland together almost fifteen years before. The admiral, Nixon said, symbolized the "greatness" of the nation and its military, "because this man, who is controversial, this man, who comes up with unorthodox ideas, did not become submerged by the bureaucracy, because once genius is submerged by bureaucracy, a nation is doomed to mediocrity." He then awarded Rickover his fourth star, promoting him to full admiral. Rickover liked Nixon, despite his wrongdoing, and feared the divisions that split the country. "The times are perilous," he warned the small group. During his long career, the nation had gone through many periods of danger, he said, but they were met by citizens who "faced each crisis with a deep feeling of responsibility." He asked that "all accept responsibility and work for the restoration to the country of quiet and harmony."[1]

Not long after that day, the Naval Academy opened its largest academic building, a massive academic and laboratory facility for its engineering programs. Congress passed a resolution calling on a reluctant Navy to name it for a living naval hero, a rare tribute. At the dedication of the new H. G. Rickover Hall, a bust of the admiral greeted midshipmen passing through its entryway, a monument to an officer who was still very much on active duty, still determining the fate of many if not most midshipmen who would study there.

The Navy leaders may have thought that the time was finally coming when they would bid the admiral farewell. But they were wrong. Rickover had no intention of releasing his grip from the Navy's throat. And, unexpectedly, he found a renewed sense of vigor through a new life companion.

Following Ruth's death, Rickover had not reached out to the petite, amiable, and efficient nurse, Eleonore Ann Bednowicz, who had tended him after his first heart attack. She called him once while he was in the hospital recovering from his second heart attack. She was now posted as the education coordinator at the Great Lakes Naval Hospital, from which she traveled to the Washington, DC, area for a meeting in fall 1974. While there, she stayed with a mutual friend who suggested that she invite the admiral over for dinner. He readily accepted. After that evening, Rickover phoned her daily and saw her whenever possible. Finally, while on an inspection tour of a contractor's factory floor, he stopped to call her. That was a fittingly unromantic setting and means for proposing to her. She hesitated for a week. She was thirty years younger than Rickover, and while Rickover valued her devout Catholic faith, he was Jewish, even if unobservant. But both were dedicated naval professionals; they shared a biting sense of humor and sharp intellects; each possessed a strong will. She accepted.

The couple traveled to Chicago incognito. The press got wind of the matrimony in the offing and tried to track them down. Somehow, the couple avoided the cameras and reporters. The *Chicago Sun-Times* called their January 19, 1974, wedding "the best kept secret since the Manhattan Project."[2] Held at Saint Celestine Church in Elmwood Park, Illinois, outside Chicago, the ceremony brought Rickover's thirty-three-year-old son, Robert, together for the first time with his father's family, including his sister Augusta and nieces. After a two-week honeymoon in the eastern Mediterranean, the newlyweds returned to Washington. Too many memories of Ruth filled the apartment on Connecticut Avenue. They moved to an apartment in a modern complex in Crystal City overlooking the entrance to the building housing Naval Reactors' offices. Rickover went to work with a renewed spring in his step. Before walking into his office in the morning, he waved up to Eleonore in the window of their apartment. His home life also changed. Evenings the couple invited guests for small dinner parties, even attending receptions and concerts, something Rickover had never done previously.

On February 25, 1974, a month after their wedding, Rickover gave one of his annual "Rickover lectures" to the Joint Committee on Atomic Energy. Members' questioning turned jocular at one point. A committee member raised the "issue" of a man who "becomes the father of the nuclear Navy and then he gets married." Rickover quipped back, "When you meet a very charming, gracious, witty, intelligent and beautiful woman, you must break the rules."[3] Ever the rule breaker, Rickover would need all his energy for another battle against a different foe, one not part of the government yet beholden to it—and him.

Sometime in the late 1970s, Admiral Thomas B. Hayward, the chief of naval operations after Holloway, sent Rickover a paper dealing with a nuclear ship contractor that required his signature. It came in the wake of Rickover's accusations that several shipyards were overcharging the Navy for cost-overrun claims. According to Vice Admiral Thomas Kilcline Sr., who was attached to the CNO's office at the time, Rickover refused to sign the paper. The frustrated CNO asked his vice chief, Admiral Robert Long, a former nuclear skipper, to call Rickover. "Talk to your friend," he pleaded.

Long tried, but still Rickover would not do it. But he said to Long, "You're the Vice Chief. You're senior to me, order me to."

"I don't want to order you to, Admiral, but all right, I will. I order you to sign that."

Rickover fired back, "I'll be damned if I'll sign it!"[4] He was making the point that when it came to orders with which he disagreed, rank meant nothing to him, and he was not playing ball with contractors—though perhaps he was not above playing games with the Navy.

The bit of comic theater came when Rickover's fight with contractors neared a peak of vitriol. It was a clash that Rickover viewed as a watershed in government-contractor relations that would determine whether the Navy and Naval Reactors could continue as the tough customer that kept control over contracts, quality, and progress on their ships. Or would he and the Navy cede their power and taxpayer dollars to business executives willing to let standards slide rather than sacrifice profits and, to his mind, defraud the federal government? Their fight threatened to sink the entire Navy and filled the newspapers with opinion pieces debating the relative merits of each side's case.

Historically, shipyards bid and contracted to build new vessels at agreed-upon fixed prices for their services. The contract built in a profit for the company. If the company controlled costs while fulfilling its contractual obligations, the profit could grow. But in building large, complex, long-timeline projects like ships, especially highly sophisticated nuclear-powered vessels, some of which were new classes or outfitted with untested technologies, problems that were outside the shipbuilders' control regularly arose. So did costs. Delays in the arrival of materials and components, insufficient numbers of skilled craftspeople, engineering difficulties affecting sophisticated new systems, and especially changes the Navy made in designs could lead to cost overruns amounting, in some instances, to tens of millions of dollars. As a result, Navy contracts generally included an escalation-of-cost clause to recover overruns due to deviations in orders or other issues that were demonstrably not the shipyards' fault. When contractors encountered problems for which the Navy should appropriately be held to account, they filed claims to cover the added costs. After auditing the charges, the Navy and contractor would negotiate a settlement payment.

The system had worked well until the mid-1960s. But costs

for labor and materials had spiraled upward. In the grinding push to keep up with inflation, contractors struggled to make their so-called cost-plus profit built into ship contracts. In addition, competition from lower-cost, government-subsidized shipbuilders in Asia and Europe had wiped out nearly all the nonmilitary business of the Navy's ship contractors, while the Navy stopped building ships altogether at its own yards, where costs ran 40 percent higher than at private shipyards. Nearly all the major US shipbuilders went bankrupt, consolidated with other yards, or exited the industry altogether.

Finally, by the late 1960s, only two conglomerate-owned shipyards remained to bid for contracts for the Navy's nuclear ships: Newport News in Virginia, then part of Tenneco, built both the giant carriers, other surface ships, and subs, and General Dynamics' Electric Boat in Connecticut worked exclusively on submarines. The Navy recognized that inflation was crushing their business and that, should one or both yards abandon shipbuilding, the nation would face a threat to its long-term security. As a stopgap, the Defense Department instituted a new way for the struggling yards to recoup their cost overruns. It turned the tables on accounting practices. Starting in the late 1960s, companies began to bundle together any cost problems they encountered and then charge the Navy without the shipbuilders having to prove the validity of individual parts of the claims. The Navy simply approved the total and paid the shipbuilders a lump sum to keep work moving along. That consolidated-charge process quickly opened the door to a flood of such bundled claims. Shipyard cost-overrun claims soon became a regular if cockeyed way of doing business with the Navy. When Tenneco and General Dynamics made their public financial reports, they booked their anticipated overrun claims payments as future revenue.

With little oversight to keep cost-overrun claims in check, not surprisingly the companies used them to bolster their earnings. Claims escalated into a tidal wave. In 1974 alone, the over-run claims totaled $893 million (almost $4.7 billion today), equal to the budget to build an entire additional nuclear carrier. In April 1976, claims involving seventy ships (most nonnuclear, though many of the costliest claims were) reached $1.72 billion ($7.8 billion today).[5] Rickover, renowned for his parsimonious ways with taxpayer money, was livid about participating in a contract process that, in his eyes, absolved the shipbuilders of responsibility for keeping their costs under control and working efficiently. He asked at one point during congressional testimony, "Why bother negotiating and signing contracts if they are not going to be enforced?"[6] The claims process, to his mind, turned the Defense Department into a coconspirator in legalized defrauding of the taxpayer. "As I see it," he said at another hearing, "when you make a contract, you should fulfill it."[7]

Both Newport News and Electric Boat insisted that they were not responsible for the overruns. They faulted Rickover and Naval Reactors for frequent and what they viewed as capricious design changes and Rickover's intrusive inspectors, who micromanaged quality control, squeezing the yards to the breaking point. In 1974, Tenneco's influential lobbyist Thomas ("Tommy the Cork") Corcoran, at one time a trusted adviser to President Franklin D. Roosevelt, tried to get Congress to force Rickover out. He went to see CNO Admiral James Holloway III, complaining that Rickover had "become a terrible thorn in the side of U.S. industry . . . and an impossible problem in either getting or carrying out a contract with the Navy."[8] But Rickover had enough steady friends like Wisconsin Democratic senator William Proxmire, who was making a name for himself in Congress defending the taxpayer's wallet. Rickover remained in place.

Unable to get Rickover off their backs and to make enough money, the companies took the gloves off. Tenneco's Newport

News threatened to halt work altogether on the two aircraft carriers, four cruisers, and seven attack submarines under construction in its yard. In August 1975, the company ordered work to stop on a cruiser, refusing to continue without resolution of its claims. A court finally ordered resumption of work pending a negotiated settlement.

If anything, problems and battling at Electric Boat were worse. Rickover believed that quality control had slipped badly there. During one submarine's sea trial, periscopes leaked, a pump failed, and other mettlesome and perhaps dangerous problems emerged that should have been caught earlier. In addition, EB's finances were shaky. The yard's parent, General Dynamics, claimed $544 million (almost $2.2 billion today) for government deficiencies and, anticipating payment, had already booked settlement of the claims as revenue in annual financial statements. When the Navy balked at paying the claims at Rickover's insistence, Electric Boat's general manager announced that work would stop on the vital 688s at the yard until the Navy paid up. Ratcheting up the political pressure, the company issued layoff notices to eight thousand workers.

Newport News and Electric Boat blamed Rickover for slowing up work by stalling resolutions on their claims, while inflation was making it impossible for them to produce ships at anywhere near their contracted prices. Rickover asked why government contractors should get compensated for the harm they suffered from inflation "deriving from their own mistakes" when other private businesses had no such recourse. "Isn't the taxpayer burdened enough already by inflation?"[9] At one point, he even suggested that the government purchase the yards outright and then hire other companies to operate them. Critics condemned the scheme as nationalization of the shipbuilding industry.

The Defense Department, fearing a collapse of the last of

its private shipyards, invoked a "national emergency" law to settle contractors' claims. Rickover was incensed at what he saw as systematic looting of taxpayer money by unscrupulous businessmen in cahoots with the Navy brass and Defense Department leadership. In testimony on June 7, 1976, he described the yards' claims as "absurd" and the currently proposed settlement as "one of the biggest ripoffs in the history of the United States." He scorched the two yards' corporate parents for unpatriotic attitudes toward national defense and unethical business practices. "The conglomerates," he declared, "wouldn't care if they were building ships or manufacturing horse turds. Their goal is to make money, no matter how." (The *New York Times* censored "turds," substituting "collars.")[10]

When reports of Rickover's ships and horse turds comment reached the corporate heads, they were ready to explode. They began a game of chicken, with the nation's defense at stake. The president of Newport News formally notified the Navy that it would have to remove the partially completed hull of the carrier *Vinson* and the five 688-class submarines under construction in the yard unless full compensation of its outstanding claims was made promptly. In an atmosphere of crisis and acrimony, in early July, Rickover, CNO Holloway, and the deputy secretary of defense, the Texas oilman William Clements, who had been tasked with resolving the matter, sat down in Clements's Pentagon office. Clements warned the seventy-six-year-old Rickover that history would not look kindly on him if he scuttled the future fleet. Finally, the three men agreed to Rickover's suggestion that the Navy set up an ad hoc three-person claims-settlement review board, with neither the companies nor Naval Reactors putting a member on it. Afterward, Rickover held his tongue. "I don't want to get into an argument," he said, brushing off a reporter's question. "I think," Clements said later, "Rickover realizes his usefulness in settling these claims has reached point zero."[11] The board eventually paid the Newport News and Electric Boat claims for substantially less than the original charges.

But Rickover's public distress over the claims had not faded away. He was convinced that by agreeing to break the terms of the two shipyards' contracts without scrutinizing the individual claims, the Navy gave up the leverage it possessed to force the companies to meet standards of either quality or business responsibility. Effectively, he declared to anyone who would listen, the tough customer and the contractor had traded places. And the shipyards, for their part, returned the enmity. Their battles were not over and eventually grew into an all-out war that battered and ended numerous careers, including Rickover's.

14

The Longest-Serving Officer

"THERE WAS A LOT of Hyman Rickover in Jimmy Car-
ter," wrote Carter's chief domestic adviser, Stuart Eizenstat.[1]
He was not being entirely complimentary. Even before Carter
won the White House in 1976, his administration was closely
identified with Rickover.

Carter, a former nuclear-trained engineering officer, had
followed Rickover's writings and other public statements since
leaving the submarine force in 1953. He invited Rickover to his
1971 inauguration as Georgia governor. The admiral demurred;
he did not remember Carter. But that restarted their relationship. After Carter became governor, they spoke by telephone
from time to time, often about education.[2] Four years later,
Carter handwrote a note to Rickover telling him, "well before
any public announcement is made," that he was planning a run
for president. And, he said, "I do not intend to lose." He asked
for Rickover's "advice and counsel in developing a clearer con-

cept of what our defense establishment should be." He added, "You have had a great and beneficial effect on my life—more than you could know." He signed it, "Jimmy."[3]

The fifty-two-year-old Carter's 1976 election began one of the more unusual presidential-advisory relationships in US history. Although the seventy-six-year-old Rickover was a four-star admiral with a long and distinguished, albeit controversial, record, he headed a fourth-echelon division within the Navy. His days were passed far from his titular bosses in the Pentagon E-ring and the secretary's office in the newly created Department of Energy. But Carter did not want Rickover's views on defense procurement and reactor engineering in the White House; he wanted his wisdom. Within two weeks of Carter's inauguration, the president and his wife, Rosalynn, welcomed Rickover and Eleonore to the White House for a casual lunch. Photographs show Carter beaming a toothy smile while standing in shirtsleeves and cardigan alongside a poker-faced Rickover in a dark business suit. The two wives immediately took to each other. While Rosalynn showed Eleonore around the family quarters, the two men sat down to talk. They "established" what Carter wrote later was to be "a close friendship from the beginning of [his] presidency."[4]

Carter insisted that Rickover not discuss parochial Naval Reactors matters with him. "He told me," Carter recalled, "that he would never mention to me anything that related to budget allocations or priorities for any ship in the nuclear Navy."[5] Rickover's longest and bloodiest career fights were effectively out of bounds in the president's presence. In fact, Carter proved no friend of the Navy. With inflation spiraling fast, he slashed defense expenditures, depleting both crew and materiel on many ships and aircraft squadrons—though submarines continued to receive strong support. He did not want another nuclear carrier at all and vetoed the 1978 defense appropriation bill because it added one. Rickover took the fight for the carrier with his usual forcefulness to Congress. But he kept his word, refraining from trying to influence the president directly on any Navy matter—that is, until an appropriate moment presented itself. In return, Rickover became someone Carter trusted as counsel on many matters.

Carter, like Rickover, was ambitious, driven, supremely confident about his intelligence, demanding, and detail oriented— a notorious micromanager, sometimes to his detriment. Both took pride in their self-denying parsimoniousness and personal rectitude. And each was an outsider who was sometimes looked down on by Washington political insiders, a rejection they held up as a badge of honor. Alongside a mentor, Carter found in Rickover a father figure, a man much like his strict, hardworking, and difficult-to-satisfy late father. Carter wrote about his youth, "my greatest ambition [was] . . . to please my father." Placing Rickover figuratively and sometimes literally at his ear, he asked the admiral to tell him when he went astray.[6] After leaving the White House, Carter acknowledged about Rickover, "I never really felt like his boss."[7]

Rickover believed that his influence on the new president could, he told Eleonore, "do the country some good." It might prove the "crest"—his word—of his career.[8]

Shortly after that first lunch, Rickover dispatched a speech he had first delivered a year before to Carter. "Thoughts on Man's Purpose in Life" was a sort of summation of his life philosophy, offering moral and civic reflections that resonated deeply with Carter. Rickover laid out what could be called his philosophy of responsibility. Responsibility went beyond the workplace. Unending individual responsibility formed the core of his conception of an ethical life, which was, to his mind, the only life worth living. Personal responsibility informed a life's meaning through the family and community, work and the pursuit of excellence; it undergirded US society and democracy's ability to endure. When individual citizens lose their willingness to take responsibility for their actions, Rickover believed civilizations begin to crumble.

And Rickover saw a dangerous decline in Americans' ambitions "for doing a job right." He blamed the country's unprecedented material wealth for its growing spiritual emptiness and ethical laxness. A malaise had overtaken a nation that once took pride in building a better future. "The unwillingness to act and to accept responsibility is a symptom of America's growing self-satisfaction with the status quo," he stated. "The result is a paralysis of the spirit, entirely uncharacteristic of Americans during the previous stages of our history." He feared that Americans, having abandoned established religions that helped build community and maintain individual integrity, "are now living on the accumulated moral capital of traditional religion. It is running out, and we have no other consensus of values to take its place," leaving only the pursuit of wealth and material pleasures. But materialism undermined the nation "because man can now obtain on earth what previously was promised him when he reached heaven." Without shared values and individuals willing to do the hard work, take responsibility for what they did, insist on high standards, and "maintain the values alone which give society the capacity to survive," the United States' future was in danger. "A free society can survive only through men and women of integrity." Carter was a man of deep but not dogmatic religious faith who constantly questioned the morality of his thoughts and acts. As he set out to lead the nation, Rickover's words surely resonated when he read, "I believe it is the duty of each of us to act as if the fate of the world depended on him." In Carter's case, it did.[9]

Every few months or more frequently at the president's invitation, Rickover returned to the White House. Sitting together in the Oval Office or the private family quarters upstairs, the two men discussed many subjects. They ranged from ways to respond to rising dependence on foreign sources of oil to the sources of crime and poverty in urban areas. They talked about the question of federal funding for abortion among the poor, which Carter opposed and Rickover favored; Rickover told the president that there were already too many people in the world. Rickover bucked up the president's spirits when his legislative efforts seemed to flag. He told him, "As long as a man is trying as hard as he can to do what he thinks to be right, he is a success, regardless of the outcome." He was surely reflecting on his own career as well.

On April 8, 1977, Rickover visited the White House, where he expressed his support for the president's decision to make the advancement of human rights a stated goal in US foreign affairs for the first time. Within days of that meeting, the president sent him a note asking for his help with "energy principles." He was looking for expertise for an upcoming national address about the ongoing energy crisis. Gas shortages had driven up prices, leading to long lines at the pumps; the energy crisis undercut the economy, and dependence on foreign oil posed a national-security threat should Arab nations again embargo oil exports. Carter wanted to institute a national energy policy to reduce demand and boost alternative forms of energy. Rickover warned the president that Americans were not ready to make sacrifices to conserve energy. But he offered up several ideas for the speech, which Carter delivered on April 18 in a prime-time address from the Oval Office.

The president told the nation that solving the energy crisis was "the greatest challenge that our country will face during our lifetime." He laid out a national energy policy designed "to reduce demand through conservation," along with "a shift to plentiful coal, while taking care to protect the environment, and to apply stricter safety standards to nuclear energy." He also urged speeding up development of renewable sources of energy, including solar power. Among other sacrifices he envisioned, Americans who drove large gas-guzzlers would face higher taxes. "Many of these proposals will be unpopular," he acknowledged. But what made the speech memorable was his declaration that these pragmatic steps to address the energy crisis amounted to "the moral equivalent of war."[10] The speech became known as the "Moral Equivalent of War" address. Both Carter and Rickover viewed the energy crisis as a moral crucible for the nation and a test of its democracy.[11] Rickover suggested the "moral equivalent of war" phrase—taken from the philosopher William James.[12] Carter would later regret what he called "an excessive statement," and political opponents mocked the phrase—some labeling it "MEOW" for its toothlessness. But Carter would turn to Rickover's ideas and moral fervor as inspiration for other important speeches.

On May 27, 1977, the president and First Lady flew to Cape Canaveral, where they spent the day with Rickover on the nuclear submarine *Los Angeles*, lead ship in the new 688 fast-attack sub class. They steamed about thirty-five miles out into the Atlantic before submerging. With the Carters on board, Rickover and the captain put the ship through extreme maneuvers, including a dead-officer drill, a regular exercise during sea trials in which Rickover would point to an engineering officer during maneuvers and declare, "You're dead." Another officer needed immediately to take over the "dead" man's duties. The watch performed flawlessly. At one point, with the sub moving at flank speed, Carter took the throttle. He also manned the diving controls.

Later, sitting in the wardroom, Carter and Rickover spent two hours talking about the decline in the Protestant work ethic and the possibility of eliminating nuclear weapons. "I was surprised," wrote Carter, "when I asked him how he would react to a total elimination of nuclear weapons—and nuclear power production—from the earth. He said it would be one of the greatest things that could happen."[13] A few years later, Rickover would repeat that view but with a pessimistic outlook about humanity's fate.

Front pages across the land carried photos of Rickover seated next to Carter at the diving controls aboard the *Los Angeles*. Carter declared to reporters, "There is no finer ship." Never one to pass up an opportunity to strike at his usual targets, Rickover stood with the president and growled, "The Defense Department and the Navy have almost consistently been against submarines, nuclear submarines."[14] Back at the White House, Carter wrote a note to Rickover: "Your nuclear submarines are, I believe, the finest exhibition of superb engineering ever created by man."[15]

Just days later, at dinnertime on May 31, 1979, Rickover and Eleonore were at home when he answered a knock at the door. It was the president, Mrs. Carter, and their daughter, Amy. They came to the Rickovers' apartment at Eleonore's invitation for a surprise dinner for Rickover. Somehow the president and his entire motorcade and Secret Service detail managed to arrive at Rickover's door without the admiral knowing a thing about it. When Rickover opened the door to the president, he acted as if he were not surprised, but Carter insisted to Eleonore, "He is." After dinner, while the Carters' daughter Amy did homework and the wives went off together, Rickover and the president spent three hours in conversation. As usual, they talked about many topics, from race and education to politics and energy. Perhaps because they were in Rickover's home and not at the White House, Rickover expressed his views about building another nuclear carrier, then being debated in Congress. Carter favored including a conventional carrier in the current defense appropriation bill. Rickover told him that he should "cancel his request for any carrier other than a nuclear one." He told the president that "if there were to be another carrier, it should be nuclear powered."[16] The following fall,

Carter, while still voicing opposition to the nuclear ship, said he would not veto its funding this time around.

In July 1979, many seemingly intractable problems plagued the nation. Inflation was running at a rate of 13 percent per year. Unemployment was also rising. Gasoline lines stretched far down the blocks, with little obvious progress in finding solutions to the energy crisis. Carter was determined to address the nation about its many troubles. He retreated to Camp David, where for ten days he consulted with various people from civic, religious, business, labor, and other groups, as well as ordinary citizens. On July 15, he came back to the White House, where he gave a televised address to the nation. It came to be known as the "Malaise Speech," despite his never having used the word.

Viewers may have expected a more typical political laundry list of proposals for addressing the nation's woes and optimism about solutions. Carter did suggest several policy steps to reduce dependence on foreign oil, bolster conservation, and control inflation. But at the very start, he said, "It's clear that the true problems of our nation are much deeper—deeper than gasoline lines or energy shortages, deeper even than inflation or recession." Instead of a typical policy speech, Carter delivered a civic religious homily on "this crisis in the growing doubt about the meaning of our own lives and in the loss of a unity of purpose for our nation." Americans, he said, faced a "crisis in confidence," which struck "at the very heart and soul and spirit of our national will." In language that Rickover could have written, he said, "In a nation that was proud of hard work, strong families, close-knit communities, and our faith in God, too many of us now tend to worship self-indulgence and consumption." He declared that "all the legislation in the world can't fix what's wrong with America." Many sources and individuals fed into Carter's address. But his focus on the loss of trust in government and other public institutions and his condemnation of the unbridled pursuit of material wealth and the associated spiritual decline were vintage Rickover. So, too, was his appeal for individual sacrifice and responsibility rather than relying on a political solution. Those phrases and his closing call for "a rebirth of the American spirit" echoed his conversations with Rickover.[17]

In January 1979, Carter formally extended Rickover's active-duty status for another two-year period. A few months later, on April 9, 1979, the world's first atomic-powered submarine, the *Nautilus*, departed Groton on its final voyage. It steamed south and through the Panama Canal. From there, it cruised north to the Mare Island Naval Shipyard, where, on May 26 — its last day under way on nuclear power — inactivation procedures began. It had served the Navy for a quarter century, making 2,507 dives and traveling 513,550 nautical miles (591,000 miles).[18]

Carter and Rickover had expected to work together into a second presidential term. But battling headwinds from multiple foreign and domestic sources, Carter lost badly to Ronald Reagan in the 1980 election. Carter wrote Rickover after his defeat, "I've never gone wrong by following your advice."[19]

The incoming administration wanted Rickover gone. Even before Reagan's inauguration, John F. Lehman Jr., the secretary of the Navy designate, let it be known that one of his "first orders of business . . . would be to solve, at last, the Rickover problem."[20] The Naval Reserve aviator and former Nixon White House appointee was just thirty-eight years old, the youngest ever to hold the post and less than half Rickover's age. Lehman's *father* was seven years old when Rickover entered the Naval Academy. "Rickover's legendary achievements were in the past," he contended. "His present viselike grip on much of the Navy was doing it much harm." There were few issues confronting Lehman that he did not blame on Rickover: In Lehman's eyes, Rickover had forced the Naval Academy to become an engineering school that turned out technologists who could not communicate concepts and lacked the education for assessing and leading organizations and making decisions beyond their limited technical perspective. He satirized Rickover's nuclear Navy as a "cult" that created a "monastic atmosphere—austere, disciplined, with a deep reverence toward the reactor within the holy of holies, and for its high priest and prophet, Admiral Rickover." He also thought budget problems in building and maintaining a navy that he wanted to grow to six hundred ships could be traced to Naval Reactors' doorsteps. Among other issues, he considered Rickover's long-standing refusal to automate control functions within propulsion plants anachronistic, necessitating large teams of skilled operators— as many as six hundred on a carrier—all at great expense. And he believed Rickover's stranglehold on the shipyards and the "capricious demands" he made on them led contractors to distrust the Navy and ultimately flee its business or go broke, leaving the Navy with few competitors to hold down prices. He even accused Rickover of having sparked the bureaucratization of the Pentagon, despite his famous decades-long battle with the Defense Department's systems-analysis "whiz kids" and bureaucratic bloat. Lehman claimed that the systems-management bureaucracy had taken root as a counterweight to Rickover's own technocratic Navy.

Above all, Lehman decried Rickover's "parallel chain of command" that showed "by example that duly instituted authority exists to be ignored, deceived, and flouted." His "commissariat" and "Gestapo-like" grip on the ships of the nuclear Navy trumped the line officers who commanded the ships and the higher-ups who ordered operations. "That," he said, "was intolerable if the Navy was ever going to be put back on an even keel." To build the ships to pursue a unified, two-ocean Cold War strategy, Lehman intended to bring the nuclear Navy to heel, though Rickover charged that it was never considered "an inherent part of the Navy" in the first place.[21] Lehman wrote that his mission was to return "the powerful role of NR to what it was originally intended to be—the guarantor of nuclear safety and quality control, rather than the Vatican of a military priestly order."

As soon as Lehman moved into his new Pentagon office, he began his campaign "to retire Admiral Rickover respectfully but forcefully." But doing so would require placating Rickover's supporters, who were still a force to be reckoned with. Lehman understood what he faced in trying to bring down a naval pope. Many had tried; all had failed.

And Rickover was not ready to go. At age eighty-one in January 1981, he had already served in the Navy for almost sixty-three years. Rickover had now been on active duty far longer than anyone in history—only Army general Omar Bradley by virtue of the permanent active-duty status attached to his five-star rank officially had served longer in the US military. Rickover wanted to remain for at least one more two-year term.[22]

The admiral's colleagues and fellow Navy officers painted a mixed portrait of the man in this period. According to his biographer Francis Duncan, he still arrived at his desk each morning at eight and worked steadily—except for fifteen minutes jogging in place at lunchtime—until seven at night, as well as on Saturdays. Duncan thought that his short-term memory was not what it once was. But he worked without tiring, his tart voice still sprayed vinegar and piss, and his authority over his reactors and their operators reaching out to the farthest shores and ocean deeps remained redoubtable. As Rickover's "line-locker," his chief liaison to the wider Navy at the time, then-captain Zach Pate had an office down the hall from the Kindly Old Gentleman, the KOG. He saw, he said, "no diminishment in power, control, or interest. There was no decline in the power of his mind."[23] William Hughes Jr., who had captained several subs and overseen officer evaluations at the Idaho

Falls prototype, headed NR's evaluation team for nuclear ships in the Pacific Fleet. "I had no sense," he remembered, "that he had lost his capacity to do the job."[24]

But others thought Rickover could no longer carry the heavy load. Some hinted at senility. "Even his good friends in Congress," said Vice Admiral Thomas Kilcline, "realized it was time, but no one wanted to tell him."[25] And there were fewer and fewer of those friends left. The Joint Committee on Atomic Energy had been dissolved, its oversight and policy work dispersed to other committees. Early supporters Sabath, Durham, and McMahon were long gone; Mendel Rivers had retired; so too had Chet Holifield and Carl Vinson and many others who had protected him since before the *Nautilus* went to sea. Only Scoop Jackson remained among the "old guard" and William Proxmire among a later generation. Most of the rest had lost reelection, retired, or died, while Rickover continued on and on.

Following Lehman's February 5, 1981, swearing-in ceremony, he began to assemble his forces. Few inside the new administration objected to pushing out someone so closely identified with Carter. According to Lehman, "Reagan himself had no strong feelings one way or the other," but Vice President George H. W. Bush "was ready to see him retire." Most defense contractors had backed Reagan's campaign for president. They used their newfound access to the White House, wrote Lehman, "to pee in the Admiral's well." The key to shoving him overboard, though, was unshackling Congress from him. Lehman went methodically through the list of Rickover's most influential remaining backers on Capitol Hill, meeting with many of them multiple times over the next few months. Most agreed with him, he found, and those who opposed forcing Rickover out, like Proxmire, were not doing so "with great vigor." But "no one wished to support his retirement openly."

By the end of summer, Lehman determined that Congress would not act to stop him.

Remarkably, it was the Navy brass that began to get cold feet. They were scared off because, Lehman recalled, "they didn't really believe I could pull it off." And they worried that if Rickover were forced out, his loyal top civilian aides would resign as one, leading to NR's collapse. The press got wind of Lehman's campaign. The betting odds, wrote pundits, favored Rickover. "His authority," declared the *New York Times*, "isn't as absolute as it used to be, but he still has plenty of firepower." When push came to shove, the *Times* doubted the upstart Lehman could bring the hoary admiral down: "The decision is nominally up to Mr. Lehman, but he apparently lacks the political stature to make a ruling stick."[26]

But others were working in parallel, or in concert, with Lehman against Rickover. In April 1981, a retired admiral, the only type who dared challenge Rickover, John T. Hayward, wrote in the Navy's leading journal, *Proceedings*, "As an engineer, he (Rick) has few superiors. As a man to fight a war or to prepare a Navy to fight a war, he has much too narrow a vision. No one has been killed by a propulsion plant, nor have many ships been sunk by one." Rickover's vision for the Navy still gave priority to his reactors. "Events," he concluded, "have overtaken him."[27] Also around this time, publishing plans became public for a Rickover biography by Thomas B. Allen and Norman Polmar, the latter a longtime consultant to the Navy and author on naval affairs who was known for his support for building more lost-cost conventional ships, including diesel-electric subs, rather than fewer expensive nuclear vessels.[28] Advance notice made the book sound like an indictment of the Navy's "unaccountable man," as the authors labeled him, an officer, they wrote, who, his past accomplishments aside, engineered his own power at the expense of the very people and military branch he claimed to serve.[29] The book was set for publication in January 1982, the month when Rickover would come up for reappointment. Rickover sent a letter to the publisher's board threatening to sue "should there be any inaccuracies in the book," though that failed to sway them from releasing the book.[30] He did succeed in keeping the Navy-affiliated Naval Institute Press from copublishing it and stopped a Hollywood producer from making a movie based on it. But even before the nearly eight-hundred-page book appeared, the authors' damaging intent was apparent.

Others with axes to grind also ensured that their concerns about the admiral received wide press coverage. The contractors wielded big axes. On July 26, the 688-class attack submarine *La Jolla* left Electric Boat for its sea trials. Per usual, several EB representatives joined Rickover on board. But Rickover thought they were more intent on tracking his activities than the *La Jolla*'s. He wrote to Eleonore during the trip, "they have been instructed to note all that I do and report it at once — so an issue can be made of it."[31]

At the end of *La Jolla*'s full-power test run on the second day, Rickover ordered an emergency stop, or "crashback." That maneuver, standard during sea trials, throws a sub racing along at flank speed into full reverse power to come to a quick stop, akin to a fully loaded freight train rolling at top speed slamming its powertrain into reverse. For the seven-thousand-ton 688 moving through the deep at better than thirty knots, a crashback taxed its propulsion plant to its limits. The maneuver had its risks: after reaching a full "dead in the water" stop, it needed to return immediately to forward thrust, not travel in reverse. A botched crashback risked angling the sub's stern steeply up or down, forcing an abrupt recovery maneuver with the potential for diving too deeply or surfacing out of control. During the *La Jolla*'s sea trial, Rickover twice ordered crashbacks without calling for forward thrust at the proper instant. Both times the sharp upward stern tilt forced the captain to order steep dives, sending the sub beneath the depths at which it had been tested so far, followed by sharp upward climbs to right it.[32]

P. Takis Veliotis, EB's general manager, learned about the crashbacks from his "spies" and sent a July 31 letter to CNO Admiral Thomas B. Hayward, in which he accused Rickover of putting the sub at risk and endangering lives. Hayward responded to Veliotis two weeks later that he did not think the maneuvers, which never approached dangerous depths or the surface, posed any grave risk to the sub. But EB forwarded Veliotis's letter to the press after that. Before the end of August, stories appeared in newspapers across the country, carrying Veliotis's charge that Rickover had "imperiled" the sub. One headline read, "It's Time to Put Adm. Rickover on the Beach." The forces to oust Rickover were mounting.

By November, Lehman sensed that congressional support for Rickover had mostly evaporated. Reagan gave his approval for Lehman to act. His plan called for Rickover to retire while the president would ask that the admiral remain on active duty for two months beyond his formal January 1982 retirement. Rickover would help smooth his successor's takeover and after that become a special adviser on nuclear science to the president. Lehman got the Department of Energy to agree that he should select the admiral's successor. After meeting with several possible replacements, including Rickover's own former civilian deputy, William Wegner, Lehman settled on Vice Admiral Kinnaird McKee, a nuclear-submarine commander who had been on Admiral Zumwalt's team during Zumwalt's tour as CNO and who had stood out during his rotation as superintendent of the Naval Academy.[33] Lehman asked McKee to serve as Rickover's deputy for a transitional period, but McKee scoffed at the idea. He told Lehman, "That won't work. The landscape is littered with heirs apparent. . . . The thing for me to do is go over there and relieve him as quickly as possible."[34] Although fearing a rocky change of command, Lehman agreed. He scheduled a meeting together with Secretary of Defense Casper Weinberger and Rickover for November 13 at the Pentagon, at which time Lehman planned to tell Rickover that he was done.

But press leaks smashed Lehman's plan. On November 9 at four in the afternoon, Eleonore heard the news on the radio that her husband was not going to get reappointed. Away on yet another sea trial, Rickover arrived home at ten that evening. He had not heard the news. When she told him, he shrugged, "Well, that's it."

Still, the bureaucratic Kremlinologists doubted that the decision would stick. At a brief meeting the next morning with Rickover at his office, Lehman officially told him that he was not going to be reappointed. According to Lehman, Rickover's reaction was muted. "He didn't view my position as all that important," Lehman realized. "He knew that only the President could make the [final] decision." And, indeed, later that day, a reporter asked Reagan whether, at age eighty-one, the admiral was too old for the job. The seventy-year-old Reagan looked incredulous and seemed to undercut Lehman, quipping, "You're asking me?" Then he added that "Mr. Gladstone," the four-time prime minister of Great Britain, "reached his height in England at eighty-three." According to the *New York Times*, Senator Jackson was gathering a bipartisan group to lobby for Rickover. The senator stated that Admiral Rickover was "active and vigorous" and that, to him, "this is the test."[35]

The very next day, a day rife with political irony and tension, Rickover, Lehman, and EB's Veliotis—along with Vice President Bush—stood together at Electric Boat for the launch of the *Ohio*, the lead SSBN in the new Trident-missile program. Lehman recalled the day as "most awkward," especially when Vice Admiral S. A. White, commander of the Atlantic submarine fleet, gave an effusively pro-Rickover speech, setting off loud cheering from the crowd of eight thousand. Reporting on the day, a *Washington Post* headline ran "Betting Line Favors Rickover, Whose Future Is Now in Reagan's Hands."[36]

When Rickover went to Weinberger's office at the Pentagon two days later, the secretary of defense told him that the president wanted him to stay on as his nuclear science adviser. Seven times Weinberger offered Rickover the post, and seven times the admiral replied, absolutely no. From there Rickover hurried to Jackson's office on Capitol Hill, where Senators Strom Thurmond and John W. Warner (a former secretary of the Navy) and Representative Melvin Price arrived to plan how to keep the admiral from being forced out. But in the midst of their meeting, word came that the White House had formally announced that Reagan would not reappoint Rickover.

Rickover's career as the United States' longest-serving active-duty military officer and the unlikeliest four-star admiral in the nation's history seemed at an end.

Defeated and angry, Rickover went home. He told Eleonore that he "felt as if he were kicked in the teeth" in the way he had been told. He wanted nothing to do with the meaningless presidential-adviser post. He said to her, "They must take me for a fool if they didn't think I could see through their plan. No one asked me for my advice while I was on active duty, and now to save face, they would relegate me to a room, and I would wait for the telephone to ring."[37]

An embittered Rickover went back to "that damn place" of work where, over the next few weeks, he concluded various projects, including the shutdown of the Shippingport power plant, the world's first civilian nuclear utility. Over its twenty-five-year lifetime, the small plant operated for more than eighty thousand hours and produced about 7.4 billion kilowatt-hours of electricity, enough to power more than five hundred thousand homes for a year. More important than its actual energy output, it helped establish the basis for an entire new industry.[38]

At times Rickover deluded himself into believing that he might still win a presidential reprieve. With the approach of his last day, set for the end of January 1982, President Reagan invited him to meet at the White House for what Lehman hoped would be "a straightforward, cordial meeting," an exit interview befitting a man with such a long and distinguished military career. But it proved to be, wrote Lehman, "the most incredible meeting" he had ever experienced.

Lehman prepared a briefing paper for Reagan. The president should express the nation's gratitude for the admiral's historic contributions and again offer him the advisory post. Reagan would then ask Rickover to share lessons learned during his sixty-three years of naval service. But Lehman did not understand the first thing about the pugnacious man whom he encountered waiting in the Oval Office reception room on January 8. Rickover was not going down until he had fought to the last.

Upon seeing Lehman, Rickover snapped, "You have a hell of a nerve after you fired me!" The president's staffers watched with widening eyes as Rickover proceeded to unleash a stream of invective and profanity at Lehman about his temerity in trying to push him out. "What the hell do you know about the Navy?!" he shouted so loudly that some staffers feared he might become violent.

The two men were finally ushered into the Oval Office, where the president, Weinberger, and two ranking administration staffers waited. After a period of calm while a photographer snapped shots, Reagan uttered a few words in praise of the admiral until Rickover interrupted, "Well, if all that is so, then why are you firing me?"

Reagan sputtered that he was not, but "the Pentagon has recommended that it is time for a transition."

Pointing at Weinberger and Lehman, Rickover barked, "Then they are lying." He said of Lehman, "Mr. President, that piss-ant knows nothing about the Navy. . . . He's a goddamn liar, he knows he is just doing the work of the contractors. The contractors want me fired because of the claims and because I am the only one in government who keeps them from robbing the taxpayers."

Reagan attempted to calm Rickover, but he turned on the president: "Are you a man? Can't you make decisions yourself?" After Reagan repeatedly tried to reassure Rickover that he was not being fired, Rickover interrupted, "Aw, cut the crap!" He demanded, "Are you a man or not? I thought this was to be a meeting between you and me. I want to speak to you alone." Lehman worried that Rickover might physically attack the president. But Lehman and the others left the two men there in the Oval Office.

Those ten minutes with Reagan were Rickover's last hurrah. When he finally emerged empty-handed, he walked up to a stunned Lehman "with a smile and said in the very chummiest way, 'Can I give you a ride back to the Pentagon?'" Even at this extreme, he showed his Janus faces of professional white heat and humane feeling.

Rickover returned to Naval Reactors. At the end of the month, he went to Newport News to run the *Carl Vinson* carrier's sea trials. On January 27, it passed its four-hour full-power run with flying colors. That was the last of 126 sea trials Rickover oversaw.

The next day, he went up to Capitol Hill, where he gave a final Rickover lecture to the members of the Joint Economic Committee.[39] As usual, he ranged far and wide, covering most of the subjects and themes that had been the hallmarks of his career. He spoke about systemic abuses by contractors—"They can do anything they wish"—and the ethical problems in the growing concentration of corporate power: "an environment where fewer businessmen honor traditional values." And he discussed the poor preparation of midshipmen coming out of the Naval Academy: "There is no impulse to work hard and to study hard. There are many distractions." He lambasted the Defense Department bureaucracy: "I do not know why we have a Defense Department. I really do not know. I do not know what it does. Nobody knows." And he recalled being a six-year-old on the *Finland* crossing to America, eating out of "a barrel of salt herring and loaves of bread in the hold." He expressed gratitude for the opportunities the United States had given him: "This nation provided me a refuge, a home, and opportunities for my parents and me at a time when they were not available abroad."

Asked to sum up his views of nuclear power, he surprised the committee, as he had Carter, when he expressed a deeply pessimistic view of humanity's fate and his own nuclear ships' value: "I think the human race is ultimately going to wreck itself. . . . In this broad philosophical sense, I do not believe nuclear power is worth the present benefits since it creates radiation. You might ask why do I design nuclear-powered ships? That is because it is a necessary evil. I would sink them all." Press coverage focused on those words: "I would sink them all."

He concluded, "I owe more to this country than I can ever repay." It was his last time testifying before Congress.

Two days later, Saturday, January 30, Rickover arrived at his office at Naval Reactors as he had for the previous three decades. In the afternoon, he called the staff together and told them, "I now say goodbye to you. This to me is a sad day. . . . But I remain a servant of the United States, and so long as I can I will help that great service to which I belong body and soul."

After he left that evening, workers came in and stripped his office of its simple bookshelves, desk, and conference table, his rocker, the short-legged chair in which more than fifteen thousand nuclear-officer candidates had squirmed. Then the office was made ready for Admiral McKee's arrival Monday morning.

Walking out of Naval Reactors, Rickover remarked, "I guess I'll never see this place again." And he did not. He went home at 5:45 that evening. Arriving in the apartment, he said to Eleonore, "I finished all my work."[40]

Like Falling in Love

SOMETIME IN THE LATE 1960s, Admiral Rickover was sitting in a car driven by Ensign T. R. Reid through Connecticut. While Reid worked for him, Rickover had grown as close to Reid as he would allow with a Naval Reactors staff member, even attending Reid's wedding. Rickover talked with Reid about his life of struggle. At one point, Rickover got worked up. "You take some Jew," he said, "and treat him lousy his whole life. You treat him like dirt. Watch out! He's going to do something."[1] And he did. As President Harry Truman declared at the *Nautilus*'s 1952 keel-laying ceremony, in capturing "the same source that heats the sun," Rickover had made "something new in the world." By the time in early 1982 that his sixty-three years of naval service ended, his career had spanned thirteen commanders in chief, from Woodrow Wilson to Ronald Reagan.

All his life Rickover harbored within him the boy whose family had fled antisemitism and poverty in a Polish shtetl. He

never forgot his parents' travails from the time of their arrivals
in the United States and in carving out a place in America. He
never forgot grappling to gain entry and remain in the Navy
and nearly seven decades of war against the service that gave
him opportunity and became his lifelong home. Rickover's
past, his fears, resentments, and many battles, fueled a monu-
mental drive within him—like the fiery enriched uranium inside his reactors. They fed an unquenchable, obsessive need for
power that propelled him throughout his long career and boiled
over into a never-ending crusade, fight after fight, against enemies whom he *had* to defeat no matter the cost. No man's soul
seemed more aligned with his greatest material achievement,
the invention of a new and potentially deadly form of energy
generated out of the kernel of the cosmos, the nucleus of the
atom. And no man seemed more out of step with the organization that made his life's work possible. But the world knew
that when Rickover harnessed the power within the nucleus of
the atom, he had unleashed a revolution. The four-star admiral
Rickover was unlike any person ever to wear—or more often
refuse to wear—the uniform.

Less than half a year after his forced retirement, on May
20, 1982, the US Department of the Interior designated Rickover's seminal engineering triumph, the USSN *Nautilus*, a National Historic Landmark. After its deactivation and conversion at Mare Island, history's first nuclear-powered vessel was
towed upriver from its birthplace in Groton, Connecticut. The
Nautilus opened to visitors on April 11, 1986, at the Submarine
Force Library and Museum.[2] The ship was open to all eyes, *except* for its engineering compartments housing the nuclear reactor and propulsion machinery that of course made the sub
such a revolutionary triumph. They remain classified almost
seventy years after the *Nautilus* first got "underway on nuclear
power." But that unseen stainless steel, Zircaloy-2, and hafnium
reactor inside the hull inaugurated the practical use of atomic

power, propelled the first underwater polar-ice-cap transit, re-imagined the warship, and reworked the global strategic equation. Today, it serves first and foremost as a monument to one man's genius for engineering power.

Ousted from Naval Reactors, Rickover was at a loss in retirement. The Navy offered all four-star admirals a temporary "transition office" at the Washington Navy Yard for the first months of their retirement. After Rickover's epic White House blowup, Weinberger did not want to extend him any special privileges, but Lehman convinced him to include a secretary and driver, along with naval aides, with the possibility of six-month extensions of the arrangement, "assuming he behaved responsibly," the Navy secretary admonished. In August, Congress passed legislation that made those special privileges permanent, "one of the final exercises of the classic Rickover touch," Lehman remarked.[3] Rickover's friends in Congress were eager to honor him one last time. Congress voted without objection to award him a second Gold Medal. He became the only person other than US president and war hero General Zachary Taylor to receive the honor twice. His friends on Capitol Hill also pushed the Navy to name an aircraft carrier for him, but the Navy would agree only to christen a submarine on the ways in his honor. The fast-attack *Hyman G. Rickover* (SSN 709) launched at Electric Boat on August 27, 1983. In Rickover's speech that day, he commented, without mentioning the man's name, on the recent indictment of EB general manager P. Takis Veliotis, his former nemesis.[4] Veliotis faced federal charges for having taken kickbacks from suppliers and running up fraudulent claims against the Navy. Rickover called on EB to act after this "as a responsible supplier and not as a contractor trying to dominate the customer."[5]

With little to do at his Navy Yard office, Rickover grew despondent, found Francis Duncan, who met with him during his retirement while researching a book on his work developing the first nuclear reactors.[6] Rickover's war with the Navy still raged on in his heart. On an otherwise bare office wall, he hung a photo of Lehman and, above it, a portrait of Benedict Arnold, the Revolutionary War traitor.[7] To escape his doldrums, he and Eleonore, in the company of a young former federal attorney, Joann DiGennaro, traveled extensively in the Middle East, China, and Japan. Wherever they went, his fame brought them attention and invitations to meet with political and scientific leaders.

After months of searching about for a cause, his energy and interest lighted on educational reform. He worked together with DiGennaro to establish the Admiral H. G. Rickover Foundation, seeding it with his speaking fees. A tribute gala in his honor gave the foundation a large financial boost. It also demonstrated the continuing reverence in which he was held outside the current administration.

The "Salute to Admiral Rickover" at a Washington, DC, hotel on February 23, 1983, brought together five hundred people, paying $1,000 each. Guests included a rare gathering of the three living former presidents: Nixon, Ford, and Carter. Not surprisingly, Reagan was out of town and did not send a representative or tribute. The president most identified with Rickover, Jimmy Carter, spoke of his memories of Rickover as "omnipotent, omniscient and omnipresent." He repeated that next to his father, Rickover, "above all other men," had had an impact on his life. Nixon recalled being moved when, after pinning on the admiral's fourth star, Rickover saluted him, "who had only been a lieutenant": "Tonight . . . we are proud to salute him." After a standing ovation, Rickover spoke about his personal life, which he almost never did previously in public.[8] He told the guests about his family's arduous journey to America, his education, and how the Navy lifted him out of poverty. "I was in the Navy more than 63 years, longer than any naval officer in our history," he said. "Nevertheless, I do not believe I have done enough for my country. I did what I wanted and was paid well for my work." He quipped, "I obeyed all orders that I agreed with," which set off much laughter. And he ended, "Admirals never die. And they do not fade away."[9]

With the evening's receipts and the earnings from his speeches, the foundation set to work. Rickover became most active in its Rickover Summer Science Institute, later the Research Science Institute (RSI). The program brought together around fifty or more top math and science high school students from the United States and abroad. At first, they came to Washington, DC, for classes and to intern in government laboratories and meet with Rickover. The foundation, which is known today as the Center for Excellence in Education, still sponsors math, science, and engineering programs for high school students and teachers.[10]

Rickover did not fade away from the spotlight, although for unhappy reasons. His legacy as an indefatigable brawler for ethical business practices on behalf of the taxpayers took a gut shot from revelations that first appeared in July 1984.[11] Not long after Veliotis's indictment, he fled the country for his native Greece. When General Dynamics sued him, he went to the Justice Department with evidence that the company had fraudulently padded its overrun claims—just as Rickover had long charged. But the mud also splashed Rickover. Investigators from the House Energy and Commerce Committee looking into the scandal found that company officials had provided Rickover with numerous gifts and special favors over the years.

Starting in 1977, the Defense Department had banned its military and civilian officials from receiving gifts of any value from anyone doing business with the federal government. But over the years, the "rig-for-Rickover" list to prepare for his comfort on sea trials with select foods, clothing, books, stationery, dry cleaning, chauffeured cars, barbering, and other services came mostly at the expense of the shipyards. And the list had bloated. Rickover began calling on the shipbuilders to prepare special personal gifts outside the trials, mostly trinkets but some bizarre and brazen. Following up on the congressional inquiry, Navy investigators out of the secretary's office eventually found that over the last two decades of his career, Rickover had received $19,000 worth of gratuities to commemorate boat launchings and keel-layings. These included sterling-silver trays; fourteen-karat-gold discs; silver-plated, engraved mint-julep cups; engraved plaques including one that Rickover gave to President Kennedy that he kept on his desk; chrome-plated tie clasps—items that Rickover presented to dignitaries who participated in the events, supporters of his program, and staffers.

Far more damning were the personal gifts, which Rickover asked for and the company felt compelled to give while shielding them from public scrutiny. The report found that General Dynamics "loaned" him a video-cassette recorder and television monitor, which Rickover never returned, as well as gifts of shower curtains that he had seen at a hotel, a set of *Encyclopaedia Britannica*, twelve mahogany and teak boxes made from deck boards of the *Nautilus*, at least fifteen pairs of nautilus-shell bookends, and twelve gold-plated fruit knives with handles made from water buffalo horns. Perhaps most jarring was the revelation that in 1977 Electric Boat bought $1,125 worth of jewelry for him, including a matching set of jade earrings and pendant. The jewelry was hand-delivered to his Naval Reactors office. When Rickover said he did not like the box holding the jewelry, General Dynamics dispatched a different one. He gave the jewelry to Eleonore. The company had falsified the receipts for the jewelry to cover up any evidence of the purchases.[12]

Rickover denied any memory of the jewelry, though the transactions were well documented. He said to a *Washington*

Post reporter that the "trinkets" had no influence on his relations with the contractor. "Did anyone ever suggest that I stopped taking them on?" he asked. "Did anyone ever suggest that I did not try to get the best deal I could for the government? What did they hope to gain by giving me the gifts?"[13] Demonstrably he was right. But the damage was done.

Eventually, a Navy board looking into the many gifts given to Rickover assessed their total value at $67,628.33. General Dynamics was fined ten times that amount and lost two contracts. Lehman sent Rickover a letter of censure. Rickover's response was, "I can emphatically say that no gratuity or favor ever affected any decision I made." He insisted to the end, "My conscience is clear on this subject."[14]

Despite the stain on Rickover's reputation, his influence on the Navy remained pervasive. Numerous and successive chiefs of naval operations, labeled by Norman Polmar, a Rickover critic, the "submarine mafia," came from the nuclear program.[15] Congress made sure that Rickover's standards and methods became permanently enshrined within the Navy. A 1984 law designated that Naval Reactors would retain cradle-to-grave responsibility for all Navy reactors and that every future NR chief must hold four-star rank and serve in the post for eight years—an unprecedented intrusion into Navy affairs.[16] Decades after Rickover's death, his presence remains stamped on the nuclear Navy and the whole Navy. In fact, a cottage industry has developed to study his leadership methods and engineering organization.[17]

Rickover did not live to see the end of the Cold War. But the Soviet Union spent lavishly trying and mostly failing to overcome US technological superiority in nuclear submarines and ships. Although the reasons for the demise of the Soviet Union remain subject to academic debate, the strain of massive defense spending helped push the Soviet economy to the brink.

Intimately aware of the situation, Rickover's successors, Cold War submariners, and foreign-affairs analysts were certain that US nuclear ships had sometimes provoked the Soviets but in the end helped to stave off nuclear confrontation and contributed significantly to the end of the Cold War.[18]

The Navy continues to sail in nuclear ships. As of 1990, all US Navy submarines were nuclear powered. Since 2009, when the Navy retired its last conventionally fueled aircraft carrier, the nation's carriers have all been nuclear. But Rickover lost the war for nuclear surface escorts. No additional nuclear-propelled combatant ships have been built since the last of Rickover's vessels was taken out of service in 1999.[19]

But the naval culture he built remains. "Admiral Rickover's legacy is generational," Admiral James F. Caldwell Jr., Naval Reactors director, said at the May 11, 2018, keel-laying ceremony for the next *Hyman G. Rickover* (SSN-795). "It lives on in the hearts and minds of the officers and sailors that serve in the United States Navy."[20] The new and most advanced fast-attack submarine was scheduled for commissioning in the second half of 2021 or early 2022.

On July 4, 1985, a month after Rickover had delivered his undaunted response to Lehman's censure letter, he suffered a stroke. He lost use of his right side and had difficulty speaking, though he remained coherent. He recovered enough to return home but suffered a second stroke two weeks later. With Eleonore's nursing care, he again went home. Over the coming months, he began to receive people, some among them his old colleagues from Naval Reactors whom he had previously barred from social contact. But his health problems compounded. He fell and broke a rib, then contracted pneumonia. His decline hastened. He became bedridden.

Over the course of several of Rickover's hospitalizations, Eleonore came to know Captain Bruce Kahn, a Navy chaplain and rabbi who "walked the deck" visiting patients at the Naval Hospital in Bethesda.[21] Whenever Rickover was asked about his religion, he typically snapped, "It's none of your damn business!" Even his son, Robert, believed he had converted.[22] But Eleonore was emphatic with Kahn that her husband had never converted from Judaism. Yet while lying in the intensive-care unit, Rickover made it clear to Eleonore that he had no interest in seeing the Jewish chaplain. In early July 1986, the Navy informed Kahn that the admiral's condition was grave and instructed him to make ready for Rickover's death. With Eleonore nearby and a large contingent of press on a "death watch" in the street outside Rickover's Arlington condominium, the admiral expired early in the evening on July 8, 1986. At Eleonore's request, the Navy sent Kahn to the Rickovers' home soon after the admiral's death. She took him to her husband's bedside and asked him to say a prayer. Looking at Rickover's tiny body, he had a vision of the admiral leaping up and grabbing him, shouting, "I did not want a prayer, dammit!" Kahn said the traditional Jewish blessings over his body.

Rickover had never been without a book nearby. At the end of his life, no longer able to read, Eleonore had sat at his bedside and read to him. Beside his bed, Kahn saw that the last book they were reading together was a history of Poland's Jews and the Holocaust.

As the body was being readied for transport, Kahn went to the admiral's study. He sat down in a chair to make notes in preparation for Rickover's burial. Kahn slid immediately to the floor. It was the infamous short-legged chair in which thousands of nuclear-power candidates had sat and suffered through their Rickover interviews.

Keeping with the Jewish tradition of a speedy burial, within two days after Rickover's death, he was interred at Arlington National Cemetery next to Ruth's grave. Kahn officiated. Thirty-three people gathered at Rickover's graveside, including Francis Duncan and Admiral Bruce DeMars, the Navy's chief of submarine operations and later McKee's successor as chief of Naval Reactors, plus three or four others outside Eleonore's family. None of Rickover's family attended, not even his son. Former president Jimmy Carter asked to be there, but Eleonore said that the event was for family only.

On July 14, the Navy held its official memorial for Rickover at Washington's National Cathedral. More than a thousand people filled the vast gothic Episcopal church. The Catholic chief chaplain of the Navy led the ecumenical service, during which Kahn read from Psalms. Carter was asked by Eleonore to recite John Milton's "On His Blindness," the sonnet Rickover had memorized as a boy, with its final line replete with meaning: "They also serve who only stand and wait." "Second only to my own father," Carter told the gathering, "Hyman Rickover made my life."

Admiral James D. Watkins had grown close to Rickover over the preceding few years. The nuclear-power officer and, until the end of June, chief of naval operations delivered the eulogy. "The admiral," he joked, though with much truth to it, "would surely chide us all today for even bothering to attend this service, and ask us why we weren't back at work doing something more constructive." He recalled a line from Voltaire that Rickover often quoted: "Not to be occupied and not to exist, are one and the same thing." Watkins affirmed: "Admiral Rickover was *occupied*."[23]

Rickover begins "Thoughts on Man's Purpose in Life" with that quote from Voltaire and then writes, "Man's work begins with his job; his profession. Having a vocation is something of a miracle, like falling in love." That miraculous love occupied him at every instant of his life.

ACKNOWLEDGMENTS

ADMIRAL RICKOVER'S LEGACY IS a living one. The exceptional men and women who serve or served in the Navy express great pride, fondness, and sometimes discomfort about their connections to Rickover. I have had the privilege of speaking to dozens of them while researching this book. Many spoke at length about their memories of Rickover the man. Others related to me his continuing presence within the Navy. I am especially indebted to Vice Admiral George W. Emery (USN, Ret.), a nuclear submariner who led a distinguished Navy and business career and who today explores topics in naval history in his own right. He shared his remembrances of life under the admiral, showed me his collection of letters Rickover wrote, and generously read the entire book in manuscript. His many pithy comments saved me from numerous boneheaded and embarrassing errors and gaffes. Another veteran naval nuclear engineer, Douglas Pinnow, read and commented on technical sections, again providing helpful corrections. I apologize for any errors that slipped through; all are my fault.

Others from the Navy who spoke to me, often at length, sent
me their own writings, or guided me include, without rank, L. B.
Barton, James Bryant, Alfred R. Calabrese, David Campbell, John
Crawford Jr., Barry C. Danforth, William Gaines, James Guti-
errez, Frank Hood, William Hughes, Richard Itkin, Raymond
Jones, Bruce Kahn, Peter Koester, Daniel Kohnen, David Kohnen,
Zack T. Pate, Al Perry, T. R. Reid, and Ernest Eugene Tissot Jr.
I spoke with others who did not wish to be cited. Dale Lumme,
Clair Sassin, and especially David Winkler of the Naval Histori-
cal Foundation assisted me in many ways. Rickover's son, Robert
Rickover, spoke with me at length and shared photographs of his
father. Two of the greatest naval historians, John Hattendorf and
Paul Kennedy, advised me at various stages.

I am grateful to the knowledgeable and helpful staff and archi-
vists of the Naval Historical Foundation, the Naval Historical Archive Collection at the Naval War College, the Navy Department
Library at the Washington Navy Yard, the Naval History & Heritage Command, the Submarine Force Library and Archives, and
the Naval Institute Press. In particular, my thanks go to Wendy
Gulley and Gary O'Shea of the Sub Force Library, Stacie Parillo
of the Naval War College archives, Eden Marie M. Picazo of the
NHHC, and Jacqline Barnes and Janis Jorgensen of the Naval
Institute Press. Chris Zendan, Public Affairs Officer, SUBASE
New London, smoothed the way for me, as did Eric Durie of the
Navy Office of Information East and Jodie Cornell with the Com-
mander, Submarine Forces and Commander, Submarine Force
Atlantic. Sidney Davies of the General Dynamics Electric Boat
public-relations office sent me information and photographs.

Robert Harris and David Fishman of the Jewish Theological
Seminary, Megan Lewis of the US Holocaust Memorial Museum
Library, Steven Seegel of the University of Northern Colorado,
Beverly Chubat of the Chicago Jewish Historical Society, and
Mordechai Millunchick of Congregation Adas Yeshurun in Chi-
cago guided me to information about Rickover's shtetl and Chi-
cago childhood.

I owe a particular debt to my ingenious cousin and friend

Joanna Shear. Her research came up with Rickover's true birthdate, something unknown even to him. She also identified various other documents from his earliest years in the United States.

Numerous wise and generous friends encouraged me in myriad ways. They include Edward Rugemer, who first led me to connect to Jewish Lives and Yale University Press, Nathaniel Philbrick, Elissa Lines, Skip Lehman, Lee Branch, and Tim Cole. Historian and friend Daniel Headrick read and provided insightful comments on the manuscript.

My gratitude goes to the Jewish Lives team: Ileene Smith initiated the book, John Knight edited the manuscript, Andrew Katz copyedited it, and Heather Gold and Eva Skewes shepherded the various aspects of producing the book.

Without knowing it, my son Charlie, my daughter Rebecca Sananes, and my students at Quinnipiac University helped me refine skills for communicating the past in what I hope is a clear and lively way. The youth baseball teams that I coached while at work on this book helped distract me from its demands. Thanks to all of you.

Jodi Cohen, my wife, never flagged in her encouragement and patience when I disappeared on research trips and became absorbed in writing about this peculiar and demanding man. She helped our family and many others live through the pandemic with grace and optimism. She steadies me in these stormy times and reminds me to laugh, dance, and keep my heart open. I dedicate this book to her.

Introduction

1. Harry S. Truman, "Address in Groton, Conn., at the Keel Laying of the First Atomic Energy Submarine," June 14, 1952, American Presidency Project, https://www.presidency.ucsb.edu/do cuments/address-groton-conn-the-keel-laying-the-first-atomic -energy-submarine.

2. Several sources describe this event. I have relied on E. E. Kintner, "Admiral Rickover's Gamble," *Atlantic*, January 1959, https://www.theatlantic.com/magazine/archive/1959/01/admiral -rickovers-gamble/308436/; Francis Duncan, *Rickover: The Struggle for Excellence* (2001), 129–30; and John W. Simpson, *Nuclear Power from Underseas to Outer Space* (1995), 52–57. See also Richard G. Hewlett and Francis Duncan, *Nuclear Navy, 1946–1962* (1974), 184–86; and Theodore Rockwell, *The Rickover Effect* (1992), 133–37.

3. Researcher Joanna Shear resolved the question of Ricko- ver's disputed birthdate. On the author's behalf, she requested Chaim Rykower's original birth record directly from Maków-

Mazowiecki's town leader (copy in author's possession). The handwritten entry for Rickover's birth gives a date of December 12, 1899, which is December 24, 1899, in the now standard Gregorian calendar. This confirms his actual birthdate. According to authorized biographer Francis Duncan, Rickover believed when he applied to the USNA that he was born on January 1, 1900, but later learned, incorrectly, that his actual birthdate was January 27, which is the date inscribed on his gravestone at Arlington National Cemetery. See Duncan, *Rickover*, 4.

4. Kintner, "Admiral Rickover's Gamble."

5. "Rickover, Father of Nuclear Navy, Dies at 86," *New York Times*, July 9, 1986. See also Edward L. Beach, foreword to *Rickover and the Nuclear Navy: The Discipline of Technology*, by Francis Duncan (1990), x; Kintner, "Admiral Rickover's Gamble."

6. On the role of submarines in the Cold War, see Owen R. Cote Jr., *The Third Battle: Innovation in the U.S. Navy's Silent Cold War Struggle with Soviet Submarines*, Naval War College Newport Papers 16 (2003).

7. Hyman Rickover, "Nuclear Power and the Navy," remarks to the Navy League of the United States, San Francisco, October 27, 1955.

8. "Hymie Rickover and His Atomic Submarines," *Mad*, no. 7 (July 1959): 6.

9. H. G. Rickover, *Education and Freedom* (1959), 21.

10. Rockwell, *Rickover Effect*, 323.

11. Hyman Rickover, transcript of interview with Diane Sawyer, *60 Minutes*, 1984, http://www.people.vcu.edu/~rsleeth/Rickover.html.

12. Rickover, *60 Minutes* interview.

13. Duncan, *Rickover and the Nuclear Navy*, 234.

14. John F. Lehman Jr., *Command of the Seas* (2001), 111; Norman Polmar and Thomas B. Allen, *Rickover: Controversy and Genius, A Biography* (1982), 479; Elmo R. Zumwalt Jr., *On Watch: A Memoir* (1977), 64; Duncan, *Rickover*, 220–21.

15. Hyman Rickover, "The Role of Engineering in the Navy," speech to the National Society of Former Special Agents of the

Federal Bureau of Investigation, Seattle, August 30, 1974, http://gmapalumni.org/chapomatic/extras/Rickover.htm; Rickover, *Education and Freedom*, 68.

16. Charles K. Duncan, *The Reminiscences of Admiral Charles K. Duncan, U.S. Navy (Ret.)* (1981), vol. 2, #9, 815.

17. Duncan, *Rickover and the Nuclear Navy*, xxi.

18. There are multiple examples, but see James L. Holloway III, *Aircraft Carriers at War: A Personal Retrospective of Korea, Vietnam, and the Soviet Confrontation* (2007), 168; and Admiral (Ret.) Harold E. Shear, letter to the editor, *New York Times*, July 11, 1986.

19. Rear Admiral Dave Oliver, USN (Ret.), *Against the Tide: Rickover's Leadership Principles and the Rise of the Nuclear Navy* (2014), 98.

20. See Thomas Nilsen, Igor Kudrik, and Alexandr Nikitin, "The Russian Northern Fleet Nuclear Submarine Accidents," Bellona Report 2:96 (1997), http://spb.org.ru/bellona/ehome/russia/nfl/nfl8.htm#O5.

21. Department of the Navy and National Nuclear Security Administration, *United States Naval Nuclear Propulsion Program* (September 2017), https://www.energy.gov/sites/prod/files/migrated/nnsa/2018/01/f46/united_states_naval_nuclear_propulsion_program_operating_naval_nuclear_propulsion_plants_and_shipping_rail_naval_spent_fuel_safely_for_over_sixty_years.pdf.

22. On Rickover's transformation of the Navy's culture, especially its officer preparation, see especially Mark R. Hagerott, "Commanding Men and Machines: Admiralship, Technology, and Ideology in the 20th Century U.S. Navy" (PhD diss., University of Maryland, 2008).

23. Hyman Rickover, *American Education—A National Failure: The Problem of Our Schools and What We Can Learn from England* (1963), 23–24.

24. Rickover, *Education and Freedom*, 32.

25. Duncan, *Reminiscences*, vol. 2, #9, 829.

26. Edward L. Beach, "Life under Rickover: Stormy Duty in the Silent Service," *Washington Post*, May 27, 1977.

27. Duncan, *Reminiscences*, vol. 2, #9, 830.

28. Jimmy Carter, *Why Not the Best? The First Fifty Years* (1996), 57.

29. Jimmy Carter, "Presidential Medal of Freedom, Remarks at the Presentation Ceremony, June 9, 1980," *Public Papers of the Presidents of the United States: Jimmy Carter,* book 2, *May 24 to September 26, 1980* (1981–82), 1060. See also Stuart E. Eizenstat, *President Carter: The White House Years* (2018), 21; "3 Ex-Presidents Join in Dinner Honoring Rickover," *New York Times,* March 1, 1983.

Chapter 1. The Lucky Bag

1. *Finland* passenger record, copy in author's possession; Duncan, *Rickover,* 5, 316n2.

2. The translation of the Rickover name varies on the ship manifests and immigration forms and includes "Rikower" and "Ricover." On the processing and experience of immigrants, see Ronald H. Bayor, *Encountering Ellis Island: How European Immigrants Entered America* (2014).

3. "The Man in Tempo—3," *Time,* January 11, 1954.

4. Duncan, *Rickover,* 4–6; "The Education of Hyman Rickover," *Washington Post,* March 6, 1983, a partial transcript of a speech Rickover gave at his retirement dinner.

5. On the shtetl life of the Russian Empire, see Samuel Kassow, "Shtetl," *The YIVO Encyclopedia of Jews in Eastern Europe* (2010), http://www.yivoencyclopedia.org/article.aspx/Shtetl. On Maków's Jewish life, demographics, etc., see "Maków Mazowiecki," *Virtual Shtetl* (POLIN Museum of the History of Polish Jews), https://sztetl.org.pl/en/towns/m/582-makow-mazowiecki/; "The Jewish Community of Maków Mazowiecki," Beit Hatfutsot Database, https://dbs.bh.org.il/place/makow-mazowiecki; Max Pianka, "A Visit to the Home-Town Makow Twenty-Three Years after the Holocaust," *Maków-Mazowiecki Memorial Book* (2003), 468–70 and the hand-drawn map in same (n.p.).

6. "Education of Hyman Rickover"; Roman Vishniac, "The Inner World of the Polish Jew," in *Polish Jews: A Pictorial Record* (1947), 10.

7. On the Holocaust in Maków and the rest of northern Mazovia, see Beit Hatfutsot Database; and Martin Dean and Mel Hecker, *Encyclopedia of Camps and Ghettos, 1933–1945*, vol. 2, *Ghettos in German Occupied Eastern Europe* (2012), 4–5, 15–17.

8. *Palatia* ship manifest, copy in author's possession.

9. Many would-be US immigrants went back and forth multiple times before sending for their immediate family and other relatives and settling permanently. The travels of Rickover's father after his initial voyage are not documented except through his and family members' interviews many decades later. See Polmar and Allen, *Rickover*, 29.

10. Abram's travels courtesy of Joanna Shear. Citizenship: Naturalization Commissioner, Supreme Court of the State of New York, First Judicial District, oath referring to the first Declaration of Intention to Become a Citizen of February 24, 1898, copy in author's possession.

11. District Court of the United States for the Eastern District of New York, Petition, September 6, 1906, copy in author's possession.

12. Ruchia had only an incomplete address for her husband in a tenement on Attorney Street (listed as "Attorne" on the ship's manifest) in Manhattan's Lower East Side. Perhaps the telegraph delivery person could not find him.

13. "Education of Hyman Rickover."

14. "Mortgage Assigned to Abraham Rickower and Morris Buchner," *Brooklyn Daily Eagle*, June 6, 1906.

15. "Education of Hyman Rickover."

16. Duncan, *Rickover*, 6; *Brooklyn Daily Eagle*, March 4, 1908, 16; *Brooklyn Daily Eagle*, June 8, 1908, 14.

17. Abraham's employment at Edward Rose & Co. listed on September 12, 1918, draft registration card, in author's possession. In later years, he managed a clothing factory; see "Gunmen Spray Acid on Clothing in Factory Raid," *Chicago Tribune*, April 8, 1932.

18. On Lawndale's Jewish community, see Irving Cutler, *The Jews of Chicago: From Shtetl to Suburb* (1996), 101, 209 ff. On Lawndale synagogues, see "A Walk to Shul: Chicago Synagogues

of Lawndale and Stops on the Way," *Chicago Jewish History* 27, no. 2 (Summer 2003): 1, 8–9. Most Lawndale synagogue records have been lost, according to Rabbi Mordechai Millunchick, director, Yeshurun/Anshe Kenesses Israel, email to author, January 8, 2019.

19. Clay Blair Jr., *The Atomic Submarine and Admiral Rickover* (1954), 35.

20. Duncan, *Rickover*, 7.

21. Polmar and Allen imply in their 1981 biography, *Rickover* (29–30, 37–38), that the earlier date was Rickover's actual birthdate and that four years later he changed it to the later date to improve his chances for admission to the Naval Academy. Rickover originally believed his birthdate was January 1 and then changed it to January 27. See Duncan, *Rickover*, 7–8.

22. "Education of Hyman Rickover"; T. R. Reid, telephone interview by the author, July 9, 2018.

23. Duncan, *Rickover*, 8–9, photo insert, 2.

24. Polmar and Allen, *Rickover*, 35–36; Duncan, *Rickover*, 8, 9.

25. "Marshall and M'Kinley High Cadets Enroll," *Chicago Tribune*, March 21, 1917. For his dreams of serving, see Duncan, *Rickover*, 11.

26. Sabath, who died in November 1952, was a vocal early supporter of the Navy's atomic submarine program and, before death, active in helping Rickover during his promotion struggle.

27. Duncan, *Rickover*, 9. Rickover told Clay Blair Jr. a somewhat different version of events (*Atomic Submarine*, 35–36).

28. Duncan, *Rickover*, 10–11; Polmar and Allen, *Rickover*, 38–39.

29. Duncan, *Rickover*, 10–11; Rockwell, *Rickover Effect*, 21; Kintner, "Admiral Rickover's Gamble."

30. For Rickover's first days in Annapolis, see Thomas L. "Tim" Foster, "Technology and Leadership: Hyman G. Rickover," in *The Art of Command: Military Leadership from George Washington to Colin Powell*, ed. Harry S. Laver and Jeffrey J. Matthews (2008), 182–83; Polmar and Allen, *Rickover*, 41–43; Duncan, *Rickover*, 11–14.

31. Blair, *Atomic Submarine*, 37

NOTES TO PAGES 25-33

32. Polmar and Allen, *Rickover,* 47-59.

33. Polmar and Allen, 51.

34. Duncan, *Rickover,* 14.

35. Beach, "Life under Rickover."

36. Naval Academy, *The Lucky Bag 1922,* American Jewish Archives, http://americanjewisharchives.org/exhibits/aje/_pdfs/S_29 .pdf. For the newspaper coverage, see for example "Charges Race Slur at Naval Academy, *New York Times,* June 14, 1922; "Navy Academy Incident Closed," *Riverside (CA) Daily Press,* June 15, 1922; Norine Dresser and Theodor Schuchat, "In Search of the Perforated Page," *Western Folklore* 39, no. 4 (October 1980): 300-306.

37. Naval Academy, *The Lucky Bag 1922,* 94, copy in author's possession.

38. Polmar and Allen, *Rickover,* 194.

39. Rickover, *60 Minutes* interview.

Chapter 2. Mastering Power

1. On Rickover's early Navy seagoing duty, see Duncan, *Rickover,* 18-26.

2. "45 Officers of the Navy Take Special Courses," *New York Times,* August 12, 1928. International House still exists and was the first student residential center of its kind. See International House, "Our History," https://www.ihouse-nyc.org/about-student -housing-in-ny/our-history/.

3. Duncan, *Rickover,* 27.

4. "Dr. Charles Lucke, Engineer, 74, Dead: Columbia Emeritus Professor, Department Head 34 Years, a Thermodynamics Expert," *New York Times,* March 27, 1951; Polmar and Allen, *Rickover,* 74.

5. Rickover, *Education and Freedom,* 19, 64-65. On Rickover and the Technocracy Movement, see Hagerott, "Commanding Men and Machines," 195-208.

6. Hyman Rickover to Ruth Masters Rickover, June 28, 1935, in Duncan, *Rickover,* 57.

7. Robert Rickover, telephone interview by the author, May 3, 2018.

8. Hyman Rickover to Ruth Masters Rickover, September 9, 1929, in Duncan, *Rickover*, 30–31.

9. Hyman Rickover to Ruth Masters Rickover, August 5, 1931, in Duncan, *Rickover*, 41.

10. Ruth Masters Rickover to Hyman Rickover, September 13, 1929, in Duncan, *Rickover*, 30.

11. Rear Admiral William D. Irvin, USN (Ret.), "Oddball S-Boat," in *Submarine Stories: Recollections from the Diesel Boats*, ed. Paul L. Stillwell (2007), n.p.

12. Duncan, *Rickover*, 39–40.

13. Hyman Rickover to Ruth Masters Rickover, February 22, 1932, in Duncan, *Rickover*, 43.

14. "Lieutenant Hyman G. Rickover," *Chicago Tribune*, June 3, 1931.

15. Hyman Rickover to Ruth Masters Rickover, December 1932, in Duncan, *Rickover*, photo caption, 168.

16. Hyman Rickover to Ruth Masters Rickover, February 22, 1932, in Duncan, *Rickover*, 44.

17. Irvin, "Oddball S-Boat."

18. Edward L. Beach, *Salt and Steel: Reflections of a Submariner* (1999), 179–81.

19. Hyman Rickover to Ruth Masters Rickover, March 16, 1933, in Duncan, *Rickover*, 51. On the dangers of atomic energy, see for instance Rickover's testimony to Congress in *Economics of Defense Policy: Adm. H. G. Rickover: Hearing before the Joint Economic Committee*, 97th Cong., 2nd sess., pt. 1, January 28, 1982.

20. Hyman Rickover to Ruth Masters Rickover, September 25, 1933, in Duncan, *Rickover*, 50.

21. Hyman Rickover to Ruth Masters Rickover, March 3, 1936, in Duncan, *Rickover*, 58–59.

22. "Services Held for Father of Adm. Rickover," *Chicago Tribune*, November 10, 1960; "Adm. Rickover's Mother Dies," *Indianapolis Star*, March 11, 1968; Duncan, *Rickover*, 60–61, 167, 219.

23. See for instance Oliver, *Against the Tide*, 4; Polmar and

Allen, *Rickover*, 192; John Lehman, *On Seas of Glory: Heroic Men, Great Ships, and Epic Battles of the American Navy* (2001), 312. Robert Rickover, interview.

24. Robert Rickover, interview. Robert Rickover converted to Judaism later in life.

25. Rabbi (Captain, ret.) Bruce Kahn, telephone interview by the author, September 9, 2018.

26. Robert Rickover, interview.

27. Ruth Masters Rickover, *International Law in National Courts* (1932); Hyman Rickover, "International Law and the Submarine," *Proceedings*, September 1935; Hermann Bauer, *The Submarine: Its Importance as Part of a Fleet, Its Position in International Law, Its Employment in War, Its Future* (1936).

28. Ruth Masters Rickover to Hyman Rickover, January 30, 1932, in Duncan, *Rickover*, 54.

29. Rear Admiral Charles E. Loughlin, USN (Ret.), oral history interview, 1980, https://www.navalhistory.org/2019/07/02/the -early-years-remembering-admiral-rickover.

30. Captain John W. Crawford Jr., "Passing Rickover's Muster," *Naval History*, Spring 1992, 38.

31. Hyman Rickover to Ruth Masters Rickover, June 10, 1935, in Duncan, *Rickover*, 54. On Rickover's period aboard the *New Mexico*, I have relied on Duncan, 53–62; and Polmar and Allen, *Rickover*, 83–85.

32. Hyman Rickover, "Thoughts on Man's Purpose in Life," speech at luncheon meeting of the San Diego Rotary Club, San Diego, February 10, 1977. Accessed as pamphlet, Council on Religion and International Affairs, September 10, 1982, https://www .carnegiecouncil.org/publications/archive/morgenthau/763/_res /id=Attachments/index=0/763_2ndMML-H.G.Rickover.pdf.

33. Polmar and Allen, *Rickover*, 88–89.

34. See Marc Wortman, *1941: Fighting the Shadow War: A Divided Nation in a World at War* (2016), 90–97.

35. Hyman Rickover to Ruth Masters Rickover, August 22, 1937, in Duncan, *Rickover*, 65.

36. "Chinese Armies Retreat Mile in Shanghai Battle," *Chicago Tribune*, October 4, 1937.

37. Ruth Masters Rickover, *Pepper, Rice, and Elephants: A Southeast Asian Journey from Celebes to Siam* (1975), ix–xi, 23, 124–25, 258–59.

38. Duncan, *Rickover*, 69–70.

39. "Why the Navy Wants to Scuttle Rickover," *Navy Times*, August 17, 1958.

40. See Endowment for International Peace, *International Organizations in the Field of Public Health* (1947).

41. Robert Rickover, interview.

42. Rear Admiral Julius Augustus Furer, "Bureau of Ships," in *Administration of the Navy Department in World War II* (1959), http://www.ibiblio.org/hyperwar/USN/Admin-Hist/USN-Admin/USN-Admin-6.html.

43. Schuyler N. Pyne, *The Reminiscences of Rear Admiral Schuyler N. Pyne, U.S. Navy (Ret.)* (1972), 134–36. See also Duncan, *Rickover*, 72–73. Polmar and Allen criticize Rickover's methods while at the Electrical Section, which they assert could "eventually produc[e] a disaster" (*Rickover*, 103–5).

44. Duncan, *Rickover*, 78–79.

45. On Rickover's time at the Electrical Section, I have relied on a history of the Electrical Section commissioned and edited by Rickover, *Electrical Section History* (1946), http://www.doerry.org/norbert/references/19460226BUSHIPSElectricalSectionHistory-original.pdf. Also, see Duncan, *Rickover*, 71–81; and Polmar and Allen, *Rickover*, 97–107.

46. Rickover, "Role of Engineering in the Navy."

47. Simpson, *Nuclear Power*, 4–5.

48. Duncan, *Rickover*, 83.

49. Beach, foreword to *Rickover and the Nuclear Navy*, xiii.

50. Polmar and Allen, *Rickover*, 109, 106.

51. Rockwell, *Rickover Effect*, 30–31.

52. Rockwell, 83.

53. Hyman Rickover to Ruth Masters Rickover, November 18, 1945, in Duncan, *Rickover*, 88–89.

54. Masters Rickover, *Pepper, Rice, and Elephants*, 188–90n.

55. Duncan, *Rickover*, 90–92.

56. Joe Williams Jr., *The Reminiscences of Vice Admiral Joe Williams, Jr., U.S. Navy (Ret.)* (2002), 113; Commander (Ret.) David Trent Leighton, oral history, Naval Historical Foundation, January 18, 2011, 25–26, http://www.navyhistory.org/wp-content/up loads/2018/01/Leighton-manuscript.pdf.

57. Rockwell, *Rickover Effect*, 32.

Chapter 3. The Two Hats

1. "Navy to Test Atom Bomb. Admirals Seek Answer to Query, Is the Fleet of Today Obsolete?," *New York Times*, October 24, 1945.

2. "Nimitz Receives All-Out Welcome from Washington," *New York Times*, October 6, 1945.

3. "Hopes to Release Energy in Atoms," *New York Times*, October 18, 1924.

4. On fission's discovery and research into chain reactions, see Richard Rhodes, *The Making of the Atomic Bomb* (1986), 233–75; Richard Rhodes, "A Demonstration at Shippingport," *American Heritage* 32, no. 4 (June–July 1981), https://www.americanheritage .com/demonstration-shippingport; and F. G. Gosling, *Manhattan Project: Making the Atomic Bomb* (1999), https://www.osti.gov/open net/manhattan-project-history/publications/DE99001330.pdf.

5. On early Navy work on nuclear power, I have relied on Joseph-James Ahern, "'We Had the Hose Turned on Us!': Ross Gunn and the Naval Research Laboratory's Early Research into Nuclear Propulsion, 1939-1946," *Historical Studies in the Physical and Biological Sciences* 33, no. 2 (2003): 217–23; Hewlett and Duncan, *Nuclear Navy*; and Carl O. Holmquist and Russell S. Greenbaum, "The Development of Nuclear Propulsion in the Navy," *U.S. Naval Institute Proceedings*, September 1960, 65–71.

6. For Abelson's memoirs about his and Gunn's work separating U-235 from uranium, see Philip Abelson, *Ross Gunn, 1897–1966: A Biographical Memoir* (1998), 7–10.

7. On Manhattan Project interest in the NRL/Ableson

liquid thermal diffusion process, see Rhodes, *Making of the Atomic Bomb*, 549–54.

8. Ahern, "We Had the Hose Turned on Us!"

9. "Submarine Navy with Atom Fuel and Surface Speed Held Safest," *New York Times*, December 13, 1945. On the Abelson report and its reception by the Navy, see Hewlett and Duncan, *Nuclear Navy*, 24–28.

10. Abelson, "Ross Gunn," 10.

11. On the search for a postwar submarine mission, see Cote, *Third Battle*, 26.

12. Albert G. Mumma, *The Reminiscences of Rear Admiral Albert G. Mumma, U.S. Navy (Ret.)* (2001), 240.

13. Hyman Rickover to Ruth Masters Rickover, May 4, 1946, in Duncan, *Rickover*, 95.

14. Farrington Daniels, "Those Early Days as We Remember Them (Part V)," Nuclear Engineering Division, Argonne National Laboratory, June 1971, https://www.ne.anl.gov/About/early-days/early_days_5.html.

15. Simpson, *Nuclear Power*, 8–10.

16. Hyman Rickover to Ruth Masters Rickover, July 13, 1946, in Duncan, *Rickover*, 98.

17. Captain James M. Dunford, USN (Ret.), "My Years with Admiral Rickover," n.d., typescript in author's possession.

18. Quoted in Polmar and Allen, *Rickover*, 127.

19. Simpson, *Nuclear Power*, 10.

20. Duncan, *Rickover*, 98–99. See also Rockwell, *Rickover Effect*, 39–40.

21. Oppenheimer quote from "Elusive Dream," *Time*, August 23, 1948. Farrington Daniels, "Recollections of a Career in Science and Teaching," University Archives Oral History Project, University of Wisconsin, 1972 (interview conducted by Steven Lowe).

22. Beach, *Salt and Steel*, 169, 182; Beach, foreword to *Rickover and the Nuclear Navy*, xi. On the interservice battle over atomic strategy and mission between the Navy and Air Force, see Jeffrey G. Barlow, *Revolt of the Admirals: The Fight for Naval Aviation, 1945–1950* (1994).

23. Beach, *Salt and Steel*, 182.

24. Nimitz to Secretary of the Navy, memo, December 5, 1947, in Polmar and Allen, *Rickover*, 138–39.

25. E .B. Potter, *Nimitz* (1976), 424–25.

26. Ronald Schiller, "The Strange Case of the Man behind the Atomic Sub," *Look* 17, no. 5 (March 10, 1953).

27. On Rickover's early efforts to promote reactor development within the Navy, see Hewlett and Duncan, *Nuclear Navy*, 49–51.

28. Blair, *Atomic Submarine*, 88–91. Rockwell, *Rickover Effect*, 47–48.

29. Blair, *Atomic Submarine*, 97.

30. Beach, *Salt and Steel*, 182.

31. Captain William R. Anderson with Don Keith, *The Ice Diaries: The Untold Story of the Cold War's Most Daring Mission* (2008), 31.

32. Duncan, *Rickover*, 143.

33. On Navy and Rickover interactions with the AEC during this period, see Hewlett and Duncan, *Nuclear Navy*, 73–74. On competing underwater-warfare programs, see Duncan, *Rickover*, 156–58.

34. Duncan, *Rickover*, 104–5.

35. Doug Pinnow, interview by the author, July 5, 2019. Quote from Reid, interview.

36. Westinghouse had done some electrical work related to chemical processes in the Manhattan District during the war, though without knowledge of their atomic-bomb applications.

37. Simpson, *Nuclear Power*, 22, 23.

38. "Attending Atom School," *New York Times*, December 21, 1949, 49.

39. Rockwell, *Rickover Effect*, 45.

40. Rockwell, 18.

41. Confidential typescript memoir in Rickover Papers, The United States Navy Submarine Force Library and Museum, Groton, CT.

42. Duncan, *Rickover*, 111.

43. "Detection of the First Soviet Nuclear Test, September 1949," National Security Archive, published September 9, 2019, https://nsarchive.gwu.edu/briefing-book/nuclear-vault/2019-09 -09/detection-first-soviet-nuclear-test-september-1949.

44. "Atom Group 'Pleased,'" *New York Times*, February 15, 1951, 26.

45. Quoted in C. B. Palmer, "SSN-571—Making of the Atomic Sub," *New York Times*, October 26, 1952.

46. Quoted in Harold Helfer, "He's No Team Man, but . . . ," *Our Navy*, mid-November 1958, 35.

47. Reid, interview.

48. On his testimony, see for instance Vice Admiral Thomas Kilcline, oral history, vol. 2 (2000), 74.

49. Hewlett and Duncan, *Nuclear Navy*, 114.

50. Rockwell, *Rickover Effect*, 97–98; Hewlett and Duncan, *Nuclear Navy*, 159–62.

51. Hewlett and Duncan, *Nuclear Navy*, 163–64; Duncan, *Rickover*, 114–15; Harry S. Truman, "The President's News Conference of August 10, 1950," *Public Papers of the Presidents of the United States: Harry S. Truman, 1950*, vol. 6 (1965), 580.

Chapter 4. Rickover Made Us Do It

1. Blair, *Atomic Submarine*, 125–26.

2. Polmar and Allen, *Rickover*, 488–89. See also Beach, foreword to *Rickover and the Nuclear Navy*, xiii; and Duncan, *Rickover and the Nuclear Navy*, 241–43.

3. Duncan, *Reminiscences*, vol. 2, #9, 828.

4. Robert Wallace, "A Deluge of Honors for an Exasperating Admiral," *Life*, September 5, 1958.

5. Simpson, *Nuclear Power*, 34.

6. Blair, *Atomic Submarine*, 69.

7. Simpson, *Nuclear Power*, 37, 42.

8. Hyman G. Rickover, "Comments to the Navy Postgraduate School," Monterey, CA, March 16, 1954.

9. Simpson, *Nuclear Power*, 10.

10. Confidential typescript memoir in Rickover Papers, The

United States Navy Submarine Force Library and Museum, Groton, CT.

11. Simpson, *Nuclear Power*, 39–40, 158.

12. Palmer, "SSN-571—Making of the Atomic Sub."

13. Hagerott, "Commanding Men and Machines," 242–43.

14. Blair, *Atomic Submarine*, 130.

15. Rickover letter quote from Duncan, *Rickover*, 133. On Wilkinson and Rickover's relationship, see Oliver, *Against the Tide*, 12–19.

16. *Washington Times-Herald* and *Washington Star*, August 20, 1953, in Duncan, *Rickover*, 133–34.

17. Dunford, "My Years with Admiral Rickover."

18. Foster, "Technology and Leadership," 188.

19. Commander David T. Leighton, "Speech on Naval Nuclear Power Program to the American Society of Materials, Golden Gate Chapter: Circa January 1961," in oral history, Naval Historical Foundation, 95.

20. Hewlett and Duncan, *Nuclear Navy*, 140–42. See also H. G. Rickover, L. D. Geiger, and B. Lustman, *History of the Development of Zirconium Alloys for Use in Nuclear Reactors* (1975).

21. Schiller, "Strange Case," 25.

22. World Nuclear Association, "Nuclear Fuel and Its Fabrication," September 2020, https://world-nuclear.org/information-library/nuclear-fuel-cycle/conversion-enrichment-and-fabrication/fuel-fabrication.aspx.

23. Simpson, *Nuclear Power*, 47.

24. Hewlett and Duncan, *Nuclear Navy*, 165.

25. Hewlett and Duncan, 170.

26. Thomas R. Weschler, *Reminiscences of Vice Admiral Thomas R. Weschler, U.S. Navy (Ret.)*, vol. 2 (1995), 315.

27. Harry S. Truman, "August 6, 1945: Statement by the President Announcing the Use of the A-Bomb at Hiroshima," Miller Center, University of Virginia, https://millercenter.org/the-presidency/presidential-speeches/august-6-1945-statement-president-announcing-use-bomb.

28. Harry S. Truman, "Address in Groton, Conn., at the Keel

Laying of the First Atomic Energy Submarine," June 14, 1952, American Presidency Project, https://www.presidency.ucsb.edu /documents/address-groton-conn-the-keel-laying-the-first -atomic-energy-submarine.

29. In Duncan, *Rickover,* 119–20. See also Polmar and Allen, *Rickover,* 150–51.

30. The experiment took place on December 20, 1951.

31. Rockwell, *Rickover Effect,* 133–34; Kintner, "Admiral Rickover's Gamble."

32. Simpson, *Nuclear Power,* 46.

33. Kintner, "Admiral Rickover's Gamble."

34. Hewlett and Duncan, *Nuclear Navy,* 198.

35. Palmer, "SSN-571—Making of the Atomic Sub."

36. "Chicagoan Wins Legion of Merit for A-Sub Work," *Chicago Tribune,* July 8, 1952.

37. Rockwell, *Rickover Effect,* 120–21.

Chapter 5. Another Dreyfus Case?

1. Duncan, *Rickover,* 117.

2. Polmar and Allen, *Rickover,* 183–88 (quote, 188). Duncan gives an alternate version of events (*Rickover,* 117–18).

3. Rockwell, *Rickover Effect,* 145.

4. Clay Blair Jr., "Atomic Sub," *Time,* February 26, 1951.

5. On the promotion controversy, see Duncan, *Rickover,* 121–28; Rockwell, *Rickover Effect,* 145–57; and Polmar and Allen, *Rickover,* 183–205.

6. See Joseph W. Bendersky, "The Absent Presence: Enduring Images of Jews in United States Military History," *American Jewish History* 89, no. 4 (December 1, 2001).

7. John Crawford Jr., interview by the author, September 4, 2018.

8. Ruthven E. Libby, *The Reminiscences of Vice Admiral Ruthven E. Libby, U.S. Navy (Ret.)* (1984), #4, 235, 236. Circumcision in Polmar and Allen, *Rickover,* 194.

9. Kevin Hennessy, "How Ike Saved the U.S. from Another 'Dreyfus Case,'" *Confidential* 2, no. 5 (November 1954).

10. December 1952 issue in Rockwell, *Rickover Effect*, 154.

11. Simpson, *Nuclear Power*, 53.

12. Rockwell, *Rickover Effect*, 21.

13. Duncan (*Rickover*) and Rockwell (*Rickover Effect*) write that full power was reached on June 25. Simpson, who was there, writes that it took place on June 23 (*Nuclear Power*).

14. Rockwell, *Rickover Effect*, 148. See Rockwell's firsthand account of his and others' efforts to reverse the Selection Board decision (145–57). Various versions of the promotion controversy exist. They by and large agree on events, but some accounts disagree on Navy motives in refusing to promote Rickover. See also Duncan, *Rickover*, 123–28; Polmar and Allen, *Rickover*, 191–205.

15. Polmar and Allen, *Rickover*, 199.

16. Hewlett and Duncan, *Nuclear Navy*, 190.

17. "Demands Probe of Snub of Atom Sub Developer," *Chicago Tribune*, January 27, 1953.

18. *Congressional Record—House*, 83rd Cong., 1st sess., March 2, 1953, vol. 99, 1553.

19. Schiller, "Strange Case."

20. Rockwell, *Rickover Effect*, 156.

21. "Ex-Chicagoan Soon to Become 'Atom' Admiral," *Chicago Tribune*, May 14, 1953.

22. Vote per oral history interview with James L. Holloway, 1962, chief of naval personnel at the time, in Polmar and Allen, *Rickover*, 203.

23. Duncan, *Rickover*, 131.

24. Mumma, *Reminiscences*, 249.

25. Lehman, *On Seas of Glory*, 312.

26. Hewlett and Duncan, *Nuclear Navy*, 425.

27. The cover and article, "The Man in Tempo-3," appeared in the January 11, 1954, issue. Quote from "Revolution in United States Navy Power," *New Haven Journal-Courier*, January 14, 1954. On Blair's composition of the book at NR, see Polmar and Allen, *Rickover*, 199–200.

Chapter 6. Underway on Nuclear Power

1. Duncan, *Rickover*, 143.

2. Duncan, 131.

3. Kintner, "Admiral Rickover's Gamble"; Simpson, *Nuclear Power*, 56–57.

4. Kintner, "Admiral Rickover's Gamble."

5. For a lightly fictionalized depiction of Arco training, see Edward L. Beach, *Cold Is the Sea* (1978), 22–51.

6. Rockwell, *Rickover Effect*, 188.

7. Multiple interviews of former submariners by the author.

8. Simpson, *Nuclear Power*, 52.

9. Leighton, oral history.

10. Beach, *Salt and Steel*, 186–87.

11. Quoted in Polmar and Allen, *Rickover*, 209.

12. Hewlett and Duncan, 181–83; Simpson, *Nuclear Power*, 62–64.

13. FleetSubmarine.com, home page, https://fleetsubmarine.com.

14. "A-Submarine Held Unfit for Battle Now," *Washington Post*, January 4, 1954; "Full Speed Astern," *Time*, January 18, 1954; Captain Slade D. Cutter, USN (Ret.), oral history, US Naval Institute, 1985, 373–78; Duncan, *Rickover*, 135–36.

15. "Atomic Submarine Launched by U.S.: Summer Tests Set," *New York Times*, January 22, 1954. For events leading up to the day and on the grandstand, see Beach, *Salt and Steel*, 231–37.

16. "Atomic Submarine Launched by U.S." For video of the launch, see CriticalPast, "Launching and Christening of Atomic Submarine Nautilus by Mrs Dwight Eisenhower in Electric Boat Division, Groton," https://www.criticalpast.com/video/65675052 624_USS-Nautilus-SSN-571_Mrs-Eisenhower-christening_Com mander-Eugene-P-Wilkinson.

17. Rockwell, *Rickover Effect*, 185.

18. On the sea trials, see Rockwell, 188–95; Duncan, *Rickover*, 138–40.

19. "Atomic Sub. No. 1," *New York Times*, February 1, 1965.

20. "The Nautilus Goes to Sea: First Atomic Powered Ship," *New York Times*, January 18, 1955.

21. Rockwell, *Rickover Effect*, 191–92.

22. *Congressional Record—Senate*, 84th Cong., 1st sess., March 22, 1955, vol. 101, pt. 3, 3345–47.

23. *Hearings on Military Posture before the House Armed Services Committee*, 89th Cong., 2nd sess., May 2, 1966, 8126.

24. Rockwell, *Rickover Effect*, 210. On the SIR, see 212.

25. *Naval Reactor Program and Polaris Missile System: Hearing before the Joint Committee on Atomic Energy*, 86th Cong., 2nd sess., April 9, 1960, 18–19.

26. Duncan, *Reminiscences*, vol. 2, #9, 804.

27. Captain Eugene Tissot (Ret.), telephone interview by the author, June 28, 2018.

Chapter 7. Atoms for Peace

1. Jozef Wilczynski, "Atomic Energy for Peaceful Purposes in the Warsaw Pact Countries," *Soviet Studies* 26, no. 4 (October 1974): 568–90.

2. For Rickover's negative view of merchant nuclear vessels, I rely on Douglas Pinnow, email to the author, June 23, 2019. On failed economics, see John Wirt, "Nuclear Ship Savannah," in *Analysis of Federally Funded Demonstration Projects: Supporting Case Studies* (April 1976), A-A-50, https://www.rand.org/content/dam/rand/pubs/reports/2006/R1927part1.pdf.

3. Simpson, *Nuclear Power*, 97. On the engineering of the civilian reactor, see Simpson, 97–103; and Hewlett and Duncan, *Nuclear Navy*, 240–46.

4. Dwight D. Eisenhower Presidential Library, "Atoms for Peace," https://www.eisenhowerlibrary.gov/research/online-documents/atoms-peace.

5. Dwight D. Eisenhower, "Address before the General Assembly of the United Nations on Peaceful Uses of Atomic Energy," in *Public Papers of the Presidents of the United States, Dwight D. Eisenhower, 1953* (1960), 813–23.

6. Simpson, *Nuclear Power*, 364. See also Richard Rhodes, *Energy: A Human History* (2018), 288.

7. "Controller General Calls Costs at Atom Plant Too High," *New York Times*, March 20, 1959.

8. American Society of Mechanical Engineers, *Historic Achievement Recognized: Shippingport Atomic Power Station: A National Historic Mechanical Engineering Landmark* (1980), https://www.asme.org/wwwasmeorg/media/resourcefiles/aboutasme/who%20we%20are/engineering%20history/landmarks/47-shippingport-nuclear-power-station.pdf.

9. Simpson, *Nuclear Power*, 109.

10. "Controller General Calls Costs at Atom Plant Too High."

11. "Eisenhower Hails Atoms for Peace," *New York Times*, May 27, 1958.

12. *Naval Reactor Program and Shippingport Project: Hearings before the Subcommittees of the Joint Committee on Atomic Energy*, 85th Cong., 1st sess., March 27, 1957, 29.

13. Rockwell, *Rickover Effect*, 162.

14. Duncan, *Rickover*, 148–49.

15. European Nuclear Society, "Energy," https://www.euronuclear.org/nuclear-basics/energy/energy/.

16. "Nuclear Task Force to End World Cruise Today," *New York Times*, October 3, 1964. See also Naval Institute Archives, "Operation Sea Orbit," August 1, 2012, https://www.navalhistory.org/2012/08/01/operation-sea-orbit.

Chapter 8. Nautilus 90 North

1. On the transformation of antisubmarine warfare, see Cote, *Third Battle*.

2. Arleigh Burke to Captain Geoffrey Bennett, March 5, 1957, in David Alan Rosenberg, "Arleigh Burke: The Last CNO," Naval History and Heritage Command, September 2, 2020, https://www.history.navy.mil/content/history/nhhc/research/library/online-reading-room/title-list-alphabetically/a/arleigh-burke-the-last-cno.html.

3. Hagerott, "Commanding Men and Machines," 242–43.

4. Commander Robert D. McWethy, "Significance of the Nautilus Polar Cruise," *Proceedings* (US Naval Institute) 84/5/662 (May 1958), https://www.usni.org/magazines/proceedings/1958/may/significance-nautilus-polar-cruise. See also Tim Cole, "The Captain Comes Home," *Popular Mechanics*, September 1988.

5. Rickover, *Education and Freedom*, 158; Charles J. G. Griffin, "'Operation Sunshine': The Rhetoric of a Cold War Technological Spectacle," *Rhetoric & Public Affairs* 16, no. 3 (2013): 521–42.

6. "U.S. Missile Experts Shaken by Sputnik," *New York Times*, October 13, 1957, 185; "Soviet Movie Shows Reach for the Moon," *Time*, October 28, 1957; "World Opinion and the Soviet Satellite: A Preliminary Evaluation," USIA report, October 17, 1957, in Griffin, "Operation Sunshine."

7. Eisenhower in Anderson with Keith, *Ice Diaries*, 166.

8. Anderson with Keith, 195.

9. See Anderson with Keith for a complete recounting of the mission.

10. "The West's Good Week," *Time*, August 18, 1958; "Under the Ice Cap," *London Daily Telegraph*, August 9, 1958; "Beneath the North Pole," *Life*, September 1, 1958, 59; "Men of Nautilus Proud, Efficient," *New York Times*, February 13, 1955.

11. James S. Russell, *The Reminiscences of Admiral James S. Russell, U.S. Navy (Ret.)*, vol. 2 (1975), 348–50.

12. "Rickover to Shun 2 Launching Rites," *New York Times*, August 15, 1958; Duncan, *Rickover*, 158–59.

13. See Herbert Block, "—this splendid achievement, made possible by a man whose name I forget—," August 13, 1958, Library of Congress, https://www.loc.gov/pictures/item/2012633923/.

14. *Congressional Record*, 85th Cong., 2nd sess., August 11, 1958, vol. 104, pt. 13, 16911–17.

15. "Ticker-Tape Parade and City Hall Ceremony Acclaim Crew of Nautilus," *New York Times*, August 28, 1958.

Chapter 9. Education and Freedom

1. "Rickover to Kozlov on Peace: 'Do Something,'" *New York Times*, July 12, 1959.

2. Duncan, *Rickover*, 162; Duncan, *Rickover and the Nuclear Navy*, 175–77.

3. Rockwell, *Rickover Effect*, 266–69.

4. Duncan, *Rickover*, 163.

5. For a record of the meeting, see US State Department, *Foreign Relations of the United States, 1958–1960*, vol. 10, pt. 1, *Eastern Europe Region; Soviet Union; Cyprus*, 98. "Memorandum of Conversation," Moscow, July 25, 1959, 355–58, https://history.state.gov/his toricaldocuments/frus1958-60v10p1/d98.

6. "Soviets Let Rickover Study Atom Ship on Nixon's Plea," *New York Times*, July 28, 1959; Rockwell, *Rickover Effect*, 265–70.

7. Richard M. Nixon, *Six Crises* (1962), 286.

8. Duncan, *Rickover*, 167.

9. Testimony of Vice Admiral H. G. Rickover in *United States Senate, Report of Proceedings, Senate Investigating Subcommittee of the Committee on Armed Services and Committee on Aeronautical and Space Sciences*, February 3, 1960 (hereafter cited as Senate Armed Services Preparedness Investigations Subcommittee), 430.

10. H. G. Rickover, "Education—Our First Line of Defense," address delivered at the Harvard Club of New York City, New York, December 11, 1958.

11. Rickover, *Education and Freedom*, 18.

12. For a focused study of Rickover's work in education, see William J. Haran, "Admiral Hyman G. Rickover, USN: A Decade of Educational Criticism, 1955–64" (PhD diss., Loyola University Chicago, 1982), https://ecommons.luc.edu/luc_diss/2078.

13. Senate Armed Services Preparedness Investigations Subcommittee, 452.

14. "A Comparison: European vs. American Secondary Schools," *Phi Delta Kappan* 40, no. 2 (1958): 60–64, http://www .jstor.org/stable/20342163.

15. Rickover, *American Education*, 57–58.

16. For a transcript of Rickover's appearance on *Meet the*

Press, see *Congressional Record—Appendix*, February 2, 1960, vol. 106, pt. 2, A898–900.

17. Rickover, *Education and Freedom*, 150–51.

18. See *Report on Russia by Vice Admiral Hyman G. Rickover, USN: Hearings before the Committee on Appropriations, House of Representatives*, 86th Cong., 1st sess., 1959.

19. Hyman Rickover, "The Education of Our Talented Children," address at the Seventh Institute of the Thomas Alva Edison Foundation, New York, November 20, 1956.

20. "Rickover Hails Reds' Education: Calls It Main Challenge to U.S.," *New York Times*, August 9, 1959.

21. Rickover, *Education and Freedom*; Rickover, *Swiss Schools and Ours: Why Theirs Are Better* (1962); Rickover, *American Education*.

22. Hyman Rickover, "The Role of the Critic," address at the Tenth Institute of the Thomas Alva Edison Foundation, New York, November 19, 1959.

23. *Meet the Press* transcript, A899.

24. "Rickover Scores School Equality," *New York Times*, April 4, 1958.

25. Senate Armed Services Preparedness Investigations Subcommittee, 462.

26. See Haran, "Admiral Hyman G. Rickover," 149; "Rickover Scores School Equality."

27. Rickover, *Education and Freedom*, 155.

28. Senate Armed Services Preparedness Investigations Subcommittee, 461.

29. "Hyman G. Rickover Oral History Interview—JFK#1, 8/17/1964," John F. Kennedy Presidential Library and Museum, https://www.jfklibrary.org/asset-viewer/archives/JFKOH/Rickover%2C%20Hyman%20G/JFKOH-HGR-01/JFKOH-HGR-01.

30. Edward R. Murrow, preface to Rickover, *Education and Freedom*, 7.

Chapter 10. A Different Kind of Man

1. Duncan, *Rickover*, 177–78.

2. Rickover, *Education and Freedom*, 19. On Rickover and the Technocracy Movement, see chapter 2.

3. *Naval Reactor Program and Polaris Missile System: Hearing before the Joint Committee on Atomic Energy*, 86th Cong., 2nd sess., April 9, 1960, 23.

4. Rickover, "Role of Engineering in the Navy."

5. See Beach's account of the circumnavigation, *Around the World Submerged: The Voyage of the Triton* (2012).

6. Duncan, *Rickover*, 174.

7. Richard Reeves, *President Kennedy: Profile of Power* (1993), 58.

8. Hagerott, "Commanding Men and Machines," 265.

9. See charts in Rockwell, *Rickover Effect*, 296–97, 299.

10. Hyman Rickover, *Eminent Americans: Namesakes of the Polaris Submarine Fleet* (1972). See Vice Admiral George W. Emery, USN (Ret.), "An Admiral's Letters to His Son," *Naval History Magazine* 23, no. 5 (November 2015); also Emery, email to the author, November 8, 2018, and January 29, 2021.

11. See "The KOG," *Bubbleheads* (blog), August 19, 2013, https://bubbleheads.blogspot.com/2013/08/the-kog.html; and Patrick Tyler, *Running Critical: The Silent War, Rickover and General Dynamics* (1986), 162–63, 223–24.

12. See Hagerott, "Commanding Men and Machines," 244.

13. Hagerott, 272.

14. Duncan, *Reminiscences*, vol. 2, #9, 797.

15. Hagerott, "Commanding Men and Machines," 192.

16. Duncan, *Reminiscences*, vol. 2, #9, 789–90.

17. Rickover, *American Education*, 181–82. See also Duncan, *Rickover and the Nuclear Navy*, 86.

18. Hagerott offers an insightful analysis of the conflict, "Commanding Men and Machines," 285–89.

19. Statement by Vice Admiral H. G. Rickover, USN, in *Tour of the U.S.S. "Enterprise" and Report on Joint AEC-Naval Reactor*

Program: Hearing before the Joint Committee on Atomic Energy, 87th Cong., 2nd sess., March 31, 1962, 40.

20. Crawford, interview, November 12, 2018.

21. Polmar and Allen, *Rickover*, 418.

22. Richard G. Folsom, *Report of the Curriculum Review Board of the United States Naval Academy* (1959), 6–7, 1.

23. Associated Press, "Rickover Lashes Service Academies," *New London Day*, June 19, 1961.

24. Warren Rogers Jr, "The Rickover: Counterfire," *New York Herald Tribune*, June 24, 1961.

25. On curricular, faculty, and administrative changes at the Academy, see Hagerott, "Commanding Men and Machines," chap. 6. Calvert quote, 365.

26. Bruce M. Davidson, Academic Dean, USNA, in Hagerott, 386.

27. In fact, Jones never uttered those words; see Lori Lyn Bogle and Joel I. Howitt, "The Best Quote Jones Never Wrote," *Naval History Magazine* 18, no. 2 (April 2004), https://www.usni.org/magazines/naval-history-magazine/2004/april/best-quote-jones-never-wrote.

28. Hagerott, "Commanding Men and Machines," 286.

29. George W. Emery, interview by the author, November 5, 2018.

30. Quotes in this and the following paragraph from Hyman G. Rickover, "The Never-Ending Challenge," *Metals Engineering Quarterly* 3, no. 1 (February 1963): 1–16. For press coverage, see for example "Rickover Assails U.S. Industry over Standards of Technology," *New York Times*, October 30, 1962.

31. Norman Polmar and Kenneth J. Moore, *Cold War Submarines: The Design and Construction of U.S. and Soviet Submarines* (2004), 150.

32. "Thresher," *New York Times*, April 13, 1963.

33. Multiple works discuss the *Thresher* disaster. The clearest scenario and explanation based on the available evidence is Captain Zack T. Pate, USN (Ret.), Rear Admiral David Goebel, USN (Ret.), and Vice Admiral George Emery, USN (Ret.), "The Tragic

Loss of the Nuclear Submarine *Thresher,* 10 April 1963," *Submarine Review,* June 2018, 123–33. For the most complete account, see Norman Polmar, *The Death of the USS* Thresher: *The Story behind History's Deadliest Submarine Disaster* (2004). I have also benefited from Joel I. Holwitt, "The Loss of USS *Thresher:* Technological and Cultural Change and the Cold War U.S. Navy," *Journal of Military History* 82 (July 2018), 843–72; and Captain James Bryant, USN (ret.), telephone interview by the author, June 25, 2018.

34. "Hope Abandoned for 129 Aboard Atom Submarine," *New York Times,* April 12, 1963.

35. A 2020 court decision following a lawsuit by Captain James Bryant, USN (ret.), seeking release of remaining unclassified documents from the Court of Inquiry resulted in the decision ordering that the Navy make them available. See "Judge Orders Navy to Release USS Thresher Disaster Documents," *USNI News,* February 11, 2020, https://news.usni.org/2020/02/11/judge-orders -navy-to-release-uss-thresher-disaster-documents. See also US Navy, "Department of Navy Releases Records Related to Loss of USS Thresher," press release, September 23, 2020, https://www .navy.mil/Press-Office/Press-Releases/display-pressreleases /Article/2358204/department-of-navy-releases-records-related -to-loss-of-uss-thresher/.

36. See "Retired Submarine Commander Sues Navy to Release USS Thresher Investigation," *USNI News,* August 9, 2019, https:// news.usni.org/2019/08/09/retired-submarine-commander-sues -navy-to-release-uss-thresher-investigation.

37. *Loss of the U.S.S. "Thresher": Hearings before the Joint Committee on Atomic Energy,* 88th Cong., 1st and 2nd sess., 1963–64, viii, https://stacks.stanford.edu/file/yk130sc8375/00002075_mixed .pdf.

38. Hyman Rickover to Robert Rickover, May 6, 1963, quoted in Vice Admiral George W. Emery, USN (Ret.), "An Admiral's Letters to His Son: Sequel #4 — Tragedy: Thresher and Scorpion" (typescript in author's possession).

39. Bryant interview (June 25, 2018); Bryant, "Declassify the Thresher Data," *Proceedings* (US Naval Institute) 144/7/1,385 (July

2018), https://www.usni.org/magazines/proceedings/2018/july/de
classify-thresher-data.

40. Vice Admiral Ralph K. James, USN, oral history by Dr.
John T. Mason of the US Naval Institute (1972), 288–89; Polmar
and Allen, *Rickover*, 430–31, 433.

41. Fred Korth, former secretary of the Navy, and Vice
Admiral Marmaduke Bayne, USN (Ret.), interview, Washington,
DC, April 5, 1987, in Philip Martin Callaghan, "Effects of the USS
Thresher Disaster upon Submarine Safety and Deep-Submergence
Capabilities in the United States Navy" (thesis, Virginia Polytech-
nic Institute and State University, May 1987), 11.

42. *Loss of U.S.S. "Thresher,"* ix.

43. *Loss of U.S.S. "Thresher,"* 66.

44. On the prior problems with silver-brazed joints, see Duncan, *Rickover and the Nuclear Navy*, 58–61.

45. Captain Zack T. Pate, USN (Ret.), "Observations Related
to the Loss of USS *Thresher* (SSN 693) on 10 April 1963," in Pate,
Goebel, and Emery, "The Tragic Loss of the Nuclear Submarine
Thresher," 131.

46. *Loss of the U.S.S. "Thresher,"* 6.

47. *Loss of the U.S.S. "Thresher,"* viii.

48. In Oliver, *Against the Tide*, 40–45, 145n6, the author re-
lates causes considered and his plausible theory of a battery explo-
sion.

49. From classified portions of *Loss of the U.S.S. "Thresher,"*
172, in Duncan, *Rickover and the Nuclear Navy*, 89–90.

50. Pinnow, interview, July 5, 2019. Pinnow served as a Naval
Reactors officer and engineer, 1961–65.

51. Hagerott, "Commanding Men and Machines," 405, 296–
97.

52. Crawford, interview, August 31 and November 12, 2018.

53. Zumwalt, *On Watch*, 99.

Chapter 11. The Chair with the Short Legs

1. For Rickover's views on nuclear training and the requirements leading to command, see H. G. Rickover, Admiral, USN,

Statement before the Subcommittee on Energy Research and Production of the Committee on Science and Technology, U.S. House of Representatives, 96th Cong., 1st sess., May 22, 23, 24, 1979.

2. Duncan, *Reminiscences*, vol. 2, #8, 698.

3. On the candidate review process, see Crawford, "Passing Rickover's Muster," 35–38.

4. Rickover, *60 Minutes* interview.

5. Numerous accounts confirm Rickover's interview techniques, including author telephone interviews with Crawford, August 31 and November 12, 2018, and with Lieutenant Frank Hood, USN (Ret.), May 9, 2019. See also Frank Hood and Charles Hood, *Poopie Suits & Cowboy Boots: Tales of a Submarine Officer during the Height of the Cold War*, 3rd ed. (2020), 41–45; and Beach, "Life under Rickover."

6. Schiller, "Strange Case."

7. Captain William J. Toti, USN (Ret.), "The Wrath of Rickover," *Proceedings* (US Naval Institute) 136/6/1,288 (June 2010): 30–31.

8. Rockwell, *Rickover Effect*, 110; Blair, *Atomic Submarine*, 128–30.

9. Crawford, interview. See also Captain John W. Crawford Jr., "*Get 'Em Young and Train 'Em Right*," *Proceedings* (US Naval Institute) 113 (October 1987): 66–68.

10. Anderson with Keith, *Ice Diaries*, 21.

11. Reid, interview. See also Kent L. Lee, *The Reminiscences of Vice Admiral Kent L. Lee, U.S. Navy (Ret.)* (1990), 370.

12. Duncan, *Reminiscences*, vol. 2, #9, 794.

13. Numerous interviewee stories tell of Rickover's behavior during their interviews, but see Polmar and Allen, *Rickover*, 455–56.

14. Hood, interview. Hood was part of a pool of candidates on a day when Rickover ordered a midshipman to call his fiancée.

15. William Smedberg, *The Reminiscences of Vice Admiral William Smedberg*, in Polmar and Allen, *Rickover*, 286.

16. Crawford, "Passing Rickover's Muster," 36.

17. For Zumwalt's account of the interview, see his *On Watch*,

3. Handwritten letters, October 23, 1974, and August 11, 1976, Box 1 Correspondence, Rickover Papers, Submarine Force Library and Archives, Groton, CT.

4. Carter, *Full Life*, 192.

5. Carter, 192.

6. On Carter's father, see Jimmy Carter, *An Hour before Daylight: Memories of a Rural Childhood* (2001), 47. "My mentor": George C. Edwards III, "Exclusive Interview: President Jimmy Carter," *Presidential Studies Quarterly* 38, no. 1 (March 2008): 1–13.

7. Rickover, *60 Minutes* interview.

8. On the personal relationship between Carter and Rickover, see especially, Duncan, *Rickover*, chap. 19.

9. Rickover, "Thoughts on Man's Purpose in Life."

10. Jimmy Carter, "April 18, 1977: Address to the Nation on Energy," Miller Center, University of Virginia, https://millercenter .org/the-presidency/presidential-speeches/april-18-1977-address -nation-energy.

11. Edwards, "Exclusive Interview."

12. Jimmy Carter, *Keeping Faith: Memoirs of a President* (1995), 96.

13. Carter, *Full Life*, 193.

14. "Carter, after Nuclear Sub Dive, Declares, 'There Is No Finer Ship,'" *New York Times*, May 28, 1977.

15. Duncan, *Rickover*, 263.

16. Duncan, 273–74.

17. Jimmy Carter, "July 15, 1979: Crisis of Confidence Speech," Miller Center, University of Virginia, https://millercenter.org/the -presidency/presidential-speeches/july-15-1979-crisis-confidence -speech.

18. SubGuru, "USS Nautilus (SSN-571)," http://www.subguru .com/nautilus571.htm.

19. Bourne, *Jimmy Carter*, 474–75.

20. John F. Lehman, *Command of the Seas* (2001), 1. For Lehman's version of Rickover's final retirement, see 1–36. All Lehman quotes, unless otherwise indicated, are from these pages.

21. *Naval Nuclear Propulsion Program*, February 20, 1974, 6.

22. Duncan, *Rickover*, 277.

23. Zach Pate, telephone interview by the author, November 19, 2018.

24. William Hughes Jr., telephone interview by the author, November 30, 2018.

25. Kilcline, oral history, 75.

26. "Lining Up on the Question of Rickover's Retirement," *New York Times*, June 7, 1981.

27. Vice Admiral John T. Hayward, USN (Ret.), "Comment," *Proceedings* (US Naval Institute) 107, no. 4 (April 1981): 21–22.

28. See Polmar and Moore, *Cold War Submarines*, 210.

29. Polmar and Allen, *Rickover*, 653.

30. "Rickover Losing Fight to Stop a Biography," *New York Times*, June 26, 1981.

31. Hyman Rickover to Eleonore Rickover, July 27, 1981, in Duncan, *Rickover*, 284.

32. On the crashback controversy, see Tyler, *Running Critical*, 295–300; Duncan, *Rickover*, 27–85; and Polmar and Allen, *Rickover*, 654.

33. For McKee's memories of the transition, see Admiral Kinnaird McKee, USN (Ret.), "Relieving Admiral Rickover," *Shipmate*, April 2000, 9–12.

34. Admiral Kinnaird McKee, oral history, Naval Historical Foundation, June 13, 2000, pt. 2, 81–82, https://www.navyhistory.org/wp-content/uploads/2014/01/ADM-McKee-Oral-History-Part-2_June-2000.pdf.

35. "Rickover's Allies Prepare to Resist His Retirement," *New York Times*, November 11, 1981.

36. "Betting Line Favors Rickover, Whose Future Is Now in Reagan's Hands," *Washington Post*, November 13, 1981, https://www.washingtonpost.com/archive/politics/1981/11/13/betting-line-favors-rickover-whose-future-is-now-in-reagans-hands/05d c65a3-c57f-415b-b5f6-83784b59c83f/.

37. Duncan, *Rickover*, 290.

38. United States General Accounting Office, *Nuclear Research and Development: Shippingport Decommissioning—How Appli-*

cable Are the Lessons Learned? (Washington, DC: GAO, September 4, 1990), https://www.gao.gov/assets/220/213114.pdf.

39. Quotes in this and the following paragraphs from *Economics of Defense Policy: Adm. H. G. Rickover,* January 28, 1982, 6, 8, 15, 63, 61, 50, 14.

40. Duncan, *Rickover,* 292–93.

Epilogue

1. Reid, interview.

2. Submarine Force Library and Museum Association, "History of the USS Nautilus," https://www.ussnautilus.org/history-of-uss-nautilus/.

3. Lehman, *Command of the Seas,* 7–8.

4. Tyler, *Running Critical,* 3.

5. "Rickover Launched," *Dolphin,* September 2, 1983.

6. On Rickover's retirement life, see Duncan, *Rickover,* 295–301. Duncan's *Rickover and the Nuclear Navy* was published in 1990. His biography of Rickover came out in 2001.

7. Tyler, *Running Critical,* 3.

8. "Education of Hyman Rickover."

9. "Rickover at 83: Three-Gun Salute," *Washington Post,* March 1, 1983. AP report in *Ithaca Journal,* March 1, 1983, Rickover Papers, Submarine Force Library, Groton, CT.

10. Center for Excellence in Education, https://www.cee.org/.

11. "Rickover Linked by House Panel to Gifts from Ship Builders," *New York Times,* July 19, 1984; *Federal Securities Law and Defense Contracting—Part 1: Hearings before the Subcommittee on Oversight and Investigations of the Committee on Energy and Commerce, House of Representatives,* 95th Cong., 1st sess., February 28 and March 25, 1985.

12. "New Navy Report Outlines Gifts, Favors Provided to Adm. Rickover," *Washington Post,* June 5, 1985.

13. Tyler, *Running Critical,* 4–5.

14. Duncan, *Rickover,* 302.

15. See Polmar and Moore, *Cold War Submarines,* 53.

16. Public Law 98-525 of October 19, 1984 (42 USC 7158).

17. For Rickover studies, see among others Robert Bovey, "Science and Technology in the Naval Reactors Program, 1949–1959," in *Science and Technology in Development Environments—Industry and Department of Defense Case Studies* (2004); and Admiral William J. Fallon, USN (Ret.) and Ms. Amy Roma, Esq., "The Nuclear Energy, Naval Propulsion and National Security Symposium," *Pull Together: Newsletter of the Naval Historical Foundation* 57, no. 3 (Fall 2018). See also Paul E. Brierly III and J.-C. Spender, "Culture and High Reliability Organizations: The Case of the Nuclear Submarine," *Journal of Management* 21, no. 4 (1995): 639–56.

18. Author communications with Vice Admiral George Emery, USN (Ret.). See among others Sherry Sontag and Christopher Drew with Annette Lawrence Drew, *Blind Man's Bluff: The Untold Story of American Submarine Espionage* (2016).

19. Ronald O'Rourke, "Navy Nuclear-Powered Surface Ships: Background, Issues, and Options for Congress," Congressional Research Service, September 29, 2010.

20. For video of the ceremony and speeches, see GD Electric Boat, "SSN 795 Rickover Keel Laying Ceremony," YouTube, May 16, 2018, https://www.youtube.com/watch?v=t52IDvyqnCE.

21. Bruce Kahn, telephone interview by the author, September 14, 2018.

22. Robert Rickover, email correspondence with the author, September 17, 2018.

23. Duncan, *Rickover*, 311–13; "A 'Teacher' Recalled at Rickover Rite," *New York Times*, July 15, 1986.

INDEX

Barbra Streisand: Redefining Beauty, Femininity, and Power,
   by Neal Gabler
Leon Trotsky: A Revolutionary's Life, by Joshua Rubenstein
Warner Bros: The Making of an American Movie Studio,
   by David Thomson

FORTHCOMING TITLES INCLUDE:

Franz Boas, by Noga Arikha
Mel Brooks, by Jeremy Dauber
Alfred Dreyfus, by Maurice Samuels
Anne Frank, by Ruth Franklin
Betty Friedan, by Rachel Shteir
George Gershwin, by Gary Giddins
Allen Ginsberg, by Ed Hirsch
Herod, by Martin Goodman
Abraham Joshua Heschel, by Julian Zelizer
Jesus, by Jack Miles
Josephus, by Daniel Boyarin
Louis Kahn, by Gini Alhadeff
Maimonides, by Alberto Manguel
Louis B. Mayer and Irving Thalberg, by Kenneth Turan
Golda Meir, by Deborah E. Lipstadt
Arthur Miller, by John Lahr
Robert Oppenheimer, by David Rieff
Ayn Rand, by Alexandra Popoff
Sidney Reilly, by Benny Morris
Philip Roth, by Steven J. Zipperstein
Edmond de Rothschild, by James McAuley
Ruth, by Ilana Pardes
Jonas Salk, by David Margolick